D1230544

Jacques Offenbach

Offenbach at thirty: cellist of the salons. Drawing by Laemlein

Collection Viollet

ML
410
.O41F37

JACQUES OFFENBACH

Alexander Faris

Charles Scribner's Sons

NEW YORK

Copyright © 1980 by Alexander Faris
First U.S. edition published by Charles Scribner's Sons 1981

Copyright under the Berne Convention

All rights reserved. No part of this book
may be reproduced in any form without the
permission of Charles Scribner's Sons

1 3 5 7 9 11 13 15 17 19   I/C   20 18 16 14 12 10 8 6 4 2

Printed in Great Britain

Library of Congress Catalog Number: 80 5794
ISBN 0-684-16797-2

TO

CLIFFORD MAKINS

Contents

··⚸··

Illustrations

Illustrations

ACKNOWLEDGEMENTS

One of the pleasures of writing this book has been in the friendly and enthusiastic co-operation afforded me by several descendants of Offenbach. M. Pierre Comte-Offenbach supplied information on familial and personal matters; Mr James Buckley and Mr William Buckley gave me access to scores, documents and photographs, as did M. Michel Brindejont, who also kindly allowed me to quote extensively from his father's book *Offenbach mon Grand-Père*. I am enormously grateful to these four great-grandsons of the composer, not only for spending so much time and trouble in searching for answers to my battery of questions, but also for many instances of the kind of generous hospitality — some of it, delightfully, at Étretat — for which their great-grandfather Jacques Offenbach was so renowned.

My warmest thanks go, too, to many other people: Shane Fletcher gave up holiday time to carry out research in Paris and elsewhere, as did my sister, Dr Harriet Rhys-Davies, who also contributed the medical comment in Appendix B. David Llewellyn researched tenaciously in London and compiled the bibliography. Helmut Hunder uncovered new sources of information in Germany. Adam Warren gave me scholarly guidance in the nuances of the French language, and I was supported by a redoubtable succession of experts in German — Michael McGregor, Evelyn Tracey, Frederick Vine and Ulrich Ewert. To the Arts Council of Great Britain I owe thanks for financial assistance while I was engaged in research for the book.

I am indebted to David Redston for the stylish design and execution of the musical examples; to Ann Melsom for a thoughtfully conceived and meticulously compiled index; and to Victoria Bacon for an impeccable typescript.

I am most grateful for the counsel of the eminent conductor and Offenbach scholar Antonio de Almeida. My chapter on *Les Contes d'Hoffman* draws on his research and on the work of Dr Fritz Oeser. I also greatly valued the perceptive comments of my friends Stephen Dodgson and Carlo Ardito on musical and literary aspects of the book.

A pleasant surprise for anyone writing his first book is the unfailing helpfulness of library staffs everywhere. I thank those at the British Library, the Bibliothèque nationale, the Archives nationales, the Archives de l'Opéra, the Archives de la Préfecture de Police, Paris; the Bibliothèque de la Ville, Bayonne; the Österreichische Nationalbibliothek, the Universitätsbibliothek Düsseldorf, and the Stadtmuseum Bad Ems.

I am most grateful to the following publishers and institutions for permission to use copyright material specifically acknowledged in the Notes: Constable & Co. Ltd, George Weidenfeld & Nicolson Ltd, University of Chicago Press, Librairie Plon, Librairie Académique Perrin, Bibliothèque nationale, Archives nationales, and Archives de l'Opéra.

A great Fleet Street professional, Clifford Makins, goaded me into starting this book after I had hesitated for several years, then stood by till the completion of the task with wise and affectionate advice. There is no repaying a debt of that kind, but I have dedicated the book to him as an expression of friendship and warm gratitude; and as a reminder of many hours profitably wasted in conversation.

Family

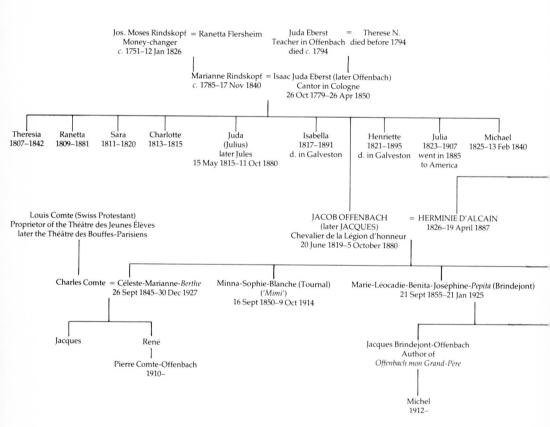

Living generations are not fully represented

Tree

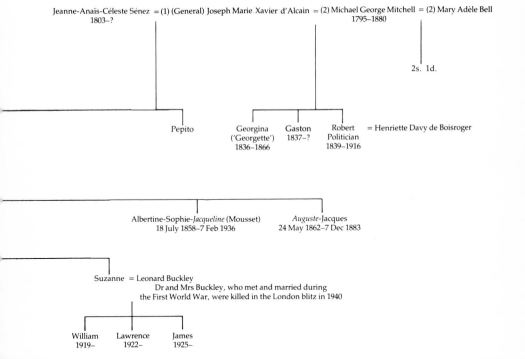

Jeanne-Anaïs-Céleste Sénez = (1) (General) Joseph Marie Xavier d'Alcain = (2) Michael George Mitchell = (2) Mary Adèle Bell
1803–?   1795–1880

2s. 1d.

Pepito

Georgina ('Georgette') 1836–1866   Gaston 1837–?   Robert Politician 1839–1916   = Henriette Davy de Boisroger

Albertine-Sophie-*Jacqueline* (Mousset)
18 July 1858–7 Feb 1936

Auguste-Jacques
24 May 1862–7 Dec 1883

Suzanne = Leonard Buckley
Dr and Mrs Buckley, who met and married during
the First World War, were killed in the London blitz in 1940

William 1919–   Lawrence 1922–   James 1925–

CHAPTER I

Father and Sons
1819–1840

On the morning of 5 October 1880 the elderly comic actor Léonce called at the apartment of his old friend Jacques Offenbach, at 8 boulevard des Capucines, near the Paris Opéra. The door was opened by Mathurin, Offenbach's manservant.

'How is he?'

'Monsieur Offenbach is dead; he died quite peacefully, without knowing anything about it.'

'Ah! — he will be very surprised when he finds out.'

Offenbach was born in Cologne on 20 June 1819; he was thus the close contemporary of Mendelssohn, Chopin, Schumann, Wagner, Verdi and Gounod, for they were all born within the same twelve years. His father, Isaac Juda Eberst,[1]* was a Jewish cantor and music teacher, who as a young man had left his home at Offenbach-am-Main and wandered from town to town earning his living as a cantor in the synagogues and as a fiddler in the cafés. He became known on his travels as 'der Offenbacher', and began to use the name of his native town as a surname. At the beginning of the century he married Marianne Rindskopf, daughter of a money-changer and lottery-office keeper in Deutz. Their second son, the seventh of their ten children, was registered at birth as Jacob Offenbach.[2]

The family lived frugally in a small house among the second-hand shops in the Grosser Griechenmarkt. To augment his cantor's fees Isaac taught singing, violin, flute and guitar. He also wrote poetry and composed, his works including settings of the Psalms and the Jewish liturgy, and he wrote with fervour about religion and the emancipation of the Jews. The whole family was musical, and Isaac soon started teaching his son Jacob to play the violin. As Offenbach later recalled:

* Notes begin on page 223

17

Father and Sons: 1819–1840

At seven I didn't play too badly, but already my mind was on composing, rather than on scales and exercises. Three years later my father came in one night, followed by a cello he had just bought. As soon as I saw the instrument, I said I wanted to learn that instead of the violin; my parents refused, on the pretext of my health — they were rather worried about my frail appearance. I pretended to give in, but from then on I would watch for them to leave the house; as soon as the street door closed I would get hold of the cello and practise it eagerly in my locked room.

A few months later they took me to a house where some friends used to play quartets every week. Everyone had been there for some time except the cellist, who hadn't turned up yet. They were getting impatient, and disappointed at having to put off playing Haydn for another week, when I went up to my father and asked him in a whisper if he would let me take the place of the latecomer. I knew I could do it.

My father burst out laughing, and the master of the house asked what caused the sudden fit of merriment.

'Why not let him try it?'

'But he has never touched a cello.'

Blushing, I confessed my disobedience. Without wasting time on scolding me he put the longed-for instrument in my hands, and I played my part to the applause of the whole company.[3]

The family gave up a few comforts so that Jacob might have cello lessons. His teacher, Herr Alexander, was an eccentric who dressed the part of an artist with an exaggerated but threadbare elegance that fascinated the local children. He had private means, but was said to be the biggest miser in town and insisted on payment in advance for the lessons. He had, however, been a fine player in his day, and gave his pupil a good grounding. When the time came for more advanced tuition Jacob went to Bernhard Breuer, a well-known composer of music for the Cologne carnivals, who taught the young Offenbach composition as well as the cello. The sacrifices made by Isaac and his family to pay for Jacob's lessons had their reward when three of the children, Julius, Jacob and Isabella, were able to form a trio — violin, cello and piano — which performed in the local bars and restaurants. In order to impress the public with the virtuosity of Jacob's playing Isaac gave the boy's age as two years less than it was. Thereafter, Offenbach, who may himself have been misled by this ruse, claimed wrongly that he had been born in 1821.

It became clear to Isaac that a boy of Jacob's promise deserved more than Cologne could offer by way of education and opportunity. Anti-semitism was, moreover, strong in Cologne. He therefore decided to take Julius and Jacob to Paris and to try to get them into the Conservatoire there. They received contributions towards their expenses from some well-disposed music lovers, and from the municipal orchestra, with whom they gave a farewell concert on 9 October 1833, before setting off on the four-day journey to Paris. On arrival, Isaac took the boys to see Cherubini, then director of the Conservatoire, to whom he had letters of introduction, confidently expecting that he would accept his sons as pupils. 'I am extremely sorry,' Cherubini declared, 'but we cannot accept foreigners; our institution is only for Frenchmen.'

Greatly dismayed, Isaac reminded Cherubini that he had brought the boys all the way from Cologne to give them a chance to develop their

1. Offenbach at fourteen: pupil at the
Paris Conservatoire

musical talents in Paris, and asked if he would at least hear the 'thirteen'-year-old play the cello. An appointment was made for the next day, and father and son arrived to find Cherubini and twelve professors waiting for them. A cello and a piece of sightreading were produced. Jacob had played about half a page when Cherubini went over to him, took his hand, and said, 'You are a pupil of the Conservatoire.'

The incident was recounted many years later by Offenbach's sister Julie, who remembered hearing the news as a child of nine. 'My father wrote home about all this, and my mother let her tears fall on the stove as she read it.'[4] Family satisfaction was all the greater in that, ten years earlier,

Cherubini had turned down the twelve-year-old Franz Liszt as a pupil on the grounds that he was not French. This rebuff was said to have 'hit the wonder-boy like a thunderbolt'. Isaac added in his letter that he had taken Julius to see Paganini, who had agreed to teach him. There are no accounts of Julius' lessons with Paganini, but Jacob was duly enrolled at the Conservatoire in the class of M. Vaslin.[5] After one year he left at his own request. No one knows why; but it was the first hint the young Offenbach gave of the rebellious attitude towards contemporary French music and its institutions that determined the course of his career and to some extent the nature of his music.

In choosing Paris for his sons rather than Berlin or Vienna, Isaac must have had more in mind than that city's reputation as a centre of music. The emancipation of the Jews was an incidental part of the secularization of France that began in the eighteenth century and was hastened by the French Revolution. The *philosophes*, Voltaire, Montesquieu and others, with their friend at Court, Madame de Pompadour, were a political force, one of whose achievements was the improved status of religious minorities. From 1784 onwards Jews no longer had to pay a personal tax. After the revolution the courts that had jurisdiction over matters of religious faith were abolished. The new freedom of thought that attracted liberals to France had therefore a particular significance for Jews. French literature, music and theatre benefited from the injection of new blood. The first of the talented Halévy family arrived in Paris before 1800; Meyerbeer came in 1826 for a performance of his opera *Il Crociato*, and settled. Heinrich Heine followed in 1831; before long he was thought of as a French poet, just as Offenbach was later (perhaps questionably) to be regarded as one of the most typically French composers.

The Offenbach boys, who now called themselves Jacques and Jules, found cheap lodgings in an attic in the rue des Martyrs. They earned a little by singing in a synagogue choir, and Isaac procured a few pupils for Jules. During the remaining months that he spent in Paris Isaac occasionally fulfilled his familiar function as cantor, while Jacques played in one or two orchestras before getting a regular job at the Opéra-Comique. Later he recalled those days:

In 1835 Halévy's *L'Éclair* had barely opened at the Opéra-Comique when *La Juive* made its appearance at the Opéra. I had been in Paris for a short time, and was naturally very curious to go and hear this *Juive*, about which so much was said for and against. Towards six in the evening I had stationed myself unobtrusively in the forecourt of the Opéra, and was waiting impatiently for the composer of these works. A little before seven M. Halévy actually arrived; with the nerve of the brat of thirteen that I then was [*recte* fifteen], I went up to him, and though my voice was anything but assured, asked him if he could get me in to hear *La Juive*.

'It's very simple,' he replied 'and I'm all the more delighted that you've asked me, since, if I remember right, it was you who played the bass part at my first rehearsal of *L'Éclair*.' Which was true, for I had just joined the orchestra of the Opéra-Comique.

'Do you want to see well?' said M. Halévy.

'I want above all to hear well, maestro.'

'Then come with me.'

We climbed to the third circle. He was admitted to a box, and there, all ears, we didn't miss a note of this magnificent score. How far away that performance seems now! Twenty years have passed, and this work, almost fought over when it appeared, now has its place among the masterpieces.[6]

After this meeting Fromental Halévy befriended the brothers. 'I see your sons quite often,' he wrote to Isaac; 'the young gentlemen sometimes come to ask for advice, which I am most happy to give them; the younger, in particular, seems to me destined for real success in his career as a composer, and I shall consider it a pleasure to play my part by encouraging and helping him in his studies and his writing.' Jacques found this letter years later among his father's papers and kept it in his wallet for the rest of his life.

Meantime he found his work in the pit at the Opéra-Comique tedious and repetitive. To liven things up he and his young partner Hippolyte Seligmann used to play pranks. One evening they each played alternate notes of the cello part in front of them. Another time they tied some of the music stands together with a cord which they pulled in the middle of the performance. Such behaviour was punished by fines, which swallowed up much of Jacques' salary. This did not help the budget in the rue des Martyrs, where Jacques and Jules now shared a Bohemian existence with another pair of brothers called Lütgen, the sons of a violinist acquaintance of Isaac's in Cologne. The four friends lived in the manner of all young men of their kind, except that, as it offended Jacques' sense of *amour-propre* to be seen doing the shopping, he used to carry the groceries home in a violin case.

In a world without radio or gramophone records popular music thrived in public places. In 1836 two colourful figures — the rival conductors Jullien and Musard — enlivened the Parisian scene. As each was a composer, conductor and impresario, they had something in common with the dance-band leaders of the 1920s and 1930s and they also exhibited some of the gimmickry of certain pop groups of recent times. Musard introduced the *chaise-cassée*, a piece of music in which, at a certain point, a chair was smashed. In later developments the chair was replaced by a pistol-shot and finally a small mortar. Jullien riposted by using fireworks and a salvo of artillery blanks. Musard was a scruffy little man with a face disfigured by smallpox, but was immensely popular. Jullien was a twenty-four-year-old Adonis with whom the women fell in love; he cultivated dandyism to the point of changing his yellow gloves several times in the course of a concert. This nonsense apart, he introduced to the public an enormous quantity of well-written light music, as did Musard. Since between them they could not possibly compose enough music themselves to satisfy their audience, they frequently employed other composers. Jullien had studied under Halévy, from whom Offenbach may have brought an introduction when he submitted some of his dance-music to the young conductor. Jullien's orchestra of sixty players performed during the summer at the *café-concerts* in the Jardin Turc on the boulevard du Temple. In the fresh air or under shelter the public could drink, dine, dance, watch the life on the boulevard or listen to the concert, as they pleased. It was here that, at the age of seventeen, Offenbach had great success with one of his first waltzes, *Fleurs d'hiver*.

Sheet music was big business in Paris; albums of waltzes were sold by the thousand, and there were also several successful weekly musical journals which could boost their sales by printing new popular music between the reviews and the tittle-tattle. Offenbach's name and music began to appear in these publications. The reviews were not always complimentary. Offenbach wrote a waltz called *Rebecca*, based on themes from the Jewish liturgical music of the fifteenth century. 'This latest production', said *Le Ménestrel*, 'is nothing but a pot-pourri arranged from a series of melodies used in the Hebrew temples. Is it absolutely necessary to make a rowdy waltz out of a travesty of melodies consecrated by religious ritual? No; but today one must have novelty at all costs.'

Jacques soon featured in the gossip column of the same journal:

There is in Paris a very young celebrity whose existence is, alas, not suspected by the musical world. It is M. Offenbach, composer of waltzes, who has formally committed himself to dethrone Strauss and Lanner. M. Offenbach regularly composes three waltzes before luncheon, a mazurka after dinner, and four galops between the two meals. This young prodigy begs us to announce that he has just lost a white handkerchief on which he had scribbled the manuscript of a waltz. A fair reward to the finder.

It has been suggested that Jacques wrote the paragraph himself, and indeed it would not have been out of character.

Johann Strauss the elder had arrived in Paris in October 1837, and both his music and the playing of his Viennese orchestra held a new excitement for Parisians. A 'musical duel' was arranged between Strauss and Musard, in the form of a joint concert at the salle Vivienne at which the talents of the two composers could be compared. The result was inconclusive, both artists emerging with honour. Strauss's waltzes were taken up by the French orchestras, and at the newly established Concerts Saint-Honoré Strauss and Offenbach appeared as composers on the same bill. A quarter of a century later Offenbach heard the waltzes of the younger Strauss in Vienna, scented a potential *Fledermaus*, and encouraged the thirty-eight-year-old composer to change course and start writing operettas.

Although the success of Jacques' waltzes was promising, the income from them was not enough to live on. He received a pittance from his father, and had one pupil. But he now had the good fortune to meet Flotow, the future composer of *Martha* and *Stradella*. The young Freiherr Friedrich Ferdinand Adolf von Flotow was a son of the landed gentry of the grand duchy of Mecklenburg. He took a liking to this compatriot, his junior by seven years, who was up against hard times. Flotow was a talented composer whose social background had given him an easy entrée to the aristocratic salons of Paris. In an affectionate memoir[7] of Offenbach, whom he outlived, he describes how he introduced him to the salon of the comtesse Bertin de Vaux. The comtesse said she would be happy to let Offenbach play at her next soirée, but as the programme was already long his item would have to be a short one. Unfortunately Jacques' repertoire consisted only of a few long concert pieces by Romberg. Flotow and Offenbach therefore quickly collaborated on the composition of some short pieces for cello and piano, in the course of which Jacques impressed his friend with his facility for inventing attractive melodies. (For all his talent Flotow was not a natural melodist. The great success in *Martha* was, in fact, the borrowed Irish air *The Last Rose of Summer*.)

Offenbach was known to Flotow as Jacob Eberscht (*sic*)[8]. When the pair presented themselves at the comtesse's soirée Flotow was surprised to hear his friend give the unfamiliar name Offenbach. After three attempts at this name the servant who was announcing them settled for 'Monsieur Jacques Offenbak'. 'Later,' wrote Flotow, 'when my friend was so popular that every street-urchin knew his name, in Paris it was always "Offenbak".' (It is still pronounced this way in France.) 'My friend was a great success and soon became a favourite in the house of the comtesse de Vaux.' Favourites, too, at the fashionable parties, were the little duets on which the two friends collaborated in such haste.

Thus successfully launched in the salons, Jacques lost no time in planning a concert. With eleven of his colleagues, including his brother Julius, and with the comtesse de Vaux as his sponsor, he faced the public for the first time on 27 January 1839 in the music-rooms of Pape's instrument shop. He was well received. *Le Ménestrel* recorded enthusiastically that a Chopinesque *valse mélancolique* by Offenbach was much applauded.

Before long Offenbach was approached by Anicet Bourgeois to write music for a vaudeville, *Pascal et Chambord*. He was excited by this first opportunity to compose for the theatre. But there were disappointments. 'To my great despair', he remembered, 'I had to cut half the finale because of Grassot, whose dreadful voice got on my nerves.'[9] The piece turned out to be a hack comedy about troopers in the Napoleonic wars and a baby of disputed fatherhood. It was presented at the Palais Royal on 2 March 1839 and sank without trace. The score is lost, but if Offenbach followed his usual practice he probably salvaged some of it for later use. Whenever one of his operettas flopped he regarded its score as a store-cupboard of ideas for the future. The Barcarolle in *Les Contes d'Hoffmann*, for instance, had appeared seventeen years earlier as the *Elfenchor* in *Die Rheinnixen*, and there are many other examples of this practice.

Offenbach hoped that after *Pascal and Chambord* he would begin to make a living as a composer. He was bored with playing the cello, though he was in demand as a teacher. The failure of the piece was therefore a double setback. He and Jules were always running out of money. All his life, however much Jacques earned, his expenditure always outstripped his income. One day when he found that he only had five centimes, a man came up to him in the street, and, having asked him if he was M. Offenbach, handed him twenty francs, explaining that he owed it to Jules, and asking him to pass it on. Jacques spent it on a partridge and a bottle of St Julien at the Café Anglais on the way home to his hungry brother.

Isaac Offenbach, who had not seen his sons for six years, now made the journey to Paris to see for himself how they were getting on. He was upset to find that Jacques had abandoned his cello-playing. So Jacques composed a cello piece specially for Isaac, and played it after dinner at a party some friends gave for his father. It delighted the company, and rekindled Jacques' love of the instrument. He wrote an 'École du violoncelle', a series of graded cello studies, for his pupils. Urged by Isaac, he also began to plan concert tours in Germany and England, and in the next few years met with great success as a travelling virtuoso.

But first the brothers went home to Cologne to see their mother, their five surviving sisters (two of the girls had died in childhood) and their brother Michael, the youngest of the family. There was an emotional meeting; Jacques' mother could hardly recognize in this thin long-haired young man the son who had left home at thirteen. There were special cakes, a bottle of Rhine wine, and family visitors. The *menorah*, or seven-branched candlestick, was brought into use. These things remained in

Flute
& Piccolo

Oboes

Clarinets
in A

in A
Horns
in D

Bassoons

Trumpets
in A

Trombones

Timpani

Solo
Cello

Violins
1

Violins
2

Violas

Cellos
and Basses

2. Opening of the *Grande scène espagnole*, suite for cello and orchestra, composed at the age of twenty-one

By kind permission of Mr William Buckley

the memory of the schoolboy Albert Wolff, a neighbour and friend of the family, who later worked in Paris as a journalist and became a lifelong friend of Jacques and his wife Herminie.

Jacques and Jules stayed three months in Cologne, during which time they gave a concert at the Casino. Then Jules went off to Bordeaux, where he had been appointed conductor at the Opéra, and Jacques returned to Paris. Ten months later they were in Cologne again; their brother Michael had died and their mother was ill. They stayed for several months. Jacques was good at cheering up his mother with his jokes, and spent some time composing a *Grande scène espagnole*, for violoncello and orchestra, to include in the programme of another concert. The *Kölnische Zeitung* was complimentary.

On 17 November 1840, a few days after the concert, their mother died. Jacques and his father both wrote some touching, if rather maudlin, verse[10] in her memory and the brothers returned to France.

CHAPTER II

Jacob and Jacques
1841–1848

····◊····

The year before he died Richard Wagner, who had earlier feuded bitterly with Offenbach, wrote a letter to Felix Mottl in which, after enthusing about the stage music in the finale of the first act of *Don Giovanni*, he went on to say: 'Look at Offenbach. He writes like the divine Mozart. The fact is, my friend, the French have the secret of these things. I don't envy them in many respects. Nevertheless one has to acknowledge this truth that leaps to the eyes: Offenbach could have been like Mozart.'[1]

The music that Offenbach was writing in his early twenties, would hardly have inspired Wagner's comment. It was simple and craftsman-like, but undistinguished. Only when he was more mature did the strength and fecundity of his melodic invention allow him to get away with a persistent simplicity of style that many composers would not have risked. But his compositions were attracting some attention, even if the attention was not always complimentary. In 1842 he gave a concert in the salle Herz, the contemporary Parisian equivalent of London's Wigmore Hall. For this event he composed settings of six fables by La Fontaine (*La Cigale et la fourmi*, etc.). Among the hostile critical comments was one suggesting that Offenbach's music was making fun of the fables' morals. Other critics (with some justification) commented that the pieces were loosely constructed. When Offenbach later resurrected some of the music for use in his operettas (*La Laitière et le pot au lait, Le Financier et le Savetier*) his better developed dramatic instinct led him to tighten up its structure.

In another salle Herz concert a year later the handsome and excellent tenor Gustave Roger contributed to the success of a duet called *Le Moine bourru* ('The Peevish Monk') in which the words by Plouvier satirized Hugo and *Notre-Dame de Paris*, and the music parodied grand opera, a favourite ploy of Offenbach's, and one which made him unpopular with the highminded dignitaries of opera houses. It was the wrong time to antagonize such people. They were the only authorities who could

27

commission dramatic works from young composers, and Offenbach's ambition was to write for the theatre.

As a cellist he was still as popular as ever. Jacques and Jules played on the same bill with the 'ten-year-old' prodigy Rubinstein (who must also have had a father who subtracted two years from his age). Jacques played some works of his own, and a *Grande fantaisie sur des thèmes russes* won general acclaim. But he was criticized for indulging in musical jokes. He would make his cello simulate the kazoo and other instruments, and in the eyes of some people this cast doubts on his artistic sincerity. His virtuosity, however, was not in question. On one occasion *L'Artiste* said 'He will be, indeed he already is, the Liszt of the violoncello.' 'Encouraged by success,' wrote Nadar in a memoir, 'he began his 3,997 visits to the various directors of the Opéra-Comique who were entrusted with the encouragement of the young.' For over fifteen years Offenbach met with consistent rebuffs in that quarter, possibly because of the influence of revered masters like Meyerbeer, who were so often the targets of Offenbach's parody. He made no secret of the fact that he found their music pretentious. 'Because he was a gifted ironist,' wrote Debussy many years later (1903), 'Offenbach was perhaps the only man to perceive the false, overblown quality of such music. Above all, he was able to expose the hidden element of farce which it embodied, and to exploit this. We know how successful he was. But no one realized what he was about, because it was so much taken for granted that Meyerbeer represented the great art at which one was not allowed to smile.'

In France as in England, drawing-room ballads were all the rage. Offenbach and Roger made a great hit with a song entitled *Rends-moi mon âme*. In the verse the poet laments that his life is no longer like a tranquil and pure lake reflecting the blue sky and the clouds by day, and the sparkling stars at night: 'I do not know what has breathed o'er me, but my whole being is troubled to its depths.' The refrain goes:

Rends-moi mon âme, jeune fille
Rends-moi mon âme, jeune fille
Rends-moi, rends-moi mon âme
Rends-moi, rends-moi mon âme
Jeune fille, jeune fille, rends-moi mon âme!

But another ballad was less vacuous, and in the circumstances more touching. It was entitled *A toi*, and was dedicated to Mademoiselle Herminie d'Alcain, stepdaughter of Michael George Mitchell[2], a new English acquaintance of Offenbach's, who lived in Paris with his French wife and family. Madame Mitchell was the widow of a Carlist general. She had a daughter and a son, Herminie and Pepito d'Alcain, by her first marriage, and three more children by Mitchell: Georgina, Gaston and Robert.

Jacob and Jacques: 1841–1848

Mitchell invited Jacques to a party in honour of a hero of the latest uprising in Spain. Jacques, as yet unknown to the family, arrived to find that he was not expected, and that his host was not yet home. But he was made welcome, and began to amuse the company with his chat about the musical world and his own work. Before long he was playing the piano and singing, without much of a voice, but entertainingly none the less. All this made a profound impression on the sixteen-year-old Herminie. Perhaps that was Jacques' intention, for he soon became a regular visitor at the Mitchell household. The Mitchells were taken aback when, after only six months, the young Offenbach asked permission to marry their teenage daughter. They had three reasons for doubting the wisdom of the match: Herminie was too young, Jacques was unlikely to be financially secure for a long time to come, and thirdly he was not a Catholic, a matter which was of particular concern to Madame Mitchell. Herminie's parents played for time by making conditions. Jacques was due to visit England in the spring of 1844, and Mitchell, who attached great importance to this tour, indicated that there could be no question of consent to the marriage until Jacques had proved that he could make a success in London, thereby implying that a musician who could succeed in England could succeed anywhere. In the meantime Jacques began to receive instruction in the Catholic faith.

The ballad *A toi* contained the germ of one of Offenbach's most moving later songs, that of the King of the Boeotians in *Orphée aux Enfers*. It began with this phrase:

Ex. 1

29

But this song lacked the strong features of the later one: the arresting rhythmic figure in the accompaniment, the tonic pedal-point, and, above all, the inspired extension of the final phrase that gave the Boeotian king his eloquence:

Ex. 2

Here was the essential romantic Offenbach, whose natural good taste led him to avoid false sentiment, and to compose popular music that had rhythmic backbone, and was at the same time simple, sensuous and passionate.

Much of French nineteenth-century music owed its colour to exotic influences — the Bohemian, the Spanish, the oriental. The polka was the latest import, and for his last concert before leaving for London Jacques composed for the cello a *Danse bohémienne*. In the same programme were a fantasy on themes of Rossini, and *Musette, air de danse*, a seventeenth-century pastiche; also a cello elegy, *Deux âmes au ciel*, in memory of King Louis-Philippe's son, the duc d'Orléans, and his wife Princess Marie, who had been killed in a carriage accident in 1842. The King wrote Offenbach a letter of acknowledgement. After a two-bar introduction, the melody of *Deux âmes au ciel* begins conventionally:

Ex. 3a

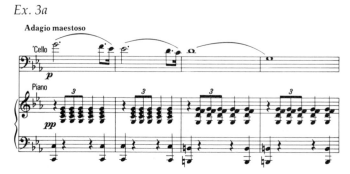

Later, it becomes 'più appassionato':

Ex. 3b

Thus when he left for London in May 1844 Jacques had an extensive repertoire of his own compositions for the cello. He was immediately well received. *The Musical Examiner*, after printing some inaccurate biographical notes, continued:

This season he has ventured into the great vortex, or musical whirlpool of London, and has 'got off' with immense applause, wherever and whenever he has appeared. He is certainly an artist of first-rate ability, and, we might add, *agility*, on his instrument, and, moreover, a man deserving the respect of every musician for his acquirements, and of every gentleman for his deportment. Herr Offenbach has been heard at several of our most fashionable concerts, and has, moreover, played with success at Court, before Her Majesty and Prince Albert, from which illustrious personages he received, in addition to the highest marks of admiration, a valuable *cadeau*.

The Court appearance was arranged by John Mitchell, almost certainly a relative of Jacques' prospective father-in-law. In addition to managing the St James's Theatre, popularly known as 'the French theatre', John Mitchell was Queen Victoria's concert agent; he was, indeed, the originator of the theatre ticket agency system. Later, when Offenbach's Bouffes-Parisiens was the talk of the European capitals, the French company appeared at the St James's, and the Queen attended one performance.

On 8 June 1844 Jacques wrote to his friend Émile Chevalet:

Last Thursday I played at Windsor in front of the Queen, Prince Albert, the Emperor of Russia, the King of Bavaria, etc. The élite of the Court, in fact. I was a great success. But in spite of all the honours I am receiving I much prefer my beautiful Paris and would rather be among my real friends, enjoying your pleasant little soirées. Here, all is magnificent but cold; there, on the other hand, everything is gracious, enticing and warm, specially if one has some good friends. Also, my dear Émile, I am longing to shake your hand again and to be back in my beloved Paris, which contains all that I hold most dear, all that I love. You can understand that, can't you, dear Émile? I am sure you will spread about the news of my appearance at Court, if you can. . . . Last week I was invited to dinner at the Society of Melodists, whose president is the Duke of Cambridge. Well, my dear fellow, as you can imagine, there was some music after dinner. I played my *Musette*; they made such a row, banging on the table for a full five minutes, and shouting 'Encore!' at the tops of their voices that I had to play the same piece again. You will see from all this that I have had just as much success here as in Paris. And I am beginning to be just a little proud. When I get back to Paris I won't be able to see you any more, accustomed as I am to mix only with lords, dukes, queens, kings, emperors! Emperors, my friend!!! I can't stoop any more to talk to a simple bourgeois, but since I can write to him, you see, I am, taking the opportunity. Adieu, my dear Chevalet. My very best regards to the charming Mme Chevalet; and you, my friend, I will allow you — mark this — I will allow you to kiss my hand.

Affectionately
Jacques Offenbach[3]

32

There was an occasional carping notice for his playing. After one concert Jacques was in trouble with the finger-wagging critic of *The Athenaeum*, forerunner of *The New Statesman*:

> . . . M. Offenbach follows a pernicious fashion in playing, on the violoncello, that which was not meant for the violoncello; 'transcribed' is a new musical term we find it hard to recognize, even when a Liszt represents, on the piano, Beethoven's Pastoral Symphony, or an Ernst, on the violin, Schubert's wondrous *Erlkönig*. Moreover, the song without words, by Mendelssohn, does not move at the funeral pace chosen by M. Offenbach. We dwell on this particular example, because the offender is both too highly gifted and too young to be permitted to wander from true artistic taste without protest.

With his letter of thanks from Louis-Philippe, his jewel from Queen Victoria, and — for the time being — plenty of money, Jacques was now an acceptable suitor for the hand of Herminie d'Alcain. The comtesse de Vaux acted as his godmother when he was baptized a Catholic, and Jacques and Herminie were married on 14 August 1844. They set up house in a tiny apartment in the passage Saulnier in Montmartre. Immediately, in a modest Bohemian way, they began the regular entertaining for which they were later famous in the musical and theatrical world. When Jacques eventually had his own theatre, he always lived nearby, and on Friday nights — 'les vendredis de Jacques' — friends would come round for a late party after the show. Male members of the cast would be part of the company; no actress ever entered the Offenbach household socially.

But he had as yet no chance to write for a theatre, let alone own one. His career was slow to advance. The director of the Opéra-Comique, M. Basset, was implacable in his refusal to commission an Offenbach work. Money was not plentiful. Times became hard for Jacques and Herminie just as they were starting a family. Their first daughter was born in September 1845, and was christened Céleste-Marianne-Berthe.

If the management of the Opéra-Comique was hostile, Offenbach had won his serious admirers among the critics, and they spoke up for him. He supplied them with good ammunition for their attacks on the authorities. In April 1846 he put on a concert of operatic fragments designed to show off his ability as a dramatic composer. The critic of *La France Musicale* wrote:

> Let me say straight away that if, in organizing this concert, Offenbach wanted to prove his ability to write scores for the Opéra-Comique, he has completely achieved his purpose, for one could not imagine music more melodious, witty, lively and lucid than his; for the sake of melody, and to bring dramatic situations to life, this young composer has the

good sense to sacrifice the element of art that the schools call technique. No doubt he will earn the blame of those gentlemen who compose dry-as-dust music for showing that all their technique gets them nowhere. But, unlike them, he will be able to please the public, and that is not to be despised.

After special praise for certain numbers, including 'a ravishing séguedille', *Sarah la blonde*, and a comic duet, *Meunière et fermière*, the writer continues: 'As I left this delightful evening I predicted that Offenbach would soon be invited to write a score for the Opéra-Comique, and I would be extremely surprised if this opinion did not prove correct.' Basset was cornered by such pressure from this and other critics, and finally commissioned Offenbach to do a one-act operatic setting of a piece called *L'Alcôve* which had been a successful vaudeville at the Palais Royal in 1833. The work was ready in a few months and Roger privately promised Offenbach that he would play the leading role. But when Jacques tried to deliver his score he found that Basset had made himself permanently unavailable. His reason may have been that Offenbach had again been parodying the august — this time Félicien David and his symphonic ode *Le Désert*. David was a Saint-Simonist. These believers in an industrial Utopia were full of their project for a Suez canal, and the desert was therefore a live topic. David's work idealized the desert as the symbol of eternity and denigrated city life; Offenbach wrote a burlesque in which these attitudes were turned upside-down. It delighted the boulevardiers who saw it in the comtesse de Vaux's salon.

Weary of attempting to reach Basset, Offenbach gathered enough resources to mount a 'concert of a new kind' which included a performance of *L'Alcôve*. The audience liked it, and *La France Musicale* asked why on earth Offenbach was being ignored by the Opéra-Comique when they were accepting so many mediocrities. It still made no difference to Basset. But Jacques had a lucky encounter with Adolphe Adam, then forty-three and the successful composer of the ballet *Giselle* and the comic opera *Le Postillon de Longjumeau*. Adam warmly praised the music of *L'Alcôve*. He had recently acquired a theatre[4] of his own which he was soon to open as the Théâtre-Lyrique. He commissioned Offenbach to write a three-act opera. This seemed to be the breakthrough Jacques had longed for. But Adam then began to have money problems, and there were all sorts of delays. His theatre did not open till November, and the production of Offenbach's opera was put off till the spring of 1848.

But by February 1848 France was in revolution. It was another upheaval in the long French struggle for a stable republic, this time with a twentieth-century flavour, for the riots were about automation, redundancies, overmanning, and the right to work. The workers fought the middle class. It was no time for Adam to put on an opera by Offenbach or anyone else. He wrote:

> On 24 February I climbed to the theatre terrace. They were fighting in the rue du Temple, and I saw the passing wounded being directed to the hospitals. At three o'clock some aides-de-camp rode by: 'There is a new government, friends,' they cried; 'shout Vive le Roi!' Nobody shouted anything, but the rioting stopped. Everyone around me was greatly relieved. 'You'll see,' I said to them, 'this is the end of the Monarchy. . . .'[5]

Adam was right. The French insurrection and its counterpart in Sicily inspired a series of mimic revolutions throughout western Europe. A wave of opposition to foreign oppression or domestic injustice (according to the country) spread to Germany, Austria, Czechoslovakia, Poland, Switzerland, Hungary and Italy. England and Belgium, more highly industrialized, were less seriously affected. Jacques Offenbach, however, was not interested in revolutions. He was very poor. He and Herminie scraped together enough money to take their daughter Berthe back to Cologne, where they took a furnished room, and Jacques got hold of an old piano. Though Germany, too, had its revolutionary outburst, there was no fighting in Cologne. But there was a wave of jingoism, and Jacques — now calling himself Jacob again — cashed in on it with two songs, *Der Deutsche Knabe* and *Das Vaterland*, the first in praise of German boys, the second of German girls (who were held to be superior to the Latins). On 14 August 1848 there was a concert to celebrate the six hundredth anniversary of Cologne Cathedral, at which Jacob inappropriately chose to play his fantasia on Rossini's *Guillaume Tell*.

He was introduced to Heinrich Dorn, the Kapellmeister of Cologne, who used to come round and hear his compositions. Dorn remembers Offenbach playing a new number from 'his three-act opera *La Duchesse d'Albe*' for which he was trying in vain to obtain a production. Henseler guesses reasonably that this was the work, with a libretto by Saint-Georges, that Offenbach had earlier written for Adolphe Adam. Another new friend was the writer C. O. Inkermann-Sternau, whom Offenbach asked to adapt a one-act French libretto into German. Inkermann did the work, whereupon, it is said, Offenbach produced a finished score 'with unbelievable rapidity'. No wonder; the libretto was *L'Alcôve*, and the score was already written. All the composer had to do was to copy out the music with the German text underneath. Offenbach's motive for this subterfuge is not clear, unless he wanted to conceal the operation from his French publishers. The work was performed on 9 January 1849 under the title *Marielle, oder Sergeant und Commandant*. It received one cool notice from a little revolutionary newspaper, *Der Wächter am Rhein*, whose editor, the

Theater in Köln.

Sonntag den 7. Januar,
neu einstudirt:

Der Wildschütz.

Komische Oper in 3 Acten, von Alb. Lortzing.
*** „Baculus" Hr. Seebach, als Gast.

Dinstag den 9. Januar:

Concert und Oper

von
Jacob Offenbach.

Unter gefälliger Mitwirkung der Frl. Schloß und
des verehrlichen Männer-Gesang-Vereins.
Erste Abtheilung:
Arie und Lieder, gesungen von Frl. Schloß.
Lieder und Chöre, vorgetragen vom Männer-Ge-
sang-Vereine.
Mehrere Violoncell-Piecen, componirt und vorgetragen von Jacob Offenbach.
Zweite Abtheilung,
zum ersten Male:

Marielle,

oder

Sergeant und Commandant.

Komische Oper von C. O. Sternau. Musik
von Jacob Offenbach.
Unter Leitung des Componisten.
Zu dieser seiner Benefice-Vorstellung ladet er-
gebenst ein
Jacob Offenbach.

Hierbei eine Beilage.

Herausgeber: Jos. DuMont.
Verleger und Drucker: M. DuMont-Schauberg.
Expedition: Breitestraße Nr. 76 u. 78.

3. The *Kölnische Zeitung* announces the première of the German
version of Offenbach's first *opéra-comique*
Courtesy of the Universitätsbibliothek Düsseldorf

poet Carl Cramer, was later alleged to have given Offenbach the idea for *Orphée aux Enfers* (see Appendix A).

In February 1848 Louis-Philippe abdicated. The provisional revolutionary government set up a republic, and introduced universal male suffrage, increasing the electorate from 250,000 to 9,000,000. It was a political miscalculation; the Republicans overlooked the conservatism of the French peasantry. When the new Assembly decided in November that a president with executive powers should be elected by plebiscite, the Second Republic 'committed a delayed suicide'.[6] There was a sprinkling of presidential candidates. To the enlarged electorate one name meant more than any other: Bonaparte. On 10 December 1848 Prince Louis-Napoleon Bonaparte, nephew of the Emperor Napoleon I, became President of the French Republic. Without knowing it the Republicans had acquired a dictator. France was uneasily quiet; but to Offenbach it still seemed a more promising place than Germany. He decided to go back and resume life as Jacques.

CHAPTER III

Cellist, Composer, Impresario
1849–1855

····⊰⊱····

The revolutionaries of 1830 fought for a republic and ended up with a monarchy. The revolutionaries of 1848 fought for and gained a republic, only to see it turn into an empire before their eyes. Offenbach returned from Germany to a Paris that was temporarily peaceful. But while the rival factions in the Assembly were jockeying for power, their elected president, Prince Louis-Napoleon, 'the methodical dreamer in the Elysée Palace'[1], was quietly making his plans; plans which were to culminate in the bloody *coup d'État* of December 1851 — code-name 'Rubicon' — by means of which the President became first dictator and then Emperor. Ambitious as Caesar, Louis-Napoleon saw himself as a man of destiny. The Elysée Palace began to assume the opulence of décor that was later to characterize the interiors of the Second Empire. The presidential ménage took on the trappings of grandeur, and the apparatus of an imperial court came into being before the advent of the Empire itself. Enormous presidential receptions were held twice a week, and Offenbach was well-enough known to be invited to one of these. It was here that he met briefly for the first time the Prince-President of whose future Empire he was to be entertainer-in-chief.

Offenbach was now thirty, of medium height and very thin, with a high forehead, a beak-like nose, and long blond hair of which he was immensely proud. There was a touch of the dandy about him, and he sported a monocle, which was later replaced by pince-nez. He was still thought of as the talented young cellist of the salons, with some successful minor compositions to his credit. He had, however, made no advance in his chosen career as a composer for the theatre. Disheartened at having to continue playing for fashionable parties, he even neglected his cello technique, and was scolded by a Republican critic because he contented himself with playing just well enough to satisfy the bourgeoisie and the aristocracy. He augmented his meagre income by supplying small items of musical interest to the papers. His hopes were raised momentarily when an influential friend secured him an introduction to M. Perrin, the new director of the Opéra-Comique, but nothing came of the meeting. The doors of the musical theatre were closed to him.

The theatres of Paris were administered at that time by the Ministry of the Interior. In 1806 Napoleon I had established a hierarchy of theatres, each with its own type of repertory, from which it was not allowed to stray. In order of status the theatres and their functions were:

I. *Théâtre-Français*: the Emperor's theatre — comedy and tragedy. The company that performed in this theatre was, and still is, called the Comédie-Française;
and
Odéon: the Empress's theatre (a subsidiary of the Théâtre-Français) — comedy only.

II. *Opéra*: Imperial Academy of Music — 'consecrated' to song and dance.

III. *Opéra-Comique* — all kinds of comedy and drama, with songs, ariettas and ensembles;
and
Opéra-Buffa (a subsidiary of the Opéra-Comique) — Italian opera only. This theatre came to be known as the Théâtre des Italiens. It subsequently put on operas of all schools and nationalities, and acquired the same status as the Opéra-Comique.

IV. Various secondary theatres: *Gaîté*, *Ambigu-Comique*, *Gymnase*, *Variétés*, *Vaudeville*, etc.

Ironically enough it was not one of the 'lyrical', or musical, houses, but the Théâtre-Français that gave Offenbach his first theatrical appointment. In 1850 the Comédie-Française was in a state of anarchy. 'The public had forgotten the way to the Théâtre-Français,' wrote Arsène Houssaye; '*that theatrical republic was heading straight for ruin.*'[2] The constitution of France's principal theatre was laid down under the *Décret de Moscou*, so called because Napoleon I had worked it out while waiting outside Moscow in 1812 for the Russians to surrender. The company was a co-operative, comprising *sociétaires*, senior actors who were shareholders; and *pensionnaires*, who were salaried juniors. There was no director; the *sociétaires* were responsible for the administrative and artistic direction of the theatre. This laudably democratic idea had turned out to be disastrous in practice (and indeed it was bizarre that Napoleon I should have invented a rulerless democracy). 'One actor wanted this, another that; this one wanted to play too much, that one not to play at all.' Eventually the actress Rachel, the most influential *sociétaire* by virtue of her unique drawing-power and her immense international reputation (all of which made her somewhat unpopular with the others) decided that without a director the company would perish. She battled with her colleagues and coaxed and wheedled politicians until the President was persuaded to overrule the *Décret de Moscou* and to appoint Arsène Houssaye as director of the Théâtre-Français.

Houssaye had come to Paris at the age of seventeen to escape from a deadening bourgeois existence in the provinces. He loved people, life and the arts, and sought out and relished every experience that Paris had to offer; fighting with students at the barricades, sharing an apartment with Théophile Gautier and Gérard de Nerval, having love affairs, writing poetry, meeting the rich and famous; and all the time observing, remembering and recording. At the end of a life lasting from the year of Waterloo to the days of the Dreyfus affair he left, in six volumes of *Confessions*, the most comprehensive chronicle of nineteenth-century Parisian life. In his humorous, passionate and occasionally ruthless personality Rachel saw a born impresario. When she had her way and his appointment at the Théâtre-Français was confirmed Houssaye wasted no time:

> I rushed over to Frederick Lemaître. On the way I met Offenbach.
> 'Do you want to make a revolution at the Comédie-Française?'
> 'Yes, making a row is my job (*je suis un homme de bruit*).'
> 'Good, I appoint you conductor. There are only two violins at the Théâtre-Français; you can have four.'
> That night Offenbach was enthroned majestically in the orchestra pit.[3]

The appointment was unpopular with the members of the company, who were afraid that music would begin to play too big a part in their temple of the spoken word.

> 'No sooner was I installed', wrote Offenbach, 'than I saw that I would fight in vain against the notion that at the Théâtre-Français you have to have completely impossible music and an execrable orchestra. The *sociétaires* especially weren't interested. I had got the management to agree that they wouldn't take the curtain up before the bell rang, as was done in the cheaper theatres, and because of this we ran into insurmountable problems every night. The actors, once they were on stage, didn't want to wait; the stage manager, for his part, refused to take the curtain up, having had strict orders from M. Houssaye, and there were endless aggravations, complaints and squabbles. . . . After a while I didn't conduct any more except when a conductor was absolutely essential, or in the plays of which the music was an integral part, such as Gounod's *Ulysse*.'[4]

But it was obvious that Houssaye was revitalizing the Comédie-Française. He had the theatre sumptuously redecorated, put up the seat prices and enlarged the orchestra pit (which meant losing a few stalls, and led to another row with the actors); he varied the classical repertoire with modern works by Hugo, Dumas, and Musset. The audiences returned and when the *sociétaires* received their first dividends for years, they were happy enough to bury the hatchet. Houssaye supported Offenbach and commissioned him to compose new incidental music and entr'actes. As he later recalled:

> Offenbach worked wonders; how many operas and operettas of his own invention he played in the entr'actes! He took up in turn the violin of Lully to accompany Molière, and the violin of Hoffmann to accompany Alfred de Musset. And what a gay companion he was when his eyes didn't stray from his wife (what a respectable beauty she was!). But alas, I have seen him torn apart by cruel passions.[5]

How much Houssaye was implying is not clear. Offenbach was certainly devoted to his wife and children. Touching on the subject in a biography of his grandfather, Jacques Brindejont-Offenbach was no more specific:

> Precisely because of his love for his family the life of Offenbach (if we ignore his regular and routine peccadilloes) passed without incident between his desk, his rehearsals and his travelling; one could not make a novel out of his adventures, and today I know of absolutely nothing confidential which I have to conceal, forget or censor.[6]

Jacques now had two daughters, and Herminie was relieved to have regular money coming in, although his salary — 600 francs a year — was modest for the time. Nor did it help when Jacques' generosity got the better of him and he took pity on anyone with a hard luck story, genuine or otherwise. He was extravagant; money in the pocket was for spending and sharing. The important thing now was that for the first time his music was being performed regularly in a theatre. He had made the long-awaited leap from cellist to composer.

Early in Houssaye's reign at the Comédie-Française he arranged to present *Le Chandelier*, a romantic comedy by Alfred de Musset. In the second act there was a love song, the *Chanson de Fortunio*, which Offenbach set to music. Delaunay, the young actor playing the part of Fortunio, had a beautiful speaking voice, but it was discovered too late that, when he tried to sing, his voice became 'grating and menacing'. In the end he spoke the verses while the orchestra played the melody softly. The song came into its own years later when it was made the basis of a successful one-act operetta.

Offenbach has left us his own record of this period: 'I also wrote some music for Mürger's *Le Bonhomme jadis*, Dumas's *Romulus* and Plouvier's *Le Songe d'une nuit d'été*; in *Valeria* I wrote the verses that Rachel sang so beautifully; finally several entr'actes for the *Murillo* of Aylie Langlé, for which Meyerbeer composed the serenade.'[7] On the first night of *Murillo* Meyerbeer's serenade was encored. Offenbach's entr'actes, on the other hand, were hardly heard above the hubbub of the audience. But Adolphe Adam was in the audience, and he at least was listening. Reviewing the performance in *L'Assemblée Nationale* he wrote:

> Your Boeotian ears did not discern that among the three pieces, the Introduction, the Serenade and the Entr'acte, there was a little masterpiece of colour, originality, grace and subtlety — the entr'acte between the first and second acts. If it had been played to you in a concert at the Conservatoire you would have stamped and shouted encore. This, combined with the memory of the beautiful choruses of Gounod's *Ulysse*, proves that there is no point in casting musical pearls before . . . the stalls of the Théâtre-Français. Brindeau sings, with a charming voice and a style that reveals a good musician, a serenade which is not perhaps as perfect as the entr'acte I mentioned, *but which is not unworthy of the illustrious name with which it is signed!*[8]

The italics are those of André Martinet, Offenbach's first biographer, who adds, 'Grande fut la stupéfaction de Meyerbeer et Jacques.'

On 2 December 1851 Parisians awoke to find the army in control of the city and posters on the walls explaining that the President was determined to foil the Assembly's treacherous plans. The *coup d'État* was swift, brutal and efficient. A brief liberal opposition was overcome; in Paris alone 380 people were killed, many by firing squad without trial. There were 26,000 arrests throughout France, and most of those convicted were either temporarily exiled or deported for life. This extreme brutality was a mistake on the part of the President. It was unnecessary, was never forgotten, and later rebounded on its perpetrator. But for the present Louis-Napoleon had seized personal control of France. As a Bonaparte he had plenty of popular support, and within a year he was able to ask the people of France to vote for the restoration of the Empire. Everything was above board. The dictator held a plebiscite and won by a large majority; the people chose Caesar for their king. On 2 December 1852, again dramatizing himself by selecting the anniversary both of Austerlitz and the coronation of Napoleon I, Prince Louis-Napoleon was received in Paris as Napoleon III, Emperor of the French.

In 1853 Offenbach composed two one-act 'little operas', *Le Trésor à Mathurin* and *Pepito*.[9] He enlisted some singers from the Opéra-Comique

LA FAMILLE IMPÉRIALE.

THE IMPERIAL FAMILY.

4. Napoleon III with the Empress Eugénie and their son Napoleon Louis, the Prince Imperial

Bibliothèque nationale

to give a concert performance of *Le Trésor à Mathurin* at the salle Herz. The cast were enthusiastic, and Jacques hoped they might urge their new director, M. Perrin, to accept the piece. In a favourable review of the performance the critic of *Le Ménestrel* suggested that Perrin must surely now give the young composer a chance. When *Pepito* was given again at the Variétés later in the year, the weighty critic Jules Janin joined those who deplored the Opéra-Comique's neglect of Offenbach. Perrin finally commissioned Offenbach to write a three-act work, provisionally entitled *Blanche*, to a libretto by Saint-Georges. The idea of using this particular libretto may well have come from Offenbach himself. We know that he already had in his cupboard *La Duchesse d'Albe* — three acts, librettist Saint-Georges — which had never been produced. It would have been characteristic of him to try to sell it to Perrin under a new title. We cannot tell: new or old, the piece was never performed. A century later, Offenbach's grandson, Jacques Brindejont–Offenbach, found the manuscript of *La Duchesse d'Albe* among the composer's papers.

In 1857 a revised version of *Le Trésor à Mathurin* was presented successfully at Les Bouffes-Parisiens under the title *Le Mariage aux lanternes*. Michel Carré now appeared on the bill as co-librettist with Léon Battu. Both *Le Mariage aux lanternes* and *Pepito* contain lyrical writing of some depth of feeling. The use of the *scena* in *Pepito* shows Offenbach tackling an extended dramatic form. In *Le Mariage aux lanternes* there is one number, *Quatuor de l'Angélus*, that reveals his debt to Mozart in the lyricism of its vocal writing:

Ex. 4

One of the pleasing features of Offenbach's earlier operettas is that in them he so often combines this lyrical flair with his skill in part-writing. In comparison with his later successes there are fewer spectacular solo melodies, and more music for larger vocal ensembles, in which the music is imbued with Offenbach's love of *Die Zauberflöte* and *Così fan tutte*. On hearing such passages it comes as no surprise to learn that Offenbach's bedside book, which he took with him on all his travels, was a life of Mozart. Unfortunately most of the librettos of these early pieces are so dated that they are seldom performed nowadays, and as a result much fresh and delightful music by the young Offenbach is no longer heard. In his six major operetta successes, *Orphée aux Enfers*, *La Belle Hélène*, *La Vie parisienne*, *Barbe-bleue*, *La Grande-Duchesse de Gerolstein* and *La Périchole* — all comedies — the lyrical writing occurs for the most part in solos and duets, any music for larger groups being comic or satirical.

When later Offenbach founded his Bouffes-Parisiens, legal restrictions confined him to writing for four characters at the most. He made a virtue of necessity by composing small contrapuntal ensembles of the kind mentioned. When the restriction on the number of performers was lifted, and perhaps because he worked at such speed, he tended to abandon counterpoint in favour of homophonic choruses. There is some lyrical contrapuntal writing in later pieces, usually when the subject-matter is romantic or pastoral, but Offenbach's works in this genre have not had the staying-power of his comedies. Thus a quantity of his lyric and dramatic writing is unknown; lost to modern audiences because it is linked to the inferior librettos by which the composer was hampered, or with which he was too easily satisfied. Many of the operettas failed to last because they fell between two stools: they were neither funny enough nor dramatically strong enough to hold their own. In the end Offenbach's fame rests on six of his comedies and *Les Contes d'Hoffmann*.

This can lead to an unbalanced assessment of his work. There is little in the familiar comedies to suggest that their composer was capable of writing the stronger passages of *Hoffmann*, which is thought of as a late and isolated masterpiece. But an examination of his earlier works shows that the composer of *Les Contes d'Hoffmann* had long been developing; and failed to come to maturity sooner only because he had not found an adequate vehicle on which to exercise his powers. Although he conducted some incidental music for the play *Les Contes d'Hoffmann* in 1851, it was twenty-five years before he decided to make it into an opera. Perhaps that is no cause for regret. Offenbach realized the potential of the play eventually; in the meantime he made his dazzling contribution to the world's repertoire of light music. But in the early 1850s he was disheartened by the intransigence of the Opéra-Comique, and by the frustrations of his job at the Théâtre-Français. He continued to compose dance music which was played in the theatre and sometimes published, and he was occasionally noticed by members of the Imperial family. In an interval at the theatre Prince Jérôme enjoyed a gay schottische, insisted on an encore, and sent Offenbach a diamond tie-pin the next day. Offenbach dedicated to Princess Mathilde a collection of melodies entitled *Les Voix mystérieuses*. Unfortunately these petty social successes merely served to underline his failure to do what he really wanted.

Jacques wrote to his sister Ranetta:

Cellist, Composer, Impresario: 1849–1855

9 May 1854

Dear Netta,

Last year I wrote you a confidential letter about my situation. . . . Unfortunately my situation hasn't improved; I would almost say that it is still worse, for I can only last another six months: the golden future I dreamt about doesn't come, and every day a little more hope goes out of the window. Believe me, dear Netta, I am not exaggerating my position . . . Living gets more expensive here from day to day and money is becoming scarce . . . In my position, unlike that of some others, a certain degree of luxury is necessary. I wouldn't even be able to meet my wife's needs if she did not have such a friendly brother who gives her presents of all sorts. My wife could not make do with three evening ensembles. I had to buy her another gown; it cost me 250 francs to buy, plus 89 francs of expenses. I'm telling you that so that you can realize how dear life is. The size of my apartment doesn't allow me to have someone living there the whole time, and I am now paying 1,000 francs. My wife's sister is here, her brother pays 150 francs a month for her board. Nevertheless I'm glad she's going back to Marseille at the beginning of winter. Never mind all that; you will see that this letter is superfluous when I tell you that the project I've had for some years to go to America for a while will certainly come about at the beginning of September. My wife will then go with the children to her father's house at Marseille, and I shall store my furniture in some room so that I can get it back and not have to buy new stuff if I come back to Europe — as I expect I shall . . . As for the concert, it's very difficult; it is now well into the season; that would not hinder things, but the concerts this winter haven't done any business. Even the man who gives the best concert every year hasn't been successful. People are economizing with money and don't want to go to concerts. People who used to buy ten or twelve of my tickets have only taken two this year. The reason is this damned [Crimean] war. Above all, the rich folk have been leaving in the last two weeks, specially in the last few days. All those who have had the time and the money are going away because of the cholera epidemic. Believe me, it is a serious decision to set off for America and leave my family, but it has to be. . . .[10]

But he changed his mind. Possibly he now saw that conditions were favourable for the realization of another dream. In a later account of his years with the Comédie-Française, he wrote:

I stayed at the Théâtre-Français for five years, from 1850 to 1855. It was during this time that, faced with the continuing impossibility of having my works performed, I had the idea of starting a musical theatre myself. It seemed to me that comic opera no longer existed at the Opéra-Comique; that truly light, gay and witty music, music with life in it, in

47

fact, was gradually being forgotten. The composers working for the Opéra-Comique were creating little grand operas. I saw that here was a job to be done by the young musicians who, like myself, were fretting in vain at the doors of the opera houses. [11]

He began to keep his eye open for premises where he might establish his own theatre. At this time Paris was looking forward to a great exhibition, planned for the spring of 1855, which was to demonstrate to the world the spectacular growth of French industry and commerce, and reinforce the prestige of the new Emperor. The site was on the Champs-Élysées (Baron Haussmann had not yet redeveloped Paris, and the present avenue des Champs-Élysées was an allée, planted but unpaved). Offenbach heard that the salle Lacaze, a tiny wooden-built theatre near the exhibition site, had fallen vacant. Lacaze was a conjuror who had been given permission to build the place after his service in the Garde nationale, on the grounds that the revolution had deprived him of the location where he previously sold magic tricks. He had now gone out of business. His little barrack-room of a theatre was nothing much, but the public were bound to flock to the neighbourhood, and that was enough.

On 24 February 1855 Offenbach made his application to the Minister of State for the Fine Arts for a licence to open a theatre for the presentation of musical shows:

> I have the honour to beg your Excellency to grant a licence in my favour for an entertainment to be presented in the Champs-Élysées. My intention would be to present *harlequinades*, pantomimes in one or more acts. I would be aiming, above all, to introduce to Paris the genre of the Italian *fantoccini* (marionettes), modified to suit French taste, and to offer new and original amusements of a kind to please both those of cultivated intelligence and the general public. In addition I would put on *tableaux vivants* reproducing the most beautiful subjects of historical painting, and, finally, plays for two or three characters with new music (which would moreover apply equally to the pantomimes, harlequinades and *fantoccini*). The use in this sort of show of music composed with skill and care would not only result in giving an unaccustomed emphasis to a particular kind of popular entertainment, but would also offer a fairly wide opening to any young composers who might come along to try their strength and show what their talent is like. Now that the Universal Exhibition is opening, you will no doubt approve, Minister, the project I have outlined in brief. Putting it into action would give the innumerable foreigners who will be flooding into Paris a show in good taste, where at present there are only some more or less vulgar burlesques. [12]

Aware that there were a score of rivals in the field, Offenbach then began canvassing support. Luckily his position at the Comédie-Française and his reputation in court circles were in his favour. He hit on the ingenious idea of composing a suite of dances to be called *Le Décaméron dramatique*. He asked ten famous writers — Achard, Augier, Doucet, Dumas, Gautier, Gozlan, Houssaye, Méry, Musset and Prémaray — to supply him with short verses. He composed ten dances (waltzes, polkas, mazurkas, etc.) each dance being 'inspired' by one of the quatrains. Every dance was dedicated to a famous actress — Rachel, Dubois, Madeleine Brohan, Fix, Augustine Brohan, Allan, Favart, Denain, Nathalie, Bonval — and was published with her portrait and the appropriate verse at the head. Intentionally or not, with his flattery-by-dedication Offenbach had made allies out of twenty of the most influential figures in the theatre. Houssaye could have told him that, with the great Rachel on his side, he need not have bothered about the other nineteen.

Offenbach's applications had to satisfy the Prefect of Police, the Minister of State, the Ministry of the Interior and others. While waiting for this battery of officials to make up their minds, and trying to raise the necessary money, he amused himself by writing a little farce called *Oyayaye ou la Reine des Îles*. The story concerns Râcle-à-Mort (Scrape-to-Death), a double-bass player at the Ambigu, who is sacked by his conductor for falling asleep over his instrument. Feeling that his talents are not recognized by an ungrateful country he sets sail for America, but is wrecked on a desert island and taken prisoner by cannibals. They remove all his clothes except his hat, collar, tie and boots, and order him to entertain their queen, Oyayaye. Râcle-à-Mort sets the royal laundrywoman's bill to music, with variations in the Italian style, and has this sung to Oyayaye. But the cannibal queen is glancing at the bass-player with hungry eyes. He distracts her for a little by playing the double-bass. She is delighted but still hungry. He plays a reed-pipe, which goes down well but again only wins a temporary reprieve. Not wishing either to become the queen's dinner or to prolong his role as a naked male Scheherazade, Râcle-à-Mort uses his double-bass as a boat, and, with a handkerchief for a sail, makes his escape, cocking a snook, as he sails away, at Oyayaye, Queen of the Isles.

The piece was accepted by Hervé and opened on 26 June 1855 at the Folies-Nouvelles. By that time, however, Offenbach can hardly have had time even to go and see it. Things had come to a head quickly. The capital for his theatre venture had suddenly fallen into his lap. One of Jacques' newer friends was Henri de Villemessant, an extrovert and energetic newspaper owner who had recently founded *Le Figaro*. Villemessant was a wholehearted supporter of imaginative private enterprise, and something of a gambler. In the face of ridicule he had backed the two young

5. The composer's friend and backer, Henri de Villemessant, founder of *Le Figaro*. After a photo by Nadar

Collection Viollet

men who started Les Magasins du Louvre, one of the world's first department stores. According to his memoirs he now went to Jacques and told him he had 'raised' 20,000 francs, which may in fact have come out of his own pocket.

The carefully worded applications and the judicious string-pulling had done the trick with the authorities. On 4 June 1855 Offenbach received a licence authorizing him to open the salle Lacaze and to present shows of the following categories:

1. Pantomime harlequinades with five characters.
2. Comic plays with words and music, for two or three characters.
3. Conjuring, juggling, fantasmagoria, Chinese shadows and marionettes.
4. Physical feats and acrobatics.
5. Exhibitions of interesting objects.
6. Dance routines for five or more dancers.
7. Chansonnettes for one or two performers in or out of costume.

Article 21 of the five page document[13] read: 'This little show will have for its title: *Les Bouffes-Parisiens.*'

CHAPTER IV

The French Creation
1855–1857

······

A company was duly formed. Offenbach would draw a salary as manager and receive the royalties on his music. Villemessant was to have a backer's percentage. He had just started publishing *Le Figaro* and regarded the Bouffes-Parisiens as a twin enterprise. It was decided to open the theatre on 5 July 1855, which gave Offenbach less than a month in which to equip the theatre, recruit actors, orchestra and staff, find authors to write material for the opening programme — and compose the music.

There was a crisis when the authors who had promised to write the prologue withdrew. Offenbach could find no author available and willing to take on the last-minute job, till he remembered that Ludovic Halévy, nephew of his former mentor Fromental Halévy, was said to have ambitions as a dramatist. Offenbach rushed over from the theatre to see him, charmed him into consent, and then told him the snags — he would have to write for three performers only, and they were already cast; he must incorporate some material that was by now written and in rehearsal, and so on. Halévy accepted the conditions as a challenge; so began one of the most felicitous collaborations of nineteenth-century theatre. When Henri Meilhac later joined the team they produced, among many others, the librettos for *La Belle Hélène*, *La Vie parisienne*, *La Grande-Duchesse de Gerolstein*, and *La Périchole*. Meilhac and Halévy, whom Offenbach called 'Meil' and 'Hal', also wrote the libretto of Bizet's *Carmen*.

The limiting clauses in Offenbach's theatre licence were the result of the Napoleonic decree of 1806, under which each theatre was restricted to its own genre. The size of the orchestra was not decreed by law, but space and economics limited it to a maximum of sixteen players.[1] Thus the scale of the production was predetermined. The nature of the material was governed by Offenbach's love of satire, parody and caricature. His ideas were justified from the start by the enormous popularity of *Les Deux Aveugles*, a 'bouffonnerie musicale' about two swindling Parisian beggars. This piece was the hit of the opening night. Ironically, it had almost been cut after the dress rehearsal. None of the invited audience had laughed — a well-known characteristic of invited audiences. Villemessant and others thought that the comedy went too far and might be offensive. But Offenbach held out for giving the piece a chance. Within months this little one-act burlesque was probably the most popular single item of theatrical entertainment in Europe. All Europe came to Paris for the great exhibition, and the Bouffes-Parisiens began to build the international audience that remained faithful for decades and included such disparate admirers as Tolstoy and Thackeray.

The rest of the opening bill consisted of the prologue *Entrez, Messieurs, Mesdames* by Méry and Halévy (who used the pseudonym Jules Servières to protect his reputation as a government official), *Une Nuit blanche*, a pastoral 'opéra-comique'; and *Arlequin Barbier*, a 'pantomime' with music based on themes from Rossini's *Barbiere di Siviglia*, adapted by 'Alfred Lange', who was Offenbach. This bill was the blueprint for the Bouffes-Parisiens programmes in the early years. When a new one-acter was completed it could be inserted, and an old one temporarily dropped. In this way the company built up a large repertoire and there was always at least one old favourite in the programme.

Pradeau and Berthelier, who played the two blind beggars in *Les Deux Aveugles*, became stars. Another future star soon arrived. One day Berthelier came to see Offenbach. With him was his mistress, a twenty-two-year-old blonde called Hortense Schneider. She had recently arrived from Bordeaux and wanted an audition. Offenbach heard her sing. "Are you going to have more singing lessons?" he asked. Playing safe, she answered yes. "Miserable child! If you dare start lessons again I will smack your bottom and tear up your contract, for I am engaging you at two hundred francs a month, do you hear?"[2] Hortense Schneider made her debut at the Bouffes on 31 August 1855 in *Le Violoneux*. She was instantly adored. Within the next twelve years the world saw her as La Belle Hélène, La Grande-Duchesse and La Périchole.

The immediate success of the Bouffes had created a new problem. It was obvious that the show could outlast the exhibition, which was due to close in the late autumn. But after that nobody was going to come through the snow to the darkened Champs-Élysées. In the passage Choiseul there was a small theatre known as the Théâtre des Jeunes Élèves. For many years it had been run by Louis Comte, a conjuror and illusionist. Comte, a Swiss Protestant, had put on respectable shows for children. His son Charles was now in charge, and welcomed the idea of a change. Offenbach went into business with him and obtained a new licence. The theatre was redesigned. *Le Ménestrel* gave its readers an advance description:

The Comte theatre, entirely demolished, will be replaced by an elegant new theatre constructed to the designs of M. Lehmann. The contractor, M. Berlot, has agreed a figure with the management for which he undertakes to hand over the theatre on 2 December at midnight. The new theatre will cost 80,000 fr; it will be extremely attractive and above all very comfortable.

The body of the theatre will look like a reproduction in miniature of the Théâtre-Italien. It will have the same interior layout, except that between the open and enclosed boxes there will be a stalls circle. There will be thirty-five boxes and a dozen stage boxes; the stage boxes will be surmounted by a canopy. The curtain will be painted by Cambon. The present orchestra of sixteen musicians will be increased to thirty.[3]

The theatre was renamed the Théâtre des Bouffes-Parisiens. It was again knocked down and rebuilt in 1863, and now fronts onto the rue Monsigny, but the back of the theatre still opens into the old glass-roofed arcade of the passage Choiseul, where Offenbach's audiences used to meet and chat in the intervals.

Le Ménestrel continued: 'Works already announced for the opening include a prologue written for the occasion by our poet Méry, entitled *Bilboquet ayant fait fortune*, another piece by the same author with music by M. Ernest Lépine, and, finally, a *bouffonnerie* by MM. J. Servières and Offenbach.' The *bouffonnerie* was *Ba-ta-clan*, described as a '*chinoiserie musicale*'. Taking advantage of Offenbach's newly acquired permission to use four characters instead of three, Halévy invented Fé-ni-han, ruler of Ché-i-no-or, an oriental kingdom, and his followers Ké-ki-ka-ko, Ko-ko-ri-ko and Fé-an-nich-ton. Much of the comedy arose from their use of nonsense-Chinese, just as later Ko-Ko, Pish-Tush and Pooh-Bah heard the Mikado's retinue sing pseudo-Japanese gibberish. But if Gilbert and Sullivan got the idea from *Ba-ta-clan*, Offenbach may have known of a piece in the Cologne carnival of 1841, called *Za Ze Zi Zo Zu, oder die beflügelte Nase, eine chinesische Dummheit* ('Za Ze Zi Zo Zu or the Winged Nose, a Chinese Farce'). An extra twist in *Ba-ta-clan* is that the four principal characters turn out to be Frenchmen in disguise.

In the score Offenbach, as well as amusing himself with pseudo-oriental jokiness, wrote a parody of Bellini to which Halévy supplied an absurd Italian text (Exs. 5a and 5b).

In the finale Meyerbeer, as so often, is the target of Offenbach's satire. Fé-ni-han, about to be executed, wishes to die in the noble manner of the Huguenots, or rather, in the noble manner of *Les Huguenots*. Interrupting a noisy battle-hymn, *Le Ba-ta-clan*, which has a striking resemblance to the opening bars of *Carmen* (1875), he calls on his comrades to join him in the chorale *Ein' feste Burg*, the phrases of which are interspersed with

Ex. 5a

Ex. 5b

ridiculous vocal parodies of trumpet fanfares. Here we have Offenbach parodying Meyerbeer quoting Luther. Pelion is piled on Ossa: the essence of farce.

Ba-ta-clan became as big a hit as *Les Deux Aveugles*. This triumph was of crucial importance in the history of the Bouffes. Where *Les Deux Aveugles* had guaranteed success for a season — while the exhibition lasted —

Ba-ta-clan demonstrated that the Bouffes had survived the transplant to a proper theatre, indicating that the enterprise had a chance of becoming a permanent institution. A house style had emerged, with Offenbach's music as the unifying element. But Offenbach was more than just the composer. As an entrepreneur and artistic director of immensely strong personality he controlled the style and dramatic content of the presentations. He would often have an idea of his own for an operetta, choose a librettist, and then work closely with him on the form of the piece as well as composing the music. He even suggested song titles. Whoever his collaborator, Offenbach's own wit, his percipience of social foibles and hatred of pretentiousness were fingerprints in all the operettas.

And there was more to it than that. Offenbach saw that in the Bouffes-Parisiens he had an opportunity to restore the true tradition of *opéra-comique*, which had been vitiated by the inflated ideas of modern composers. In July 1856 he announced a 'Competition for an Operetta in One Act', the winning work to be performed at the Bouffes the following spring. With the announcement of the *concours* he circulated as a guide to the candidates a three-thousand-word article on *opéra-comique*. It was published in full by both *Le Ménestrel*[4] and *Revue et Gazette Musicale de Paris*.[5] This essay was virtually a manifesto defining the function and artistic intentions of the Bouffes-Parisiens. It began with history:

> *Opéra-comique* is an eminently French creation. Although formed in imitation of the Italian *opera buffa*, a genre personified in the middle of the last century by Pergolesi, it is different by reason of national temperament; when the French took over the form they made it their own. Where an Italian would give free rein to his verve and imagination, a Frenchman would make a point of mischievousness, common sense and taste. Whereas the Italian would sacrifice everything to gaiety, for the Frenchman wit was paramount. . . .
>
> What else is *opéra-comique*, in fact, but sung vaudeville? The term itself points to that: gay, diverting, amusing stuff. That is how the famous creators of the form understood and practised it. To prove it one only has to cast a glance over this special chapter of musical history.
>
> The first *opéra-comique* really worthy of the name, *Blaise le savetier* by Philidor, was performed at the *Foire Saint-Laurent* on 9 March 1759. There one can find the germ of the qualities that were to characterize the genre; they were developed later with brilliance by more skilful masters. Simplicity of melodic form, restraint in instrumentation: such are the distinguishing merits of the early compositions.

Offenbach detects three phases in the history of *opéra-comique*. First there came the school created by Philidor, expanded by Monsigny, consolidated by Grétry and continued by Dalayrac until, influenced by notions of political and artistic reform, the genre suddenly changed ground and broadened its scope. In doing so it lost something of its original purity:

> That was the time of the great successes of Méhul, Lesueur, Cherubini and Berton in *Montano et Stephanie*; it was the reign of the *harmonists*. They displayed a lofty disdain for 'little music'. . . . This fashion for 'grand music' — a tyranny like all fashions — obliged the two most distinguished representatives of *opéra-comique* to abandon for a while the genre that had made them famous. To obtain pardon for their initial successes Dalayrac wrote *Camille ou le souterrain* and the composer of *Le Tableau parlant* (Grétry) wrote *Pierre le Grand* and *Guillaume Tell*.

Offenbach's 'second phase' ended with Hérold, whose *Zampa* and *Le Pré aux clercs* were transitional works leading to a new mixed style:

> From this moment the light and graceful genre of the early days almost disappeared from the stage, giving way to the larger-scale works, not yet grand opera but no longer *opéra-comique*. There was a mixed genre, the *semi-seria* of the Italians, such as Weber used for *Der Freischütz*, *Oberon* and *Euryanthe*, Mozart for *Die Zauberflöte* and Winter for *La Famille suisse*. In this third phase one would include Auber, Halévy, Thomas and the young musicians who to a greater or lesser extent were the followers of these masters of *opéra-comique*.

Offenbach observes that Halévy twice reverted to his own earlier manner, notably in *L'Éclair*, 'a masterpiece of harmonic and melodic invention written on the returning tide of success of the *comédies à ariettes*'. He sums up with a sentimental but serviceable metaphor: *opéra-comique* began as a limpid little stream flowing between green banks. It widened into a great river with imposing waves. Although the stream was part of the river its nature as a stream was destroyed. The composer/impresario then takes over. Offenbach, in a strong position, can now afford to be generous to his former enemies:

> It is the duty of the official theatres to encourage the form and help it to develop. They fulfil this task zealously. The men who direct them are obviously intelligent and active. It is not their fault if the genre has taken on proportions that often make it unrecognizable.
>
> The Bouffes-Parisiens wishes to try to revive the true original genre ('le genre primitif et vrai'[6]). Our very licence puts us under an obligation to do so. So far we have concentrated on keeping to this idea, but we feel that our efforts should go further. Without any pretensions, still working in a modest and limited sphere, we think we can do a great

service to art and artists. We have had some success in reviving the form of the musical sketches of the old *opéra-comique* and the kind of farce that produced the theatre of Cimarosa and the first Italian masters. We intend, not only to go on with this, but also to mine the inexhaustible vein of French gaiety of the past. Our only ambition is to 'write short', but if you think about it for a moment that is no mean ambition. In an opera that lasts barely three quarters of an hour, where one may only have four characters on stage, and an orchestra of thirty musicians at most, the ideas and melodies have to be in hard cash. Note, too, that with this restricted orchestra — which was after all enough for Mozart and Cimarosa — it is very difficult to conceal the mistakes and lack of experience which would be covered up in an orchestra of eighty musicians.

Far be it from us to be reactionary or to disparage new techniques. We do not say that looking back to the past is the last word in progress; but, granted that the genre we are developing under the licence of the Bouffes-Parisiens is only the first step on the ladder, there still has to be a first step if we are to climb any higher. The present demands of *opéra-comique* can easily put a young composer under a strain; one has to be a writer of experience to attempt a three-act work without tripping up. With rare exceptions no one can do it successfully until his talent has matured.

The purpose of inviting young composers to take part in a musical contest is to provide creative artists worthy of the French theatre. The theatre I am making available for their efforts asks only three things from them: skill, knowledge and originality. Is that too much to ask? Perhaps, but I cannot think of a better deal for an aspiring musician.

For the contest the jury, under the chairmanship of Auber, consisted of Melleville, Fromental Halévy, Ambroise Thomas, Scribe, Saint-Georges, Leborne, Gounod, Victor Massé, Bazin and Gevaert. After the initial tests the six candidates on the short list were given a libretto to set: *Le Docteur Miracle*, by Ludovic Halévy and Léon Battu. The equal winners were Georges Bizet and Charles Lecocq, whose versions of the work were performed alternately in April 1857.

As well as encouraging young composers Offenbach went further afield in his search for material with which to enrich the programmes at the Bouffes. Adolphe Adam had been one of the first senior composers to recognize Offenbach's talent and help him. Offenbach now asked him to write a work for the Bouffes, and he responded with *Les Pantins de Violette*. It was produced on 29 April 1856, less than a week before the composer's sudden death at the age of fifty-two. Rossini was persuaded to give permission for a revival of his early Venetian disaster *Il Signor Bruschino*.

Translated and revised by de Forges, and with some musical editing by Offenbach, it met with little more success in Paris than it had had in Venice thirty years before.

But after some research in Vienna Offenbach brought off a coup that won over some former critics. In the *Revue des Deux Mondes* Scudo wrote 'Much will be forgiven M. Offenbach for laying his hand on an almost unknown little masterpiece of Mozart, *Der Schauspiel-Direktor*, an operetta in one act which Offenbach has had the happy idea of presenting under the title *L'Impresario*.'[7] With this production, the Bouffes, already an established success with the public, acquired a cachet of respectability in the eyes of the highbrows. Before long the Emperor commanded a performance of *Les Deux Aveugles* at the Tuileries. The Empress Eugénie called for an encore of the bolero. Next day the company visited the comte de Morny and entertained his guests with *Ba-ta-clan* and *Pepito*.

In the summer of 1856, rather than announcing a summer closure it made sense for Offenbach to move his company back to the Champs-Élysées. The little salle Marigny was re-opened, and although there was no Exhibition this year, the Bouffes drew a summer public from June to September. Presumably expenses were reduced by laying off some musicians, actors and staff. *La Rose de Saint-Flour*, *Les Dragées du baptême* (celebrating the baptism of the Imperial Prince) and *Le 66!* were added to the repertoire, plus a *tableau vivant*, *Les Bergers de Watteau*.[8] Offenbach's ceaseless inventiveness was keeping the company alive and fresh. By May 1857, when they set out for a season in London the Bouffes had a repertoire of nineteen Offenbach operettas and several others to choose from.

The English tour was designed to boost the company's finances, which were flagging because of Offenbach's incorrigible extravagance as a manager. Martinet recalls:

> When he saw the takings staying nearly at capacity Jacques spent money without counting. Whole lengths of velvet were swallowed up in the auditorium; costumes devoured width after width of satin. On top of the architects' estimates came the cost of the décor ordered from the official scene-painters at the Opéra. The till was open to anyone in distress; discreet and unassuming generosity became the accomplice of brash and impressive prodigality. The spectre of Clichy [the debtors' prison] began to threaten Jacques.[9]

It was decided to split the company in two; half would go to London for two weeks while the others held the fort in the passage Choiseul. For a time at least there would be two box-offices going strong. John Mitchell, had given up his active managership of the St James's Theatre two years earlier, but he undertook the administration of the London season.[10] The St James's had remained the traditional venue for French productions. In 1855 Rachel had made her last English appearances in *Horace, Phèdre, Adrienne Lecouvreur* and other works.

The opening programme[11] consisted of *M'sieu Landry* (music by Duprato), *Ba-ta-clan* and *Les Deux Aveugles*. It was a great success; the language proved no barrier to the comedy, much of which was visual. One Frenchman observed that, though the Londoners missed some of the Parisian slang and plays on words, it didn't matter. Offenbach conducted a thirty-man orchestra which had come over from Paris with the company. Such was the popularity of the venture that Jacques contracted with John Mitchell to extend the season by a month. In order to exploit the success to the full he obtained ministerial permission to close the salle Choiseul and bring the rest of his actors to England. Offenbach himself had to take charge of all these arrangements; Charles Comte was seriously ill in Paris. Jacques kept him in touch with the news. He was fond of his young partner, who was later to become his son-in-law, and wrote regular affectionate letters. Early in June there was a special event:

> Queen Victoria is coming to our theatre tonight; she has only been in London since Friday and is going back to Windsor tomorrow. She specially wanted to come to the Bouffes, and as you can imagine I am delighted. . . . On Wednesday the première of *La Rose* and Friday *Le Financier*. Goodbye, my dear friend — when are you coming over? If you see Mme Offenbach tell her I'll write to her tomorrow; if you see my dear little children, give them a big kiss from me. *Je te serre les deux mains*.[12]

Queen Victoria, still in her thirties, had up to now been a great theatregoer. In 1854 she had visited the St James's Theatre fourteen times, three of those for Donizetti's *La Fille du régiment*. But affairs of state were making her visits more rare, and her evening at the Bouffes was her last-but-one appearance at the St James's.

Finally there was a performance at Orleans House in Twickenham (*Le Ménestrel* helpfully gave its readers the correct pronunciation — TWICKNOM). Here the old Queen Marie-Amélie, widow of Louis-Philippe, wept when the little French piper in *Dragonnette* appeared with the captured enemy flag, and the company sang 'Crions en choeur: vive la France!' Offenbach had been nervous about the political wisdom of performing before the consort of the exiled King. He had taken the precaution of asking Comte to clear the matter tactfully with the appropriate minister.

The Bouffes made a brief visit to Lyon before returning to the Champs-

Élysées where the salle Marigny had been newly decorated. More unnecessary extravagance — the theatre had opened only a year earlier and
had been in use for less than six of the intervening months. There was one
more diversion that summer. Herminie Offenbach and her three daughters were on holiday at Étretat on the Normandy coast. Jacques was to join
them. But he was not a man for inactive holidays. He arranged a charity
performance of the Bouffes in aid of the poor of Étretat, after which he
wrote to Villemessant:

> The problem that worried me most was how to find accommodation for
> the company. The day before they arrived I still hadn't found a corner
> for them to lay their expensive heads . . . their dear heads, for Étretat is
> as full today as it was a month ago. Our actors had no quarters; but now
> some people who believe in doing good works of a practical kind helped
> in various ways. One of my friends was kind enough to go away for two
> days in order to give up his room for Mesmacker; Guyot received a
> traditional curé's welcome from the worthy parish priest at Étretat;
> Désiré was pigeonholed at the *mairie* between two marriage certificates.
> When I fell on my knees in front of Madame Blanquet she packed off
> one of her baldest old gentlemen and put up Mlle Tautin. As for the
> great Salomon, the theatre accompanist, he condescended to share
> with the mayor's clerk, which more than ever does credit to the
> Judgement of Salomon!![13]

CHAPTER V

Orphée aux Enfers
1857–1859

·· ⚙ ··

Offenbach could not long be content to compose only one-act works for four characters; that artistic strait-jacket was too irksome. He had in mind several large-scale projects, and was particularly keen to complete and produce *Orphée aux Enfers*, a parody of Greek mythology. He suggested it to Halévy and Crémieux, who sketched out a libretto. More than one writer subsequently claimed to have supplied Offenbach with the original conception of *Orphée*; their contradictory claims are discussed in Appendix A. But, as Siegfried Kracauer points out, there were many sources from which Offenbach might have taken the idea: 'Italian comedians and comic poets in Vienna had long since applied the legend of Orpheus to the purposes of parody, including parody of grand opera.' Wherever the idea came from, it was Halévy and Crémieux who now gave it bones and flesh.

The story, peopled with a multitude of Greek gods and mortals, demanded a large cast of principals and a chorus; it was therefore essential for Offenbach to obtain a new theatre licence that would allow him greater scope in production. He tested the mood of the authorities with a small gesture of defiance. In *Croquefer ou le dernier des Paladins*, an entertaining romp about the Crusades, he wrote for a cast of five instead of the permitted four. The extra character was a mute called *Mousse-à-Mort*, whose tongue had been cut out in a fight against the Saracens. *Mousse-à-Mort* uttered only grunts and shouts like 'hou!', 'hon!', and 'houah!', and displayed to the audience pennants carrying such legends as *'grande canaille!'* Since he did not speak it was claimed that he was not an extra character within the meaning of the act. The audience enjoyed both the non-character and the joke against officialdom, and Offenbach got away with it.

Thus encouraged, he began one of his campaigns of string-pulling and intrigue, from which he emerged victorious with a new licence giving permission for bigger productions. In *Mesdames de la Halle* (March 1858) he was able to use a large cast. The additional salaries he had to pay, however, did nothing to help the financial difficulties in which the Bouffes still found itself. The theatre was immensely popular and box-office receipts were good, but not good enough to compensate for Offenbach's extravagance. When eventually his creditors summoned the bailiffs he had to go to ground, hiding with friends and more than once taking refuge in Brussels. It was under this kind of pressure that the score of *Orphée aux Enfers* began to take shape — the score that was to save Offenbach's financial skin, and to intimate to the musical world that this witty Parisian entertainer might also be a composer of worth. In the midst of all his other troubles Jacques was suffering from rheumatism. When touring with his company earlier in the year he had enjoyed a visit to the Rhineland resort of Bad Ems. He now went back there on his own for a physical cure, a respite from financial harassment, and the necessary solitude to work on his beloved *Orphée*.

Offenbach to Ludovic Halévy, Ems, 5 July 1858:

> My dear friend,
> I don't want to bore you about my health, you must have heard about that already. Just to say that almost the whole piece is done, and I am very happy with the details, that's the essential thing. The beginning of the finale of the second scene works extremely well. I think, I'm sure, we are going to have a success. Do send me some work please. No good talking to Crémieux about it, I might as well be singing to a brick wall. So I'm counting on you. Have you seen Cambon about the last set? I heard about your change of job. Lucky you, not having to work for me any more; don't worry, I'll make sure you do; just take a new name, sign yourself Halévinsky, and no one will know who you are. I'm writing to you today because it is exactly three years since our first campaign together, you as author, myself as director. Do you remember? Lucky fellow to have your children around you at present (that is if you want them around) while I can only think about mine at a distance. 5 July is an anniversary,[1] for me at least; whatever my day-to-day worries I always look forward to it with pleasure. Goodbye, dear friend; if you can see Hector [Crémieux] give him my love. . . .
> *Je te serre tendrement dans mes bras. . . .*[2]

The job referred to was Halévy's new appointment as secretary-general to the Ministry for Algeria. He was only twenty-five and 'played the government game more seriously than one would have believed possible'. Up to now his duties had not brought him into the limelight, but he felt that if he was to be a higher official he should not endanger his respectability by writing theatre scripts. Hector Crémieux, on the other hand, was a procrastinator, and Jacques was losing all patience with him

— Jacques who not only wrote at great speed, but never stopped working ('J'ai un vice terrible, invincible, c'est de toujours travailler')[3] and who later had a writing-desk installed in his carriage so that he need not waste time. Under further pressure from Jacques, Halévy relented and agreed to go on working provided his name was not mentioned as one of the authors. When the piece was finally put on Offenbach and Crémieux felt that their anonymous collaborator must have some form of recognition. *Orphée aux Enfers* was dedicated to Ludovic Halévy because he had written so much of it.

In the late summer of 1858 Jacques returned to Paris. He had moved his family to 11 rue Laffitte, nearer his theatre. (The house is no longer there; it was knocked down to make way for the boulevard Haussmann, while the nearby mansion of the wealthy Rothschild family was spared.) Here Jacques completed the score of *Orphée*. During rehearsals he would always, however, cut, revise and rewrite with ruthless practicality anything that did not seem to work well in the theatre. He began the process of casting. Hortense Schneider was ruled out; she had recently been asking for more money than the Bouffes could pay, had slammed the door on them, and ended up earning less elsewhere. Earlier in the year she had retired to Bordeaux to have an illegitimate child. Jacques gave the part of Eurydice to Lise Tautin, a seductive and talented young actress whom he had earlier discovered in Brussels.

Two popular and witty performers, Léonce and Désiré, were chosen for Pluto and Jupiter. As an afterthought, when rehearsals had already begun, Bache was cast as John Styx. The character of the sad and unearthly former King of the Boeotians may well have been conceived specially for Bache, an eccentric actor who had not long left the Comédie-Française. Daniel Halévy describes him: 'Endlessly long and spindly, lost in a sort of mist, at one moment dragging his sentences, then rushing his delivery, Bache was a mystery, an enigma and a joy to the public.' Coming on stage 'with the bizarre demeanour of a friendly giraffe, it seemed as if he belonged to another planet, and was only a temporary visitor on this one'.[4]

Houssaye describes Bache's voice as being 'high-pitched, like that of an adolescent'. One may guess, therefore, that the *timbre* with which he sang the moving *Couplets du roi de Béotie* may have resembled that of a male alto. The song is now always performed by a tenor or light baritone, but there is no doubt that some element of the grotesque or the eccentric is essential to the successful casting of this part.

The study of Latin and Greek was then as much of a sacred cow in France as it was in England, and therefore no educated Frenchman had to be told the story of Orpheus and Eurydice. *Orphée* made an irreverent tilt at the classics, giving a lightly cynical version of the myth against the background of a gossip-columnist's exposé of the private lives of the gods on Mount Olympus. The highminded propriety of the gods was shown to be nothing but a façade, behind which were revealed their amours, intrigues and petty jealousies. Only in the occasional presence of *L'Opinion publique* did they pull themselves together and put on a semblance of correct behaviour. *L'Opinion publique*, originally conceived as a male character, ended up as a Mrs Grundy-like female who narrated and commented on the story, fulfilling the function of the Greek chorus. She was the only personage to be respected and feared by gods and mortals alike. Here there was a touch of satire on Second Empire society, its rulers and bourgeoisie. It is important, however, not to exaggerate the role of satire in Offenbach. Neither Jacques nor his librettists were setting out to ape Swift or Voltaire: *Orphée* was not *Candide*. The satire was not there as an end in itself, but for the gaiety it generated. Comedy came from the fact that the revered gods of antiquity, who would have been expected in the theatre to declaim in the language of Corneille or Racine, chatted with each other instead in the *argot* of the boulevards. True, there was some good anti-government fun, mostly of a routine type. There were topical allusions. But if Mount Olympus was an allegory of court life, the court of the day being that of Napoleon III, there is little in the allegory that would not apply equally well to the entourages of dictators of all eras.

In Offenbach's version of the story Orpheus and Eurydice are no longer the familiar star-crossed lovers, but a nagging married couple. Orpheus is not a lutenist, but a violinist who drives his wife to distraction with his atrocious playing. When Pluto, king of the underworld, turns up disguised as a handsome young shepherd and seduces Eurydice, she is delighted to get away from her boring husband. Orpheus, for his part, is happy to be rid of his wife, but is called to task by *L'Opinion publique*, who packs him off to Mount Olympus to plead with Jupiter for Eurydice's return. He arrives on Olympus to find the gods in revolt. Bored with nectar, ambrosia and virtue, they are resentful of Jupiter, who has decreed rigid rules of conduct which he himself persistently transgresses. Orpheus sings his plea to the tune of Gluck's 'Che farò senz' Euridice?', a melody which he is given to singing or playing on his violin at the drop of a hat throughout the play. (This joke was probably both funny and shocking in 1858. It still raises a laugh nowadays even if it no longer shocks.) Jupiter, to sort the matter out and appease his rebellious family, takes everybody down to Hades. There, under a more permissive regime, they fling themselves with abandon into the final bacchanal. The fact that Orpheus finally loses Eurydice worries neither the couple themselves nor anyone else.

The score of *Orphée aux Enfers* is written in a mixture of styles. It hangs together because the pastiche in which it abounds is dramatically justi-

6. *Bacchanal* from *Orphée aux Enfers*. After a painting by Gustave Doré

fied, and because the libretto is so strong. The work provides an inventory of Offenbach's formative influences. The diversity of these influences prompts the question: Did Offenbach ever become a specifically French composer? It is not altogether easy to identify a national idiom in French music of the mid-nineteenth century, which had a cosmopolitan flavour. In 1833, when Offenbach arrived as a student at the Paris Conservatoire, the director, Cherubini, was an Italian; Meyerbeer and Halévy, the most influential composers of the day, were, like Offenbach himself, the sons of Germans, and both of them had had some Italian training. Offenbach, as has been seen, regarded some contemporary French music with distaste. His music owes too much to the tradition of Mozart and Rossini to suggest any uniquely national character. He made eclectic use of the dance music of other nations to contribute rhythmic variety and vitality to his work. A few cancans did not make his music French any more than his polonaises made it Polish. In any case, the cancan was an import from North Africa; Auber, in *Gustave,* and later Offenbach, formalized it for theatrical purposes in a style that came to be thought of as French. If anything Offenbach probably lent a style to French music rather than finding a style in it. The seemingly quintessential Frenchness of an Offenbach operetta lies in the subject-matter, the social comment, and the wit of the libretto rather than in the music.

Occasionally Offenbach imitates the early composers he admires so much. When he does so, as in *Les Bergers* and in the first act of *Orphée*, his music sounds French but archaic. In his other writing he maintains a simplicity learnt from composers like Philidor and Monsigny, but his idiom is his own. He owes something to those French models, but more to his idol Mozart; Rossini once affectionately called Jacques 'the Mozart of the Champs-Élysées'. Offenbach rejects the path taken by his contemporaries and preserves in his music a sense of classic discipline suggestive of the eighteenth rather than the nineteenth century. Given the satirical, sometimes even cynical nature of the librettos, he seems at times like an eighteenth-century gentleman commenting on nineteenth-century manners. This impression is reinforced when he parodies his more pretentious contemporaries. In *Croquefer*, as in *Ba-ta-clan*, he inserted into the farcical comedy a lengthy and grandly romantic quotation from Meyerbeer. This practice of Offenbach's not unnaturally led to some friction between the two composers, but Meyerbeer later recognized that even parody can be flattering: no one parodies a nonentity. The wounds were healed, the *lèse-majesté* forgiven. The great Meyerbeer attended the Bouffes regularly, but did not like to be seen there on first nights. Jacques knew to expect him at the second performance of every new operetta. There was a ritual; Meyerbeer would book himself a stall. When he arrived at the theatre he would be greeted by Gaston Mitchell, Offenbach's brother-in-law, and taken to the composer's box. In the course of the evening Jacques would go up and talk to the grand old man. Their *bons mots* were passed on by those who could get close enough to hear them.

Orphée aux Enfers was the first full-length work to be presented at the Bouffes-Parisiens. In terms of its length and the forces involved it is a large-scale work, with six principals, a host of minor parts, a chorus and dancers. Apart from the abundance of *couplets* (songs with repeated verses) for anything from one to seven characters, there is a variety of other solos and duets, several big choruses, and two extended finales. The first scene has a strong flavour of the eighteenth century. Eurydice is in a cornfield, picking flowers for a handsome young shepherd whom she has noticed and hopes to meet again. The music, with its opening chorus of shepherds, and Eurydice's *Couplets du joli berger*, is classical in character, with a simple Arcadian charm, which is perhaps *faux-naif*.

When Orpheus, Professor of Music, enters and insists on playing his new violin concerto, the musical style changes abruptly. The *Duo du concerto* is a pastiche of a *scena* from an Italian opera. But the main violin tune, which Eurydice also sings as the climax of the number, bears

Offenbach's personal hallmark. In many of the best melodies the movement from note to note is by step, with only occasional leaps for contrast.
Offenbach, however, manages to contrive melodies that leap backwards
and forwards in a remarkably acrobatic manner while still sounding not
only smoothly lyrical, but spontaneous as well. Consider these opening
bars:

Ex. 6a

In the course of the three beats at (*a*), the melody covers a range of a
twelfth. During a single beat (*d*) it falls a seventh and rises a fifth. That it
can do so smoothly is due to the simplicity of the harmony, which is
always at rest when the melody leaps. Stripped of its decoration the
passage is essentially:

Ex. 6b

Offenbach has merely ornamented the melodic line with appoggiaturas at
(*b*) and (*c*) and a broken chord at (*d*). Note that the to-and-fro movement
within the single beat (*d*) is made possible by the fact that the compound
time-signature allows three quavers to a beat.

Offenbach loved this soaring and dipping kind of melody. An example of
distinction is *Le Jugement de Pâris* in *La Belle Hélène*, with its graceful
extended ending:

Ex. 7

When Orpheus concludes his concerto we return to countrified music, as Aristaeus, the pseudo-shepherd (Pluto in disguise) enters to the sound of the obligatory pastoral oboe.

Offenbach is a master in the use of rhythmic figures for the purpose of establishing mood. The following are the opening phrases of three tunes which are played within a few minutes of each other in the final scenes of *Orphée*. All three are in the same key. They all consist of the same notes in

Ex. 8

almost the same order. But it would be hard to imagine a more extreme difference in feeling than that between the song of the King of the Boeotians and the *Galop*. The underlying rhythmic patterns serve an emotional function by endowing the melody with a different mood in each case (Ex.8).

The *Galop infernal*, the famous cancan, was not entitled 'cancan' in the operetta. Nor did it resemble the Moulin Rouge affairs of the nineties with their chorus-lines of gartered ladies. In *Orphée* it was a frenzied bacchanal with both men and women in wild costumes, many of them designed by Gustave Doré, who later recorded the stage scene on canvas.

Since Offenbach uses the cancan so often with such invigorating effect, it is worth examining the musical ingredients that give it its high-voltage excitement. Time-signature, 2/4. A non-stop fast oom-pah, oom-pah rhythm in quaver movement, the bass thumping away in crotchets (the 'oom'), the harmony flicking the off-beats (the 'pah'). The melody, too, keeps up an almost continuous quaver movement, with only short and striking interjections of a few longer notes. Harmony: three chords only, tonic, dominant and subdominant (cf. the pop music of the 1950s). Phrases in multiples of four bars — no fancy complications. Feminine phrase-endings, the point of these being that at the end of an 8- or 16-bar phrase there is never more than one beat of repose, and often only half a beat. In the fast tempo this gives an effect of breathlessness (literally true in the case of singers and wind players). Add to this one vital feature: the cancan always goes on for a long time in relation to its own speed. The result is a sensation of breathless, unremitting, mounting energy, with a pounding beat that frequently has the audience clapping and stamping in time to the music.

The *Galop infernal* has three strong melodic motifs. They have to be strong; there is only one key-change (to the subdominant), only one rhythmic variation, a 4-bar figure of dotted rhythm on a repeated note, used as a link and in the coda. The orchestration hardly varies, other than dynamically from soft to loud. But like all good popular music the piece makes a virtue of its own limited means, demonstrating the strength of the basic material by avoiding complexity.

Orphée aux Enfers opened at the Bouffes-Parisiens on 21 October 1858. The morning after the première, the critic Jules Noriac wrote in the *Figaro-Programme*:

> Inouï
> Splendide,
> Ébouriffant,
> Gracieux,
> Charmant,

Orphée aux Enfers: 1857–1859

Spirituel,
Amusant,
Réussi,
Parfait,
Mélodieux,
l'Opéra
d'Orphée
(c'est un opéra)
sera
incontestablement (ce mot n'en finit pas)
le
plus
grand
succès
de
l'hiver.
Ceci
soit
dit
sans
blesser
Faust.
La
musique
d'
Offenbach
est
ravissante,
Mademoiselle
Tautin
aussi.
Et
Garnier
donc!
Et
Geoffroy!
Succès
pour
tout
le
monde.
Léonce,
Désiré,

Bache,
splendides!
Cent
représentations au
moins!
Gloire
et
argent
pour
Offenbach
et
pour
Crémieux
Tant mieux!

Alain Decaux[5] suggests that M. Noriac may have been paid by the line.

The public reaction, too, was good. The box-office takings shot up, levelled out — and then dropped, at which Offenbach began to rewrite yet again. A whole scene was cut, new music and lyrics were added. In February 1859 an Orphée 'remanié' was presented. The press came again. This time the critic of the *Journal des Débats*, Jules Janin, who had in the past praised Offenbach, published an extraordinary diatribe[6] against the operetta on the grounds that it was sacrilege, a desecration of antiquity and the classics. But Janin had misjudged his readers. Offenbach and Crémieux had little difficulty in casting ridicule on him in their replies. The public, intrigued by the rumpus and its attendant publicity, began to flock to the Bouffes and *Orphée* became not only a triumph but a cult. The days of the *offenbachiade* had begun.

With such an artistic and financial success on his hands it might have been expected that Jacques would take life more easily for a while. Apart from his responsibilities as an impresario, he had composed, orchestrated, directed and conducted most of the productions at the Bouffes over the past three years. But he was unable to give up his 'vice' of working, and the remainder of 1859 saw three one-act pieces, *Un Mari à la porte, Luce et Lucette* and *Les Vivandières de la Grande Armée,* and finally the full-length *Geneviève de Brabant.* This attempted parody of medieval French history did not quite come off. Offenbach's fondness for the piece led him to lengthen it from two to three acts for a sumptuous revival in 1867, again without success. One addition to the score, however, became an international hit number: the 'Gendarmes' Duet' (*Couplets des deux Hommes d'armes*).

Now, in 1859, success found Jacques in good form. He wrote to Bache: 'You have played the role of John Styx in *Orphée* with real talent. Permit me, in recognition of this success, to impose on you a condition — rather severe, it's true, but one which you will be so good as to accept out of consideration for your director. From the 1st of this month I am doubling your salary for the whole year. In acting thus, my dear Bache, I have only one object: to create another ingrate.'[7]

CHAPTER VI

Partisanship
1860–1861

······🙶······

When faced with new works of art, especially the works of foreign artists, the French have always enjoyed invigorating controversy. The spirit of the Gluckistes and the Piccinistes lives on; cabals and cliques are the breath of life. The bright young native writer or the invading foreigner has habitually found himself adopted by *aficiònados* and attacked by enemies with robustly partisan fervour, the success or failure of a new work being regarded in terms of victory or defeat by the opposing sides.

In January 1860 the battle-lines were drawn up around Wagner, who had been in Paris since September. Wagner, it was thought, saw himself as the high priest of the Music of the Future; he was said to be prescribing a new musical technology. This erroneous idea of his intentions arose out of a misinterpretation of his book *Das Kunstwerk der Zukunft* ('The Work of Art of the Future'). To Wagner's annoyance, Berlioz reinforced the misunderstanding in an article in *Le Journal des Débats*[1] in which he referred to Wagner's 'school of the future'. There was still a year to go before the disastrous Parisian performances of *Tannhäuser*. In his article, Berlioz was reviewing three orchestral and choral concerts in which were included excerpts from *Tannhäuser* as well as the first performance of the Prelude to the newly completed but as yet unstaged *Tristan und Isolde*. These concerts caused sensation and controversy. Wagner published an indignant reply to Berlioz's comments.[2] The Press on both sides was unleashed. It was said that Meyerbeer gave 500 francs to the critic Fiorentino to prevent his saying anything good about Wagner's music.

The concerts lost an enormous sum of money. The composer, having no taste for another spell in the Clichy prison, where he had ended up on a previous Parisian visit, went round borrowing from friends and supporters. It was alleged that he even tried to get money from the Emperor, but was snubbed. Wagner was by this time stuck with the label 'musician of the future'. His disclaimers would have carried more lasting conviction had he not subsequently written another book entitled *Zukunftsmusik*

Ex. 9 From *La Symphonie de l'avenir*

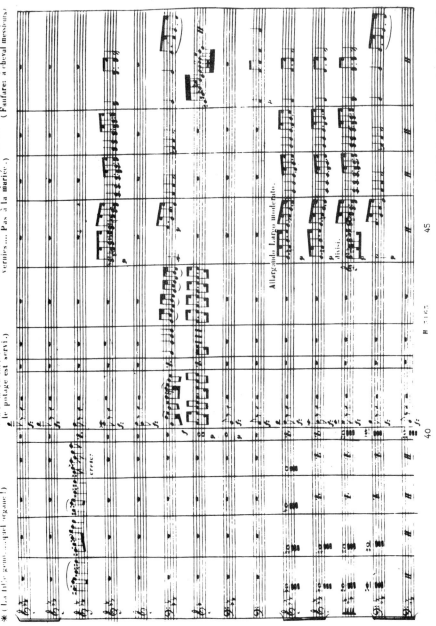

Offenbach parodies Wagner: bars 32 to 40 are probably aimed at the Prelude to *Tristan und Isolde*, bars 45 onwards at the March in *Tannhäuser*. The legend (indicated by the asterisk), 'La fille gémit . . . quel organe!' tilts at the sexual connotations of both operas.

('The Music of the Future'). Offenbach, scenting pretentiousness, seized his opportunity. At the beginning of February, with the *mardi-gras* carnival coming up, the Bouffes-Parisiens presented *Le Carnaval des revues*, in which the principal item was a sketch entitled *Le Musicien de l'avenir*.[3]

Scene, Elysium: Weber, Grétry, Gluck and Mozart are waiting for a concert to begin. Enter a gentleman who declares that he is the Composer of the Future. He denounces the musical past and proclaims a revolution. No more notes! No more harmony! No more pitch, scales, sharps, flats, naturals! No fortes! No pianos!

'No more music, then?' asks Gluck.

'Yes; but a strange, unknown, vague, indescribable music!'

The Great Masters ask to hear a sample of it. The Composer of the Future hands out some orchestral parts and begins *La Symphonie de l'avenir*[4] (see Ex. 9), a pseudo-Wagnerian tone-poem about a village marriage. The composer conducts, calling out the themes as they occur: the Nuptial March, The Departure to the Mairie, the Mother's Farewell, etc. The Great Masters are scandalized by the music. The symphony ends, and the composer insists on starting his *Tyrolienne de l'avenir* but Mozart and his fellows hound him off the stage.

Wagner was incensed by the parody, which initiated a lifelong feud with Offenbach; the latter in his turn made no bones about what he thought of *Tannhäuser*: 'To be academic and boring is not art; it is better to be piquant and tuneful!' (in *L'Artiste*, 1861). Wagner replied: 'Offenbach possesses the warmth lacking in Auber; but it is the warmth of the dunghill; all Europe is wallowing in it.'

Some ten years later, when Paris lay besieged by the Prussian army, Wagner wrote a despicable satire, *Eine Kapitulation*, in which he mocked the starving Parisians and seized the chance to dramatize his feelings about Offenbach. The perpetrator of *Le Musicien de l'avenir* is here presented as a trumpet-playing bandleader, a Pied Piper of Hamelin, encouraging people to dance as the chorus applaud his music:

> *O wie süss und angenehm,*
> *Und für die Füsse so recht bequem!*
> *Krak! Krak! Krakerakrak!*
> *O herrlicher Jack von Offenback!*[5]
>
> *(Oh, how pleasant! Oh how sweet!*
> *Perfect music for the feet!*
> *Crack! Crack! Crack-crack-crack!*
> *Oh marvellous Jack von Offenback!)*

Wagner later sent the text of *Eine Kapitulation* to Hans Richter, pretending it was the work of another author, and suggesting that he should set it to music as 'the parody of an Offenbach parody'; but the project was wisely shelved.

At the end of 1859 Offenbach applied for French citizenship. His application, which was approved by the Emperor, had to be examined by a judge-advocate and a state council. The officials turned it down, whereupon the Emperor instructed them to confer again; the dictator in Napoleon was not going to stand any nonsense from a mere council of state. The result of the second meeting was a foregone conclusion; the judge-advocate 'had nothing better to do than count the flies on the ceiling'.[7] On 14 January 1860 Offenbach was declared a naturalized French citizen.

This incident was followed by another that confirmed Offenbach's good standing at court. In the spring Napoleon III heard that a benefit gala performance had been arranged for Jacques, and promised to attend on condition that the programme included *Orphée aux Enfers*. As a memento of the brilliant occasion on 27 April 1860 Jacques received a magnificent bronze with the inscription 'L'Empereur à Jacques Offenbach' and a letter saying that the Emperor 'would never forget the dazzling evening that *Orphée aux Enfers* had given him at the *Italiens*'.

After a summer visit to Berlin, where he conducted *Orphée* while his company was successful with the same piece in Brussels, Offenbach busied himself with his outside commissions. The Opéra presented his ballet *Le Papillon*. Enemies were jealous and irate. 'Offenbach chez Meyerbeer! scandale! Offenbach chez Boieldieu! Profanation!!'[6] The critics were hostile but the public approved, and *Le Papillon* had forty-two performances — remarkable for a ballet in those times. The *Valse des rayons* was later exploited by Offenbach in other contexts including *Die Rheinnixen* (see Chapter VIII), and became a popular Apache dance in the early 1900s. The star, Emma Livry, met a grim death two years after her success in *Le Papillon*. She was rehearsing the mute title role in Auber's *La Muette de Portici* when her costume caught fire from the footlights. It took six months for the burns to kill her.

Barkouf, commissioned by the Opéra-Comique, pleased neither the public nor the critics. This *bouffonnerie* by Scribe and Boisseaux was an unfortunate choice for that theatre. Offenbach had always been critical of the type of material that formed the repertoire of the Opéra-Comique, but in going so far in another direction he was asking for trouble. The story concerns a dog, Barkouf, who is appointed Governor of Lahore by the reigning Grand Mogul. The details are such as would be found in a bad pantomime script, and Berlioz, writing in the *Journal des Débats*, was cruel enough to recount the plot in full, revealing the puerility of the whole affair. Berlioz continued:

This opera belongs to the genre that is held in high esteem in those theatres that I may not name; but why put it on at the Opéra-Comique before a public which, being unprepared for this special genre, could only be shocked by it? It didn't seem funny at all; many people were indignant; others were laughing, it's true, but only at the idea that anyone should have expected them to find it funny. Some were left baffled, they were leaping up in anger. I have never seen the foyer of the Opéra-Comique in such a state. There was a hail of waspish comments.

Members of the audience who knew their music exclaimed 'What's all this, has the composer lost his head? What are these harmonies that don't fit the tune? What is this insistent internal pedal-point that sounds a dominant, decorated — some decoration! — with a minor sixth, thereby indicating the minor mode, while the rest of the orchestra is playing the major? That sort of thing can be done, certainly, but it needs craftmanship. Here it is executed in a slipshod way, with an ignorance of the dangers involved, the like of which you've never heard. . . .' There is definitely something twisted in the minds of certain musicians. The wind which blows through Germany has made them mad. . . .Is the Day at hand? Of what Messiah is the composer of *Barkouf* the John the Baptist? . . . . 'What's going on in the orchestra?' asked one of the audience in the foyer, shattered by that unbelievably awful finale; 'I've never heard such a row.' A passer-by, overhearing, said 'It's one of those things that Punch puts in his mouth to give him a funny voice, it's a squeaker.' 'Perhaps it's a police siren that's causing the trouble,' said someone else, 'the instruments can't all have gone out of tune yet', etc., etc. [7]

Offenbach got his own back on Berlioz three years later by parodying his music in *Il Signor Fagotto* (see Chapter VIII).

Barkouf gave Jacques' enemies new cause for jubilation. As his grandson Jacques Brindejont–Offenbach wrote, 'If, as I have said, Offenbach's friends were all loyal to him, his enemies clung to him no less devotedly.' Again, Offenbach refused to waste good material. Ten years later after the failure of *Barkouf* the musical rights of the work were bought back from the Opéra-Comique, and a proportion of the score was used in *Boule de Neige* with new words by Nuitter and Tréfeu. Madame Scribe, widow of *Barkouf*'s librettist, was bought off with 25 per cent of the rights in the new piece.

An occasional visitor to the Bouffes was the comte (later duc) de Morny, 'Napoleon's illegitimate half-brother and companion in adventure'. [8] Offenbach was introduced to this powerful aristocrat, who showed signs of being stage-struck. One day Morny confessed that he wanted to compose 'une partitionette d'amateur' — a little amateur score — and needed a text. Offenbach suggested Ludovic Halévy, who with his father Léon, an established dramatist, wrote *Un Mari sans le savoir*. Morny set it to music, and it was performed at the Bouffes on 31 December 1860. The delighted composer promptly decided to arrange a special performance at the Palais Bourbon for the Corps Législatif. But the piece was too short for an evening's entertainment. Morny sent for Halévy and Offenbach. The meeting began with an embarrassed silence. 'Excellency . . .' murmured Halévy. 'Monsieur . . .' said the count. There was silence once more. Then Halévy realized what was going on: 'I was overawed, but so was M. de Morny; it was the first time I had met such an elevated personage; it was the first time he had submitted a theatrical idea to a man of the theatre. . . . I understood, and breathed more freely.'[9]

Morny shyly produced the scenario for an *opéra-bouffe* which he could not complete himself. Would Offenbach and Halévy collaborate with him? The pair could give only one answer to this flattering request; fortunately, they found the count's sketch very funny. Thus *Monsieur Choufleury* came into being. Because of the *politesse* involved, it is hard to tell who did what work on *M. Choufleury*. Crémieux and Morny's secretary Lépine (pseudonym L'Épine) collaborated with Halévy and Morny (pseudonym Saint-Rémy) on the script. Offenbach referred later to 'the operetta which I had the honour of writing with M. de Saint-Rémy, although only a small part of it is mine'. This comment, which appeared in press publicity for the Bouffes, may have been diplomatic rather than truthful, because most of *M. Choufleury*, in particular the final trio, is obviously the work of a highly accomplished musician. But perhaps Morny supplied the themes.

A few months later, after the run of *Le Pont des soupirs*, the Bouffes-Parisiens trundled some scenery and properties across the river (the actors riding in carriages bearing the Morny livery) and performed *Monsieur Choufleury restera chez lui le 24 janvier 1833* at the Palais-Bourbon in the presence of the Emperor and *le tout-Paris*.

Meantime, Offenbach had another preoccupation. One of his favourite melodies, *La Chanson de Fortunio*, had never had a proper hearing. He had composed it as an incidental song for Alfred de Musset's play *Le Chandelier* at the Comédie-Française in 1850. The actor playing Fortunio had been unable to sing it, and, instead, spoke the verses while the orchestra played the melody softly. Jacques mentioned one day to Crémieux and Halévy that he longed to find a new use for this melody. In a few hours the two writers presented him with a one-act libretto, *La Chanson de Fortunio*.

Le Chandelier was partly autobiographical. At the age of eighteen Alfred de Musset had fallen in love with a married woman, only to discover that she was leading him on so that she might use him as her 'chandelier', or candlebearer — one who diverts attention from a more serious and secret love affair. Musset used this theme of a young lover's humiliation to make a slight but rather touching romantic comedy, which is still in the repertoire of the Comédie-Française. Unfortunately Crémieux and Halévy, instead of adopting Musset's story, chose to invent a sequel to it. The crucial idea of the *chandelier* was abandoned, and the plot of *La Chanson de Fortunio* became little more than a piece of sentimental twaddle about a song which caused women to fall in love with the singer — a sort of musical love-potion. It was a pity that the authors took this course, because, apart from the eponymous *chanson* — a winner in itself — the rest of the score is good quality Offenbach, containing such enjoyable things as a highly successful bolero for the leading soprano, in which a Spanish flavour was achieved by devices soon to be used again by Offenbach's friend Bizet in *Carmen*. Here is Offenbach:

Ex. 10a

And here is Bizet:

Ex. 10b

Tam - bours de Basque al - laient leur train

La Chanson de Fortunio illustrates a problem that faces any producer wanting to put on performances of lesser-known Offenbach works today — the consistent weakness of the librettos. There exists a treasure-house of attractive scores, but the librettos are too often examples of dated comedy or over-sentimental romance. Some people have tried supplying a completely new story and script, and assembling a score out of a jumble of numbers from different operettas. Though this process has occasionally been successful it is nevertheless not an entirely satisfactory solution. It is tempting to believe that a good playwright could find at least one more Offenbach operetta with some relevance for present times, which, with a strengthened script, could be presented as a complete work.

The first performance of *Fortunio* was rapturously received. Meyerbeer wrote, 'J'aurais aimé l'avoir faite.'[10] 'It was a great come-down', writes Martinet, 'for the Jeremiahs who had materialized on the night of *Barkouf*. The man they had thought vanquished now turned out to be having a triumph. The public were applauding more than ever the fellow whose corpse they had sworn to put on show.'[11] It was another battle honour for Offenbach.

To close the 1860/61 season, Offenbach, Crémieux and Halévy created *Le Pont des soupirs*. The story, based on the *Chroniques de Venise,* is a farce involving a jealous husband, rival lovers, duels, disguises, spies' corpses in grandfather clocks, etc. Given such a plot, the score is surprisingly lyrical. It has so much ensemble singing that it almost becomes a choral cantata. The principal solo parts indicate what an exceptional range of vocal ability Offenbach could now call on within his own company. In the six years of the Bouffes-Parisiens he had assembled a repertory company of the kind of performers — able both to sing and act — that the musical theatre of Broadway was to cultivate a century later.

Lisa Tautin, a lyric coloratura and accomplished comedienne, had played Eurydice in *Orphée*, in which she had to sing some conventional coloratura cadenzas. But that Olympian role was nothing to the vocal Olympics with which Offenbach now confronted her. The title song of *Le Pont des soupirs* takes the form of an air and variations for a quartet of women — two coloraturas and two lyric sopranos. Catarina, the heroine, has lengthy coloratura passages. The following are the typical final eight bars of a 32-bar section:

Ex. 11a

The main figure is taken up by the whole quartet in the next variation:

Ex. 11b

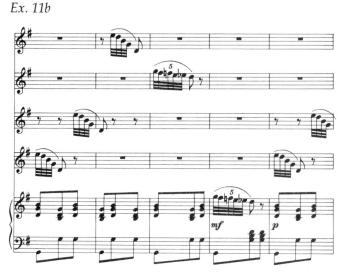

The style of the coloratura writing, and the air and variations form, suggest that the inspiration for this number may have been the trio 'Ah, vous dirais-je, maman' from Adam's *Le Toréador*, part of the soprano line of which is shown in Ex. 11c below. The fact that the two numbers are in the same key tends to support the idea.

Ex. 11c

The part of Malatromba in *Le Pont des soupirs* is written for a flexible light tenor such as Rossini uses in *Il Barbiere di Siviglia* and *Le Comte Ory*.

Offenbach gives him the following passage, which is of interest in that its style of word-setting — a busy one-syllable-to-a-semiquaver over a gentle accompaniment — was adopted by Sullivan in *The Gondoliers*.

Ex. 12a

Compare Sullivan:

Ex. 12b

The similarity of these passages is mentioned because *Le Pont des soupirs* was clearly the model for *The Gondoliers*. It would be unfair to accuse Gilbert and Sullivan of plagiarism, but they were certainly navigating the Venetian canals in similar style. The plots are different; but in both works there are choruses *à la barcarolle* for gondoliers and *contadini* singing in their addictive thirds and sixths; Offenbach has a Venetian admiral telling of his cowardice in battle; Gilbert and Sullivan have their Duke of Plaza-Toro who led his regiment from behind; the French Venetians and the English Venetians both overwork the figure:

Ex. 13a   *Ex. 13b*

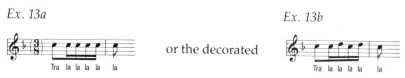

or the decorated

as an inverted dominant pedal-point (F major in both cases). In Offenbach there are two Doges in Venice at the same time; Gilbert and Sullivan have two Kings of Barataria; and in the stories of both operettas the women of the chorus take militant feminist action. *The Bridge of Sighs*, H. S. Leigh's English version of Offenbach's piece, was presented at the St James's Theatre on 18 November 1872; *The Gondoliers*, which was always to enjoy greater success, at the Savoy Theatre on 7 December 1889.

Le Pont des soupirs closed the season at the Bouffes on 29 May. Two days later the company gave their special court presentation of *M. Choufleury* — the second command performance within a year. On 15 August 1861, no doubt after some prompting from a grateful Morny, Napoleon III made Offenbach a 'chevalier de la Légion d'honneur'. The *Journal des Débats* and the *Revue des Deux Mondes* were scandalized by this award to a composer of light opera. But Offenbach paid no attention. He had arrived. And he had a new enthusiasm. Out of the profits of *Orphée aux Enfers* he had built a family house at Étretat on the coast of Normandy — the villa Orphée.

If you drive north from Le Havre along the flat cliff-top road the country is featureless for about ten miles. Then the road winds down between wooded hillsides to Étretat. Avoiding the right turn into the rue Guy de Maupassant, and keeping on across the *place*, past the *mairie* where Désiré was 'pigeonholed' when the Bouffes visited Étretat in 1857, you will find yourself in the rue Offenbach. Halfway up the hill among the trees is the villa Orphée.

It was completed in the spring of 1861. A few months later a candle left alight in a cupboard set fire to some clothes and the house burned to the ground. With characteristic resilience Offenbach immediately had it reconstructed. There Jacques and Herminie were famous for their

7. Children and grandchildren of Offenbach at the villa Orphée in
1891, eleven years after the composer's death
By kind permission of M. Michel Brindejont

hospitality. Over the years the guests included Alexandre Dumas (father
and son), Delibes, Bizet, Nadar, Gustave Doré, Villemessant, Jouvin,
Meilhac, Ludovic Halévy, Crémieux and many other celebrities. The
young Guy de Maupassant played hide-and-seek on the beach with the
Offenbach children. To convey his family and guests to the beach for the
daily bathing party Jacques acquired a char-à-banc; no ordinary vehicle,
but a replica of the one built for the Empress Eugénie. The servant
Mathurin was the coachman, and each daughter had her appointed seat.
After the first year there was the baby Auguste-Jacques on his father's
knee; and there was always a dog, whether Boum or Kleinzach.

As time passed the bedrooms were given names: 'La Belle Hélène', 'La Jolie Parfumeuse', 'Barbe-bleue', 'La Chanson de Fortunio', etc. The garden paths had romantic but less derivative names: 'Le Chemin des soupirs', 'Le Sentier de la vertu' and so on. When Jacques discovered a pair of lovers in the 'allée des Deux Aveugles' he renamed it 'allée des Deux Pécheurs' (Path of the Two Sinners), a pun on the title of his operetta *Les Deux Pêcheurs* ('The Two Fishermen'). Some of his continual punning was better than that, and was put to good use. When the local authorities imposed petty restrictions on the arrangements for a charity fête organized by the Offenbach family, Jacques designed the layout of the poster:[12]

GRANDE SYMPHONIE
DE LA

MER DE

JACQUES OFFENBACH

POUR

LES MALADES
AVEC LA PERMISSION DE

L'AUTORITÉ

showing that it is important to read the large as well as the small print.

Jacques supervised the family social life with capricious authority. If he suddenly decided at lunchtime on a family expedition, the char-à-banc would be ordered and everybody had to come. Dictatorial invitations were sent to neighbours. There was no opting out. The daughters, Berthe, Mimi, Pepita and Jacqueline, obediently present on such daytime occasions, were, however, excluded from late-night activities. They were brought up with the strictest propriety. In Paris they were not allowed to appear at the after-theatre parties until they were of age. None of them went to the Bouffes or the Variétés before she was married. On Offenbach first nights they were allowed to sit up late and wait for the news of success or failure. A family friend would take Jacques' carriage in the interval and drive home to tell them how the show was going.

At Étretat the girls' lives were supervised just as strictly. But Jacques had different rules where older women were concerned. On one occasion he found his half-sister Georgette sitting at his own customary place at the card-table playing patience. He chose to take offence at this solitary occupation. Georgette refused to stop. Jacques threatened to sweep the cards off the table. There was a struggle. Nobody was winning. In a momentary lull Jacques let down his trousers and 'calmly placed the thinnest part of his person on the table-top'. Georgette 'hit him hard', though history tantalizingly fails to relate where the blow fell. A different mood would find Jacques out in a fishing boat playing his cello in the moonlight. It was in the garden of the villa Orphée that the melody of *Dites-lui* from *La Grande-Duchesse de Gerolstein* was first heard, as Jacques played it on the cello to his family and friends. He could not escape his real vice, work. In the middle of all the social goings-on he would compose his operetta for the coming winter, sending furious letters to the librettists who couldn't keep up with him. In August 1862 he had been working at Ems with Charles Nuitter on *Bavard et Bavarde*. He was now waiting for the librettist to join him at Étretat. He wrote:

> Cher Ami
> Eh bien ! ! ! ! !
> Quand venez-vous ? ? ? ? ? ? ?
> Che fous hattend havec *un patience*
> > à vous
> > J. Offenbach[13]
> *Étretat ce 21 aout 62*

8. Characteristically impatient lines by Offenbach, in this instance to his librettist Nuitter

Archives de l'Opéra

Jacques, who wrote impeccable French, is here making fun of his atrocious German accent. He means 'Je vous attends avec *un patience*' — 'I'm waiting for you with a jigsaw-puzzle', no doubt a problem to do with fitting words to music, for which he needed Nuitter's help. But he is also punning again, on *un patience* and *impatience*.

Letters of this kind abound in his correspondence. When he was rehearsing in Paris he became even more frenzied:[14]

> *Théâtre des Bouffes-Parisiens*
> *Direction*
> Animal !
> Come to my place at 9½ hrs — it is absolutely vital complete the Finale of the 2nd act — we also have to . . . anyway, come, I'm furious! Impossible to rehearse without you.   J. O.

There was one special set of letters. When Jacques was away from home, and while his favourite child, Auguste, was still an infant, his adoring father wrote him edifying letters which were never posted, but were kept in a secret drawer with instructions that they were to be delivered to the boy on fixed dates after his father's death.

> *Ems, ten years after my death*
>
> My dear Auguste,
> I acknowledge receipt of the bill your jeweller has sent me for payment. I see among the rest an aigrette at 14,000 francs. At your age, twenty-three . . . you're doing all right. In my day the women sometimes got a feather or two, but not the jewelled kind. I have made my modest competence by the sweat of my notes. I beg you, do not send me yours, for I am not paying a penny.
>   Between you and me, don't go around with men of letters, these chaps who sleep all day and don't work at night. In short, ask me for advice whenever you want it, but never for money.
>   Your nagging old father,
>
>   Jacques.[15]

Jacques did not live to know the irony of his phrase 'at your age, twenty-three', for three years after his own death Auguste died of consumption at twenty-one.

Auguste, who was named after his godfather the duc de Morny, had hoped for a career in music. When he showed early promise Jacques did not discourage him, whatever other hopes he may have had for the boy's future. Auguste became a worshipping admirer of Bizet, whom he referred to as 'mon Dieu'. Not only was Bizet a friend of Jacques', he had married Fromental Halévy's daughter, so he was 'Ludo's' cousin, and was often present in Paris or at Étretat to encourage his young disciple. As a

9. Offenbach with his son Auguste-Jacques,
who was to die of tuberculosis at twenty-one,
only three years after the death of his father

schoolboy on holiday Auguste used to play the organ in church. The priest turned a deaf ear when the Mass was accompanied by pious improvisations on themes from Offenbach operettas.

Amateur theatricals were a favourite indoor sport at the villa Orphée, as they would also have been at any English house-party of the period. Jacques had established the tradition of family dramatics at a fancy dress ball in Paris, where he put on *L'Enfant Trouvère*, a parody on *Il Trovatore*, which had recently had its Paris première. Jacques played the lead; Ludo Halévy was a page. The orchestra consisted of Georges Bizet at the piano.

At the villa Orphée a notice would announce: 'GRANDE SOIRÉE, DONNÉE PAR LES COMÉDIENS ORDINAIRES DE MADAME OFFENBACH . . . musique de Richard Wagner . . .' (then a cast list including world celebrities like Malibran, pseudonyms for family and friends). From notices of this kind it is obvious that the entertainments were all Offenbachian burlesques and parodies. Their music and texts have not survived, but it is fair to assume that many fragments of the operettas we know today were first performed by Offenbach's children with friends such as Doré, Delibes and Maupassant, in a holiday house overlooking the English Channel.

CHAPTER VII

Tours & Troubles

1861–1862

··⚓··

In the summer of 1861 the Bouffes went to Vienna, where they had a great success with *Orphée aux Enfers,* then returned to Paris, to a bad trading year. During the season Offenbach handed over the administration to his colleague Alphonse Varney. It was an uneven winter for the Bouffes, beginning with a success of bizarre origin. A few years earlier the company had accepted for production an amusing one-act comedy by Élie Frébault with music 'by an unknown composer'.[1] Offenbach must have regretted taking the piece, for he did his best to forget about it. Frébault kept pestering him, however, and eventually Offenbach said he had lost the score, whereupon Frébault brought in lawyers. There were acrimonious exchanges of letters. In the end Offenbach had to agree to write new music. In a fit of sulky virtuosity he composed, in a few hours, a score in the decorated vocal style of the eighteenth century, full of the tricks of the trade: gruppetti, appoggiaturas, and, in Martinet's words, 'prettinesses and delicacies of every kind'. The opening number establishes the joke: urbanely elegant music set to a lyric full of uncouth rustic imagery; such matters as the sexual innocence of beans and cucumbers:

Ex. 14

Je n'ai ja-mais con-nu l'a-mour ___ Le veau qui tette en-core __ sa ___ mère ___ Le ha-ri-cot qui sort de ter- — -re Le cha-pon dans sa bas- — -se cour Le con-con-bre dans son en--fan — ce L'a-gneau qui vient de voir le jour N'ont pas __ au ___

coeur   plus— d'in-no - cen - ce   Je n'ai ja - mais con - nu l'a - mour,   Je n'ai ja-

·mais— con - nu _____ l'a - mour.

If the motive for this pastiche was mildly malicious, Offenbach could not conceal his sense of enjoyment in its execution. His little tantrum failed to annoy anyone and the public were delighted with *Apothicaire et Perruquier*. Offenbach often finds in pastiche or parody a useful approach to the treatment of an operetta subject. Because he cannot help being original the pastiche transcends imitation, and the parody emerges as an Offenbachian comment on another's style. Everything sounds fresh.

There followed *Le Roman comique*, which had some critical acclaim but failed with the public. The libretto of Crémieux and Halévy, based on Scarron's baroque novel about a group of strolling players, fell between two stools: not entirely serious, not quite burlesque. Two women singers, Mlles Olivier and Colbrun, made successful débuts at the Bouffes, and it was observed that the company was more than ever rich in talent.

Success returned early in 1862 with *M. et Mme Denis*, a one-act piece full of good things, including one of Offenbach's catchiest tunes, *La Chaconne*. 'Catchiness' is not to be confused with mere simplicity. It is a complex phenomenon, caused sometimes by neat repetitions or sequences in a rhythmic context, sometimes by a felicitous combination of accidents. When Offenbach hit on a catchy motif he had a good rule for handling it: tantalize the listener with recurring snatches of the simple motif, separated by forgettable elaborations. The trick is that the 'forget-table' bits can be the more interesting ones. In *La Chaconne* Offenbach used these passages to display the talent of Mlle Pfotzer, a coloratura soprano. The runs he wrote for her enhance the value of the original motif when it

returns in bar 29 as a relief and a contrast. The contrast is a return from
elaboration to simplicity, and a return from minor to major. The use of the
tonic minor for the middle section of a melody is a typical Offenbachian
colouring:

Ex. 15

The success of a new Offenbach operetta could still provoke bursts of spite from his opponents. During the curtain-calls on the first night of *M. et Mme Denis* the leading actor Potel called on *maestro* Offenbach to take a bow. One of the critics, Cardon, was outraged, and in *Le Figaro-Programme* he expostulated: 'Maestro Rossini, yes, *maestro* Offenbach, never. What ambitious vanity!' Jacques made short work of Cardon in his reply:

Oh Potel! my clumsy friend! now we're in a mess! M. Cardon is certainly serving us up in a tasty sauce! — Well, monsieur! temper your kind intentions and learn that *maestro* is an Italian expression applied to all composers from the greatest to the most humble, just as *maître* is used in France for every advocate from the most eloquent to the stammerer, and as *monsieur* goes for everybody, so that one has to say M. Cardon, as if he were M. Jules Janin.

I must end, M. Cardon, by conveying my gratitude for your kindness, even if it expressed itself in an attempt to give me a thorough hiding.[2]

In *Le Voyage de MM. Dunanan, père et fils,* the last new show of the 1861/1862 season, a provincial father and son, arriving in Paris, are tricked into believing they have reached Venice. This implausible situation provided the framework for a spectacular revue-like production, as suitably Venetian entertainments were laid on for the gullible pair. Playing tricks on travellers was a theme that reappeared four years later in *La Vie parisienne.* Both operettas have comic scenes in which servants are instructed in the parts they are to play in the deception. The scores, too, have a common feature. In the *Valse-mazurke* in *Dunanan* and in Métella's waltz song in *La Vie parisienne* the melody is played by cellos doubling the voice two octaves below, with a clarinet on the middle octave. In each case this slightly eerie effect comes as a colourful surprise in such a light-hearted context. The cellists must have thanked their cellist-composer for giving them something interesting to play:

Ex. 16

Dunanan uses the same orchestral pattern to begin with. A solo viola then takes over the melody, one octave below the voice, while the violins do a bit of gondoliering on their own (Ex. 17).

Dunanan originally had a scene involving a ballet of children, but when the critic of *La Presse* wrote that 'The children should be in bed at eight o'clock', a number of people agreed that the extra sleep would be better for the youngsters than would the extra money for their parents. The ballet was cut from the production. It was lucky that there was a production at

Ex. 17

all. Offenbach had been working on the music at Étretat the previous summer, when the villa Orphée burned down. The score was probably the first thing he reached for when the fire started. He sent a cable to Jules Moinaux, one of the librettists: 'Orphée burned. Dunanan saved. Everybody all right.'

In the summer of 1862 Jacques and Herminie had a son, the only boy among their five children. The theatre in the passage Choiseul was closed, and the company dispersed on tour for the summer. Half went to Brussels to bring *Orphée aux Enfers* to the Belgians for the second time. They took costumes but no scenery, and the piece was performed in the sets of another play with a devil or two painted on them. Other performers went to Vienna, where, in addition to *Orphée*, they played *Le Voyage de MM. Dunanan* and *M. et Mme Denis*. Mlle Pfotzer again went down well with her *Chaconne*. Offenbach went as usual to Ems, this time for the première of *Bavard et Bavarde*.

Once again the season's takings were not enough to pay the bills. The actor Bache was indignant. If his voice was, as Arsène Houssaye said 'high-pitched, like that of an adolescent', his prose was no less so when the management failed to pay his salary:

Tours & Troubles: 1861–1862

To His Excellency The Minister of State.

Monsieur le ministre,

The Management of the Bouffes-Parisiens Theatre, to which I belong, refuses with an unheard-of overweening presumption to pay my salary for the past month (July). And the second article of my contract forbids me, under pain of *two months* suspension of pay for each infringement, to appear at any other *theatre, concert,* or any *public or private evening performance.*

Now, not having received my monthly dues, and being unable to perform anywhere else, I have no alternative but to appeal for help to the funds set aside for needy artists, or to die of hunger.

However, I have a wife and four children! — It is a very modest salary to cover everything! Therefore I cannot wait.

Moreover, would it be wise to do so? What is the situation in this theatre?

An incompetent director, totally insolvent, landed already with *two hundred thousand francs* of the previous management's debts! — constantly augmented by his own; unable, even at the end of six

10. Offenbach performing before some contemporary composers
By kind permission of M. Michel Brindejont

months, to honour his personal guarantee! who had done no satisfactory work, and has none ready; and for whom bankruptcy is so near
that no one dares to take him in front of the competent court! ! !

There is no need for me to go into the motives that persuaded the
Varney gentleman to take over such a perilous situation from Monsieur
Offenbach; but everybody saw that it would only speed up bankruptcy;
and that later *yet another* person would be able to take over this
deplorable management.

My complaints are perhaps bitter, Minister, but as I have said, your
Excellency, I am starving! ! In this situation a man no longer consults
anything but his despair; if you do not take pity on me I truly do not
know what I can do. . . .

This letter[3] and others of its kind are in the French national archives.
Pinned to Bache's letter[3] is a note in blue crayon, a civil servant's informal
brief to his Minister: 'M. Bache, artist of the Bouffes, is asking to be paid
out of the surety — a lot of money is owed to the artists — I believe that
even the troupe in Vienna has not been paid — The surety is not enough to
pay everybody — M. Bache can therefore only expect payment in part.'
Across the corner of the page, in a strong hand, is the Minister's
instruction: 'Do not permit the Bouffes to re-open until they have paid
up.'

CHAPTER VIII

Bad Ems and Vienna
1862–1864

······

New names were appearing in Paris: the thirty-one-year-old Victorien Sardou consolidated his reputation as a playwright with *Les Ganaches* ('The Blockheads'). At nineteen Adelina Patti made her Parisian début in *La Sonnambula*. In December 1862 *Le Ménestrel* reported: 'An English musician of merit, Mr Arthur Sullivan, has arrived in Paris.'

Sardou was later to collaborate with Offenbach on *Le Roi Carotte*, based on Hoffman's story *Kleinzaches, gennant Zinnober*, and with Offenbach and Nuitter on *Don Quichotte*, adapted from Cervantes. *Don Quichotte* was never staged in Offenbach's version (see Chapter XIV) but a comedy called *Los Habladores*, attributed to Cervantes, was the source of his present success, *Bavard et Bavarde*, which opened at Ems on 12 June 1862. An expanded version, entitled *Les Bavards*, went on to Paris in February 1863, and the piece turned up later in England as *Beatrice, the Chattering Wife*. One of its successful comic devices was to have a scene of non-stop chattering followed by a scene played in total silence. Offenbach sent a telegram to Nuitter, the librettist, congratulating him on the silent scene. A good patter song, *Ah! quel repas sans égal* (Ex. 18) has a continuous quaver movement in 6/8 suggestive of the later Lord Chancellor's song in *Iolanthe*. Saint-Saëns, not usually an admirer of Offenbach's, regarded *Les Bavards* as 'a little masterpiece'.

Ex. 18

Ah! quel re‑pas sans é – gal, Quel hô‑te li‑bé‑ral D'un ac‑cueil a‑mi‑cal, Voi‑là l'i‑dé‑al;

Je pré-fère au plus beau bal, Au plus doux mad-ri – gal, Le plai-sir cor-di – al D'un pa-reil ré -gal

The Bouffes, having presumably found the money needed for per-mission to re-open, survived the winter of 1862–3 on a diet of proven successes: *Orphée, Ba-ta-clan, Chanson de Fortunio*. Offenbach enticed old audiences back to *Orphée* by supplying a one-act curtain-raiser, *Jacqueline*. But his main preoccupation was with a new project for the Opéra-Comique, a two-act comic opera, *Fédia* (or *Foedia*). According to the *Revue et Gazette Musicale* the work got as far as being put into rehearsal, but Offenbach's exasperated correspondence with Halévy indicates that it was never completed. Three years before Jacques' death it became the cause of bitterness between him and his old friend Ludo Halévy, when Jacques discovered that Halévy and Crémieux had rewritten the libretto for Charles Lecocq, his increasingly successful rival.

At the end of the season the old Bouffes was demolished and the construction of the present theatre began. Offenbach's movements were now charted in the musical press. The *Revue et Gazette Musicale* of 28 June 1863 reported: 'Offenbach stayed only long enough in Paris to see the laying of the foundations of the new Bouffes. He is leaving for Ems to produce his operetta *Il Signor Fagotto*. From there he goes to Berlin, where his three-act *opéra-comique* is to be presented; after which he will go to Vienna to prepare the production of a grand opera in four acts, *Les Fées du Rhin*. Eventually he will be coming back to Paris to devote his attention to the work that is to re-open the Bouffes: *Les Géorgiennes*.[1]

In *Il Signor Fagotto* Offenbach is thought to have been parodying Berlioz in a mock-antique passage reminiscent of moments in *Les Troyens*. *Il Signor Fagotto* preceded the first performance of Part II of *Les Troyens* by a few months, but it is quite likely that Offenbach heard part of the score at a private audition. If so, his parody must have been a riposte to the ex-coriating attack made by Berlioz on *Barkouf*. In the early 1850s, when Offenbach was writing for *L'Artiste*, he championed the cause of Berlioz when it was not yet fashionable to do so. Even when the music of Berlioz found public acceptance, Offenbach continued to praise it: 'Berlioz may console himself for his rejection by the Academy with the immense success of *L'Enfance du Christ*. . . . [he] has won the approval of the entire musical public, a section of which, up to now, used to denigrate this virile talent, which, elevated and accomplished though it was, had — for a symphonist — a serious fault, that of being French.'

But after *Barkouf* Offenbach performed a volte-face. It was possibly not just what Berlioz said about *Barkouf* that upset him, but the fact that the attack was made on that particular occasion. Offenbach's deepest wish was to succeed at the Opéra-Comique, where he had hitherto been snubbed. However much he criticized that institution, he longed to be accepted by it, and to be regarded as a serious composer rather than a buffoon of the boulevards. If *Barkouf* had been put on at the Bouffes, and

11. The Bouffes-Parisiens today. Photo by the author

had flopped, Offenbach would probably have taken its failure philosophically. But he had relied on the piece to effect his entrée to the musical establishment. The violence of his reaction to Berlioz's hostile review suggests that he had been touched on the raw; that despite his superficial self-confidence he may secretly have doubted his ability to rise above the level of the boulevard entertainer. One suspects, too, that Offenbach thought Berlioz guilty of ingratitude to his former champion in failing to soften his language about *Barkouf*, even if he disliked the piece.

Whatever the truth of the matter, Berlioz was never forgiven. Jacques Brindejont-Offenbach found among his grandfather's books a copy of Berlioz's *Memoirs* with more than 150 marginal comments in Offenbach's hand. These vary from the gently sardonic to the openly bitchy, but their sheer number reveals that even after Berlioz was dead Offenbach thought of him with with undiminished bitterness.

The Viennese journalist Friedrich Uhl once wrote that Offenbach 'would have died as rich as Meyerbeer if it hadn't been for the women and the damned card games'. A woman and a gambling session in Ems (one of the few towns in Europe where gambling was allowed) led to the creation of *Lischen et Fritzchen*. Zulma Bouffar was a vivacious twenty-year-old blonde, a talented actress with a lovely voice. In the summer of 1863 Jacques saw her in a show at Homburg, fell for her, and introduced himself. He found that she had been born in the Midi, into a theatrical family. At the age of twelve she joined a German company and was soon singing risqué Parisian songs in a Cologne brasserie. It proved to be one of the places where the young Jacob had performed in the trio with his brother and sister, a coincidence that was confirmed by Albert Wolff, who remembered seeing the girl performing there, her proud father stationed in the audience to applaud any French jokes which the Germans failed to understand. After more touring Zulma settled for a while in Brussels, where she sometimes played Offenbach roles, and eventually came to Homburg.

Jacques and Zulma became friends, and, it may be assumed, lovers. Where Offenbach's women are concerned one has to make do with hints and assumptions. The remarks of his contemporaries indicate a conspiracy of discretion, perhaps out of consideration for the much-liked Mme Offenbach. We read of Jacques being 'torn apart by cruel passions', of his 'regular peccadilloes'. He is frequently 'in love', never 'a lover'. He remained devoted to his wife and children throughout his life; but a letter to Halévy in which he says 'you must have heard everything from my wife, I won't go on about it', is taken to refer to a conjugal row about Zulma. Another letter is even more revealing. Jacques wrote from Prague to his collaborator Nuitter in Paris:

12. Offenbach dressed with his customary sartorial panache
Collection Viollet

13. The soubrette Zulma Bouffar. Offenbach brought her from Germany to become a Parisian star; Madame Offenbach had her doubts about his motives
Mander and Mitchenson Collection

It is absolutely vital that you do me a tremendous favour. Go to M. de Pêne and ask him on my behalf to put in his paper *the very same day* the following words (or something similar): 'Several artistes of the Bouffes who are not involved in *Orphée*, M. Berthelier, Mmes *Z. Bouffar* and Mariés began a series of performances this week at Nantes.' They read Pêne's paper at home, and these few words will be most timely. I must beg you and friend de Pêne to be totally discreet . . .[2]

In other words, Herminie would read in the paper that Zulma was in Nantes while Jacques was in Prague. Where Zulma actually was we do not know, but it was essential that Herminie should believe there were a thousand miles between Zulma and Jacques.

On a July evening in 1863 there was a gambling party. Over supper there was talk of Offenbach's speed in composing. Jacques made a bet that he could compose, orchestrate and rehearse a one-act operetta in eight days. He was taken on. Paul Boisselot produced a ready-made libretto, and a week later *Lieschen und Fritzchen*, a 'conversation alsacienne', was presented with Zulma Bouffar playing one of its two characters.

Offenbach had won the bet, but had cheated slightly by including an adaptation of his setting of the La Fontaine fable about the town rat and the country rat, written twenty-one years earlier.

Il Signor Fagotto and *Lieschen und Fritzchen* had their premières on successive Saturdays. The night before the opening of *Lieschen* Jacques had been at the gambling table. After an unlucky bet the croupier broke his rake as he reached for Jacques' losses. Lindheim, the young conductor from the Kursaal, asked Jacques if he might use the end of the broken rake to conduct *Lieschen*. The idea amused Jacques and the company, and after the success of *Lieschen* the rake became a talisman. Lindheim was promoted to Paris, and a year later used the same baton to conduct the first performance of *La Belle Hélène*.

After 1848 the Viennese popular theatre was looking more and more to Paris for new ideas. The Karltheater, under the direction of the playwright and actor Nestroy, had as one of its leading performers the German Karl Treumann, whose forte was playing comic parts in short sketches and farces. This sort of entertainment became increasingly popular with the appearance in Vienna in 1856 of the French comedian Levassor. Vienna had also a tradition of dramatic and musical parodies of mythological subjects. The ground was therefore well prepared for Offenbach.

Encouraged by Treumann, Nestroy planned a guest appearance of the Bouffes-Parisiens, but the project fell through because of the Karltheater's shaky financial position. In the hope that such a visit might later become possible Offenbach refused the theatre permission to mount any of his operettas with a Viennese company. Nestroy got round this with a pirated production *Die Verlobung bei der Laterne* (*Le Mariage aux lanternes*), translated by Treumann and orchestrated by Binder[3] from the French piano score. Even in this corrupt form the show was a hit. Nestroy followed it up with more piracy, finally casting himself as Jupiter in *Orpheus in der Unterwelt*. Offenbach was either powerless to stop these proceedings or unwilling to litigate in case he prejudiced his future chances in Vienna.

When Treumann took over the management of the Karltheater from Nestroy in November 1860 he immediately invited Offenbach to conduct the original versions of three of his operettas with a Viennese cast. Jacques arrived in January 1861 to a celebrity's welcome. When he was taken to meet the company Treumann introduced him in verse, and he was given a laurel wreath. The ladies of the company then presented him with a second wreath on a white satin cushion. On each leaf the name of one of the actresses was inscribed in gold.

There were three performances under Offenbach's baton — *Die Zaubergeige* (*Le Violoneux*), *Die Verlobung bei der Laterne* and *Ein Ehemann vor der Tür* (*Un Mari à la porte*). The composer won an ovation from the public and praise from the critics, who were impressed by the superiority, particularly in orchestration, of the original material over the pirated versions. One of these critics — Eduard Hanslick — was subsequently to play an important part in Offenbach's career.

As a result of his personal triumph Offenbach was invited to bring the Bouffes-Parisiens company to Vienna later the same year, and their season of twenty performances consolidated his reputation. From then on he visited Vienna regularly. Publishers asked him to compose dance music for them, but he was reluctant to compete with Strauss and others in a specifically Viennese idiom. When, however, in 1863, he was asked by the Concordia, a journalists' club, to compose a waltz for their carnival ball, he wrote *Abendblätter* ('Evening Papers'). Johann Strauss the younger had been given a similar commission, and when he heard of Offenbach's title he called his own waltz *Morgenblätter* ('Morning Papers'). It was a joke without malice; Strauss had in fact already written to Hanslick asking him to act as his intermediary in procuring *Abendblätter* for his new publishing company. At the ball *Abendblätter* was marginally better received, but *Morgenblätter* later became a classic. The two composers soon met, and it was on this occasion that Offenbach made the farsighted suggestion that Strauss should start writing operettas.

The year 1863 was nearly over. Offenbach had been active in Paris, Ems, Berlin and Vienna. A freak success in Paris had been *La Ronde du Brésilien*, a comedy duet written for Meilhac and Halévy's one-act play *Le Brésilien*. Its refrain became the hit of the day (Ex. 19).

Ems had seen *Lieschen und Fritzchen* and *Il Signor Fagotto*, which was dedicated by Offenbach 'à son ami Hanslick'. It may well have been Hanslick's influence that won for Offenbach the commission to write a full-scale work for the Vienna Opera. Certainly Wagner was the loser on this occasion. A Vienna production of *Tristan und Isolde*, planned for 1863, was abandoned partly because the tenor Ander, who had been seriously ill, was eventually considered inadequate for the part of Tristan. But Wagner reveals that there was more to the story:

> When I finally offered to write a new work solely for Vienna, taking particular account of the theatre's performers and the forces at its disposal, I received the carefully worded reply that 'the name "Wagner" had now been given sufficient consideration, and it was thought appropriate to invite an approach from another composer'. This other was Jacques Offenbach, who was now commissioned to write a work specially for Vienna.[4]

Wagner, as is well known, had his revenge on Hanslick by caricaturing

Ex. 19

Voulez vous, voulez vous, voulez vous ac-cep-ter mon bras? Voulez

vous, voulez vous, vou-lez vous ac-cep-ter mon bras? La __ fem-me __

ritenuto

ne ré-pon-dait pas

suivez

him in the part of Beckmesser in *Die Meistersinger von Nürnberg*. But this was unfair to Hanslick, whom Peter Gay has put into perspective for us in his essay 'For Beckmesser'[5] as a critic of integrity, conscientious, erudite and readable, who deserved something better than the spiteful caricature that has distorted his reputation. Hanslick was a Mozart–Beethoven–Brahms man, far too much of a conservative to come to terms with the new Wagner (though he had praised *Tannhäuser*, and had for a time been on friendly terms with the composer). He resented the fact that Wagner and Liszt, 'the musicians of the future', dared to claim Beethoven as their musical ancestor. His views on aesthetics, and on music in particular, were based on reasoned principles which Wagner found pedantic and academic. That Hanslick should have promoted Offenbach's interest at the Vienna Opera at the expense of Wagner would explain the personal animosity that further embittered the musical conflict between critic and composer. Their mutual hostility intensified to the point where Hanslick, writing of *The Ring* and *Tristan*, described Wagner's doctrine of 'the unending melody' as 'formlessness raised to a principle, opium intoxication sung and fiddled, a cult to which, as we know, a special temple has been raised at Bayreuth'. As Gay observes, 'What irritated Hanslick almost beyond the bounds of self-control was that Wagner was not merely so wrong, but that he seemed so important.'

By accident of time and place Offenbach frequently became the subject of comparison with Wagner, an exercise that now seems pointless. But both composers were in Paris in 1860, and both were in Vienna in 1863. Offenbach was the most commercially successful composer of his time, Wagner the most controversial; Offenbach was 'easy', Wagner 'difficult'. It was tempting to take sides. Even after Offenbach's death, Nietzsche was matching them against each other:

> If one understands by artistic genius the greatest freedom under the law, divine frivolity, facility in the hardest things, then Offenbach has even more right to the name 'genius' than Wagner. Wagner is heavy and ponderous: nothing is more foreign to him than moments of the most high-spirited perfection, such as this buffoon Offenbach achieves

14. Wagner as 'The Musician of the Future'

Bibliothèque nationale

five or six times in almost every one of his buffooneries. But perhaps one might understand something else by the word genius.[6]

Nietzsche's exaggeration is not complete nonsense. He touches on something of which Wagner was uncomfortably aware: his difficulty in expressing himself adequately in simple music, the feeling that eventually led him, as we have seen, to say 'Look at Offenbach. He writes like the divine Mozart. The fact is, my friend, the French have the secret of these things.' Because of this, Wagner could forgive Offenbach, the composer — and a Jew at that — who had once supplanted him at the Vienna Opera; but he never lost his contempt for Eduard Hanslick, the powerful critic who had engineered the event.

Die Rheinnixen ('The Rhine Nymphs') was the first Offenbach work to be *durchkomponiert* — 'composed throughout' — i.e. with continuous music and no spoken dialogue. Considering that the opera was for Vienna and

15. Zulma Bouffar

Collection Viollet

therefore had to be in German, Offenbach's native language, the composer set about it in a curious way. The idea was that Nuitter would write a libretto in French, Offenbach would set it to music, and the French text would then be translated into German. A justification for this cumbersome method could have been that Offenbach hoped for a Paris production later. As soon as he received an outline of the work from Nuitter, Offenbach travelled three hundred miles to Breslau to see Baron Alfred von Wolzogen, who had once written an article in praise of *Orphée* in the *Neue Berliner Musikzeitung*, to persuade him to undertake the translation into German. (Wolzogen's young son remembered their famous visitor as 'a pince-nez on a crooked nose'.)

Snippets of music with illegible French words went to and fro between Nuitter (in Paris or Étretat), Wolzogen (in Breslau) and the constantly travelling Offenbach, who kept up his usual stream of demands for alterations and faster work. Wolzogen, though he found the task difficult, was mildly amused by the whole episode. It was not the ideal way to produce a coherent work of art. The story was a mish-mash of Rhineland romanticism, with the usual clichés of that genre. Offenbach delved in his store-cupboard for old melodies. He used the song *Das Vaterland*, written in his temporary patriotic fervour of 1848:

Ex. 20

and revived the waltz from *Le Papillon*:

Ex. 21

The principal motif of the opera, occurring in the overture, in the finale, and as a central chorus of elves, was destined to be resurrected later as the Barcarolle in *Les Contes d'Hoffmann*.

In the course of his work on *Die Rheinnixen* Offenbach wrote to Nuitter asking him to borrow a copy of Berlioz's *Treatise on Instrumentation* and to have the passages dealing with horns and trumpets copied out and sent to Ems. 'The treatise of Berlioz is excellent for these two instruments,' he wrote, 'and I sometimes have to consult it — if you can't get it either from Brandus or Heugel, get me a horn method that gives it all — and the same for trumpets, although that is not so important. All this between ourselves — no need to mention the reason to Brandus unless you have to.' Offenbach was an accomplished, albeit conventional orchestrator. But he was tackling a more serious dramatic work than hitherto. It may be that, as a string player, he still felt some uncertainty about his writing for wind and brass, and was honest enough to admit to gaps in his technique, provided his rivals (Berlioz in particular?) did not hear about it.

Just before the opening of *Die Rheinnixen* Offenbach rushed back to Paris for the inauguration of the rebuilt Bouffes-Parisiens theatre. On 5 January 1864 a double-bill was presented in a bitterly cold theatre — the doors had not yet been installed and there was tenting across the entrance. *L'Amour chanteur* had a cool reception, *Lischen et Fritzchen* repeated its Ems success, and Paris was introduced to Offenbach's darling, Zulma Bouffar.

CHAPTER IX

La Belle Hortense
1864

·······

Offenbach had another sixteen years to live. Time — for him — to write fifty-one more operettas and *Les Contes d'Hoffmann*. *Les Géorgiennes*, a three-act spectacular about Amazons, opened at the Bouffes on 16 March 1864. 'Lorgnettes were to the fore', wrote Martinet, 'when the army of the *Géorgiennes* arrived; twelve adorable drummers preceding the general Ugalde, a staff of exquisite officers led by Mlles Zulma Bouffar and Taffanel, and behind Mlle Lange, the standard-bearer, two companies as sprucely coquettish as their officers.'[1] These were the forerunners of the Tiller Girls and the Radio City Rockettes. Bouffar was a great success — 'she is definitely the pearl of the theatre', wrote Halévy — and Léonce made a magnificent entrance on a cardboard elephant. The *Marseillaise des femmes* was the musical hit of the evening. Its refrain was 'A bas les hommes!' But at the end of the story, as in Gilbert and Sullivan's *Princess Ida*, the female stronghold surrendered to male predominance. A gypsy chorus in A minor and 3/8 time, going into a refrain in A major recalls the gypsy and matador music in Act II of *La Traviata*.

In the summer Offenbach went to Ems, where he produced *Le Fifre enchanté ou le Soldat magicien* (later presented in Paris) and *Jeanne qui pleure et Jean qui rit*. He wrote to his wife about his day's routine:

6.30	I got up and took the waters.
9.0	Désiré and Paul came for a lesson on *Jeanne*.
10.0	I attended the dress rehearsal of *Fortunio*.
11.0	Lunch.
Midday	Rehearsal of *Soldat*.
2.30	Visit to M. de Talleyrand, the French minister in Berlin, who had asked me to go and see him in order to present me to his wife.
4.0	My bath.
	It's now 5.0, I'm writing to you.

111

At 6.0 we dine.
This evening at 7.0 the company of *Jeanne* and *Soldat* come to
my place.[2]

Both works were a great success. Jacques went back across the Rhine to
Étretat, to his family and friends, and then suddenly to Paris to meet and
create trouble at the Bouffes. True to the predictions of the despairing
Bache (see Chapter VII), Varney had made a mess of things. His successor, Hanappier, was no better, and the theatre was yet again
threatened with bankruptcy. Since Offenbach gave up the management,
the company had been under contract to include a certain proportion of
Offenbach works in the repertoire; they had failed to do so. Offenbach
issued a writ. In an attempt at appeasement the management went to visit
him, only to find that the composer had left that morning for Vienna to
rehearse *Les Géorgiennes*.

L'*Almanach de la Musique* saw the affair from a different angle: 'We are
now assured that the direction of the Bouffes-Parisiens is to be taken over
by a great artist, Mme Ugalde. May she have success, and deliver us
forever from M. Offenbach, from his music and his absurd pretensions.'
Delphine Ugalde was the general in *Les Géorgiennes*, a part she had learnt
in two days when the original star, Mme Saint-Urbain, took ill. Her
daughter Marguerite was to be the original Nicklausse in *Les Contes
d'Hoffmann*.

Offenbach now turned again to ancient Greece for inspiration. Halévy
produced the sketch of a libretto to be called *La Prise de Troie* ('The Capture
of Troy'). Offenbach suggested collaborating with Crémieux, but, as the
recent collaboration with Meilhac, *La Ronde du Brésilien* (see Chapter VIII),
had been so successful, Halévy approached Meilhac.

Letters full of ideas from the itinerant Jacques began to pour in as usual.
'You know how the English send correspondents everywhere in wartime.
We could perhaps use this idea in our *Prise de Troie*: what about Homer as a
correspondent of *The Times*? If you can work him in as an episodic
character, do so; if not, not.' Production was planned for the end of 1864.
During the process of creation the operetta was renamed *La Belle Hélène*.[3]
Saint–Saëns reported that 'It was when Offenbach was transplanted to
the Variétés that operetta-madness and the collapse of good taste began.
When *La Belle Hélène* came on, Paris took leave of its senses; everyone's
head was turned. The most respectable women tried to outdo each other
in singing 'Amour divin, ardente flamme' ('Heavenly love, flame of
passion'). Blond rosy-cheeked children murmured softly to their mothers:
Maman, tourne vers moi un bec favorable!'[4]
The reference is to the scene where Helen, in the contrived absence of her
husband, is waiting in her apartment for the handsome young shepherd

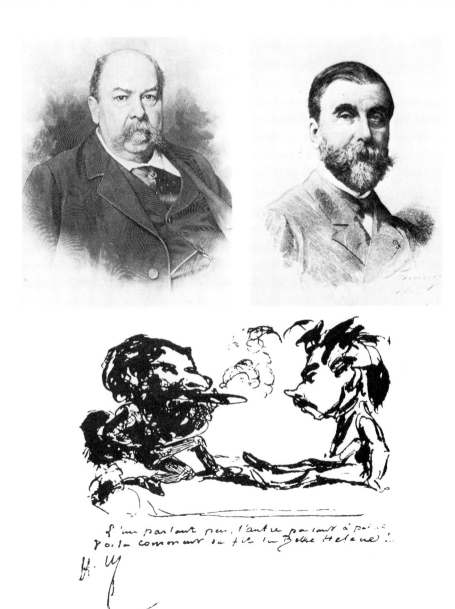

16, 17 and 18. 'Les collabos', Henri Meilhac (top left) and Ludovic Halévy (top right), the most successful of Offenbach's librettists. Meilhac drew the cartoon and wrote the caption:

L'un parlant peu, l'autre parlant à peine,
Voilà comment se fit la Belle Hélène!

(One spoke a few words, the other almost none,
That was the way La Belle Hélène was done!)

Bibliothèque nationale and *Collection Viollet*

Paris. She muses in front of a picture of Leda and the swan (Jupiter in disguise) of whose union she is the offspring: 'Here are the pair of them, my father, my mother. . . . O father, turn a kindly beak towards your child! . . . And Venus, could you not have found a less mischievous reward for the shepherd? Why, but why, O goddess, have you always picked on our family for your experiments?'

Saint-Saëns' puritanical comments typify a common attitude of the time towards Offenbach. Much of the hostile criticism directed at the composer during his lifetime was concerned not with his music, but with the moral, social or political content of the librettos. The fact that these were the work of Meilhac, Halévy or any of a dozen others made no difference: Offenbach was the butt of criticism. As impresario he determined the choice of subject; it was his attitude to life and the theatre that unified the method and manner of his diverse collaborators. His operettas were one of the artistic elements for which Paris under Napoleon III was internationally famous. Offenbach became a symbol of the Empire to such an extent that after the 1870 revolution he was *persona non grata* with the Republicans, and *La Grande-Duchesse de Gerolstein* was banned by the 'gouvernement de l'ordre moral'. He was a social, historical, almost a political figure, as much as a musical one. For that reason, in general histories of nineteenth-century France Offenbach is sometimes given more prominence than greater contemporaries such as Berlioz.

Saint-Saëns' complaint was on moral grounds. There were two common criticisms levelled at the 'Greek' operettas: first, that they were licentious; second, that they were, in Jules Janin's words, 'sacrilege, a desecration of antiquity'. Janin objected to Offenbach's frivolous treatment of subjects hitherto taken seriously: the religion of the Greeks and their classic legends. But these legends included many licentious stories; however unfrivolously Offenbach were to treat, for instance, the story of Leda and the swan, he could hardly be expected to make the antics of Venus and Jupiter conform to the morals of the Catholic Church.

Implicit in the hostility of critics like Janin was a distaste for what in the English theatre would be called 'camp'. Camp — easier to recognize than to define — might be described as the art of the knowingly artificial. It is apparent in the theatre when actors get laughs by inviting the audience to enjoy their manifest exaggerations. The acting is at two removes from reality: the actor is not only playing a part, he is also demonstrating to the audience that he is conscious of the style in which he is performing; he is deriving fun from that style and from the joke shared with the audience.

The written material that demands such performances is usually camp in itself, the author being as self-consciously mannered as he expects his actors to be. At its best camp is skilful, elegant and funny: the English Restoration comedies are high camp; so are *Orphée aux Enfers* and *La Belle*

19. Hortense Schneider as she appeared on stage as the Grand Duchess of Gerolstein
Eindhoven Collection

Hélène. (The use of the word camp in connection with effeminate mannerisms may be seen as a particular case under the above definition. It is irrelevant in this immediate context, but in one or two other Offenbach operettas, e.g. *Mesdames de la Halle*, the male actors had great success playing women's roles for comic effect).

At the storm centre of *La Belle Hélène* was Mlle Schneider, then beginning her reign as the empress of operetta. Hortense Schneider was born in Bordeaux in 1833, and died in Paris in 1920. Her father was a tailor from Strasbourg — another Jewish immigrant — her mother a native of Bordeaux. Her parents took her to the theatre where she quickly became stage-struck, dressing up, playing parts, always wanting to sing, dance and act. She worked in a shop, and attended a drama school attached to the Athénée theatre, where she studied singing and diction under a M. Schaffner, who taught her how to breathe, and to 'sing easily, without showing effort'. When she was given her chance to go on stage she was an instant success, a buxom lass with blue eyes, and red-golden hair that, in the words of her fond mother, 'put the sun to shame'.

When the theatre stopped putting on musical productions Schneider stayed on as a straight actress. She had sung in opera; but the fact that her career became directed towards vaudeville, where good acting took precedence over a classical singing style, made her an ideal artist for Offenbach works. She suffered badly from stage-fright, a problem that never left her, but no one would have guessed it from her performance. Like the young Offenbach she was given to playing pranks during performances; she would lift a supposedly heavy trunk without any sign of effort, or pretend there was a hair in her cutlet at a meal on stage. Like Offenbach, too, she was fined for such misdemeanours.

Her first lover was Cyprien Cazabonne, who 'was permitted the honour of ruining himself for her, because she had suffered too much from poverty and wretched conditions to see love any other way'.[5] Another admirer, the young actor Candeilh of the Théâtre-Français, convinced her that she should go to Paris, and gave her an introduction to Berthelier, who had just made his big hit in *Les Deux Aveugles*, and who introduced her to Offenbach on the occasion described in Chapter IV.

After her début in *Le Violoneux* she appeared in *Tromb-al-ca-zar, La Rose de Saint-Flour*, and Adam's *Les Pantins de Violette*. When the curtain fell on the first night of *Les Pantins* Adolphe Adam kissed Hortense and swore that she should play Kettly in the revival of his opera *Le Chalet*[6] at the Opéra-Comique. But a few days later Adam died suddenly. Schneider never made the move into opera.

Becoming over-confident, she demanded a new salary of 500 francs a month, a figure the Bouffes could not, or would not, pay. She left in a huff, and joined the company managed by Cogniard at the Variétés, where she was paid only half the sum she had demanded from the Bouffes. She acquired another source of income in the young duc de Gramont-Caderousse. Their affair was one of intermittent fidelity — Hortense only one of his mistresses, Caderousse only one of her lovers — but it lasted until his early death. He had tuberculosis, and had decided to kill himself quickly with wild living rather than become a slave to his illness. In the circumstances it was not surprising that he became a popular figure always in the news, whether riding his English steeplechaser, Forest King, or, in the Café Anglais, filling a grand piano with champagne to make an aquarium. In 1858 Hortense bore him a son, who, after a normal childhood, contracted a nervous malady and spent the rest of his life in seclusion, cared for by his adoring mother. When Caderousse died, he left 50,000 francs to Hortense — his only female beneficiary — and another 1,000,000 francs for their son. The will was hotly contested, but to no avail.

In Jacques Offenbach's eyes, Hortense Schneider was the only possible Belle Hélène. But there were complications. Schneider had been working at the Palais Royal. After a row about money with the manager, Plunkett, she had announced, for the hundredth time, her permanent retirement from the theatre. (She had not yet played any of the roles that were to bring her lasting fame.) Meanwhile, in support of his campaign against the Bouffes, Offenbach was pressing to get *La Belle Hélène* put on at the Palais Royal. Offenbach and Halévy went to Schneider's house. She was alone, surrounded by luggage and packing-cases, preparations for her removal to Bordeaux. A conversation took place through the closed front door: 'I have a part for you, an amazing part.' 'Too late, my love, I'm giving up the theatre.' 'A superb idea for the Palais Royal.' Schneider flung open the door and cursed the Palais Royal. Offenbach took the opportunity of a moment of calm to go to the piano (which fortunately was not yet packed) and play some of the tunes. They told her the story of the play. Hortense hesitated, then stood her ground. Hours later she was on the train to Bordeaux, feeling a qualm of jealousy for the unknown rival who would land the part of Helen. A few days later there was an exchange of telegrams:

Offenbach to Schneider:	'All off Palais Royal, possible Variétés.'
Schneider to Offenbach:	'I want 2,000 francs a month.'
Cogniard to Schneider:	'Agreed, come quickly.'
Schneider to Cogniard:	'Marvellous! I just want a week's rest.'[7]

Hortense was in Paris in two days.

Anyone who expected *La Belle Hélène* to be a mere rewrite of *Orphée aux Enfers* was in for a revelation. The setting was still Greece, but the musical style had moved halfway from Paris to Vienna. With the arguable exception of the opening chorus, eighteenth-century pastiche had been abandoned. The mood of the play is more sexual, the music more sensuous. *Orphée aux Enfers* involves sexual adventures, but *La Belle Hélène* is *about* sex. The seduction scene in *Orphée* simply sets the plot in motion, whereas the seduction scene in *La Belle Hélène* is the climax of the play.

In the plot there is a beauty contest on Mount Ida between Juno, Venus and Minerva. The prize is a golden apple, with the young shepherd Paris as judge. The goddesses offer him bribes. He awards the apple to Venus, who has promised him the love of the most beautiful woman in the world. In Act I Helen, Queen of Sparta, hears the story. Aware that she is the most beautiful woman in the world, she affects distress at her fate (indeed 'la fatalité' is invoked throughout *La Belle Hélène* to excuse every human peccadillo). Helen plots with Calchas, the high priest, to bring about this desirable fate as quickly as possible. Paris arrives, and, revealing that he is the son of Priam, King of Troy, persuades Calchas to get Helen's husband King Menelaus out of the way. Calchas orders stage thunder and announces that the gods have decreed that Menelaus must spend a month in Crete; nobody knows why Crete, or for what purpose.

In Act II Helen, about to sleep, asks Calchas to grant her a dream about the beautiful shepherd ('l'homme à la pomme'). When she wakes to find Paris kneeling at her bedside — he has entered by disguising himself as one of the guards — she allows herself to believe that this is the dream she has asked for. Paris plays along with her delusion, and in the dream duet *Oui, c'est un rêve!* — a ravishing blend of romance and comedy — the seduction proceeds with both parties willing.

Menelaus returns unexpectedly to find them together. There is general outrage, though Helen and the assembled company are quick to point out to Menelaus that a wise husband has a duty to warn his wife of his return — thereby gallantly avoiding unpleasantness. Paris is sent away, vowing that he will return to fulfil the promise of Venus (Ex. 22).

In Act III nobles and populace disport themselves on a beach. Much sport is made with nineteenth-century bathing costumes *à la grècque*, and with a test-your-strength machine. Agamemnon, looking on, bemoans the present sorry state of Greece: 'It is a huge bacchanal; Venus is working the infernal merry-go-round. Pleasure and voluptuousness are everywhere. Virtue, duty, honour, morals are carried away on the waves.' His song refers to the *haut monde* of the Second Empire. In the Greek society of the operetta Agamemnon and Menelaus are the only moral characters, and Menelaus is stupid. The rest are cynical, amoral, hypocritical; good material for comedy, with Offenbach's shrewd eye upon them.

To stop the moral decay Menelaus decides to make a sacrifice to propitiate Venus. He sends for the Grand Augur of Venus, who orders that

Ex. 22

the Queen must accompany him to Cythera and sacrifice a hundred heifers. The Augur is Paris in disguise. He reveals himself to Helen and they embark. The kings and the people, realising the trick, swear vengeance, and the curtain falls as the Trojan war is foreshadowed.

In *La Belle Hélène* Offenbach's harmony became more chromatic than hitherto. He had previously written plenty of chromatic melodies over diatonic accompaniments. A favourite device was the chromatic appoggiatura; see bars 1 and 4 of Ex. 23:

Ex. 23

But the opening three chords of the waltz in *La Belle Hélène* are in a different musical world:

Ex. 24a

Here the harmony itself is chromatic. The sequence would be unremarkable were it not for the unusual movement of the bass line. As the melody goes up a semitone from bar 1 to bar 2 the bass drops by a diminished third — technically but not subjectively a tone; Offenbach was aware of the musical function of this bass movement. It is the asymmetric stretching of the interval between melody and bass as they move from the first to the second bar that gives the opening of the waltz its seductive allure. Consider what an inferior composer might have written using the same chords, but with a different bass line altering the inversions in bars 2 and 3. The passage becomes banal:

Ex. 24b

The complete phrase looks as if it might be by Tchaikovsky:

Ex. 24c

Twenty-five years later (1889) Tchaikovsky *did* write something extra-ordinarily like it. In the next example the top line consists of eight bars of the *Sleeping Beauty* waltz transposed:

Ex. 25a

And now here are the first sixteen bars of Tchaikovsky's waltz in the original key and with his own harmony:

Ex. 25b

The affinity with Offenbach, as with Delibes and others, is easy to see; we recognize the *lingua franca* of the ballet waltz, used from France to Russia.

It would be difficult to name an operetta with more good melodies than *La Belle Hélène* (although *Die Fledermaus* would be a strong contender). The waltz has already been mentioned; the others are no less irresistible:

Ex. 26a

Ex. 26b

Ex. 26c

Ex. 26d

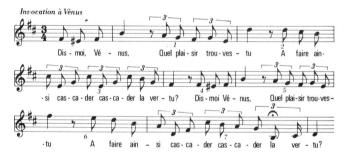

In the above invocation to Venus, Helen, with her habitual effortless hypocrisy, demands 'Tell me, Venus, what pleasure do you find in causing virtue to come tumbling down (*cascader*) like this?' The young men in the audience would shout 'Cascade, Hortense, cascade!' The music matches the words. After the melody has leapt a surprising ninth onto the first note of bar 6 it cascades down to its close: another of Offenbach's athletic, wide-ranging vocal lines. The array of melodies continues:

Ex. 26e

Ex. 26f

Ex. 26g

In *Marche de l'oie* ('March of the Goose') Offenbach joins in the emancipation of the sixth degree of the scale. Before 1800, when the sixth appears in the tonic chord it is treated as a cuckoo in the nest, an appoggiatura requiring resolution onto its neighbouring fifth. In twentieth-century light music it was to become so much an accepted part of tonic chords that they sound naked without it. Offenbach and his contemporaries are at an intermediate stage: they will end a melodic phrase on the sixth provided the next phrase contains the resolution. Though the resolution is still required, it may be postponed or concealed. The device gives new melodic possibilities, and adds impetus to the music. The discord of the phrase-ending leaves the listener in suspense: his ear demands the dénouement. Offenbach and Johann Strauss the younger use identical devices in Exs. 27a and 27b:

Ex. 27a

In bar 2 the melody note A is the sixth in the tonic chord. In bar 3 it is the ninth in the dominant chord. The A in bar 2 does not resolve until the first note of bar 4, after an intervening bar of dominant harmony. The A in bar 3

undergoes a camouflaged resolution onto the same note. In bar 2 the melody comes to rest on the chord of the added sixth, intensifying the feeling that this is now a chord in its own right that does not need to be resolved.

In the *Blue Danube* waltz (1867) Strauss uses B as the ninth in the dominant chord (Ex. 27b, bars 2–5) and as the sixth in the tonic chord (bars 6–8). The sixth does not resolve until the start of the next phrase (bar 9):

Ex. 27b

Neither Offenbach nor Strauss was yet prepared to go as far as Kurt Weill, who ends a whole melody, and, in fact, the whole opera in which it occurs, *Die Dreigroschenoper*, on an unresolved sixth[8]: *Die Drei-groschenoper*, 1928:

Ex. 27c

La Belle Hortense: 1864

The rehearsals of *La Belle Hélène* were tempestuous. Offenbach was in distress with his 'rheumatism'. It turned out to be gout. No wonder the years of taking the water at Ems had not cured it; it is ironic that it was for this reason that Ems should have been privileged to have seen the premières of so many Offenbach works.

Offenbach directed the production. Young Lindheim from Ems was the conductor. The composer sat enveloped in a heavy fur coat until something went wrong, when he would hobble up on stage to sort out the problem with speed and energy. He would get too hot, borrow a lighter coat, run out of breath, cough, eventually sit down exhausted, trying to conceal a twinge of pain. He had rows with Cogniard, who had lost faith in the show and was economizing in everything. Old scenery was repainted, second-hand costumes were patched up. The orchestra was limited to twenty-six players, too few for Offenbach.

Hortense Schneider was constantly irritable. She started a feud with Mlle Silly, who played Orestes. Mlle Silly was an accomplished performer, appropriate casting in this *travesti* part, for she appeared on the boulevards in trousers, wearing a monocle, another George Sand. The feud between Schneider and Silly lasted throughout the run of *La Belle Hélène* and longer. It appealed to the gossipy partisanship of the Parisians. The press loved it, and the two actresses supplied the papers with acidulous copy.

The dress rehearsal, in front of the customary invited audience, provided a shock. *Le Jugement de Pâris*, everybody's favourite melody, fell flat. Dupuis, playing Paris, went home mortified. Next morning there was a message for him: come quickly to the maestro's apartment. Offenbach played him two new melodies for the song, and asked him to choose. Dupuis chose the original, and made a success of it on the opening night, 17 December 1864.

Twelve hours after the curtain fell on *La Belle Hélène* Offenbach received a note from Victorien Sardou:

> That was a great success for you, my dear friend, and a delicious evening for us. I would have come to say 'Bravo!' at the theatre if I had not had to take Mme Sardou home. But this morning when I woke up I was still bravo-ing, as I remembered Dupuis' delightful air in the first act, Schneider's two romances, and the first and second act finales; moreover the whole piece was going through my head all night. Your actors served you well: Dupuis and Grenier are most amusing, Mlle Schneider performs as only she knows how, and sings with an art I had thought lost.
>
> I can't see anything short of a triumph for you and have only one regret: not to be part of it.[9]

Sardou was right; the till filled up with unaccustomed regularity. There were, however, a few sour complaints, as in the case of *Orphée*, about the desecration of the classics. Théophile Gautier, who detested Offenbach, adopted a high moral tone: 'Although a new vision of heaven has brought down their altars, these gods are still the gods of art. To try to ridicule the heroes of Homer is almost to blaspheme.' Janin wrote of 'perfidious Meilhac, treacherous Halévy, miserable Offenbach'. Meanwhile Offenbach won his lawsuit against the Bouffes.

CHAPTER X

Chef de famille

········•🜊•········

For twenty years the Offenbach family lived in a roomy apartment in the rue Laffitte. Every morning there was a stream of visitors. Mme Offenbach classified them; according to their station they waited in the drawing-room, dining-room or hall. Normally Offenbach saw everyone, writing music as he talked; but sometimes he had to be alone to concentrate. One time a visitor was told, 'M. Offenbach is not at home.' 'I insist on seeing him,' replied the visitor, whereupon Offenbach burst out of his study. 'Can't you see I'm not at home, I'm working.'

Like Mozart, Offenbach had a daily *coiffure*. Coquillard the hairdresser would arrive early. Offenbach was vain about his side-whiskers and his hair, which fell on his shoulders like a weeping willow. The household knew that the master's mood for the day depended on Coquillard's success or failure. There would be *badinage*:

> Coquillard, my good fellow, everyone in Paris thinks my hair curls and waves naturally. I am in your debt for this false reputation. Today I shall prove that I am not ungrateful. So here are my last wishes — God knows I have a horror of broaching the subject: on the day of my funeral you will lead the procession immediately behind the hearse, carrying a velvet cushion on which you will have laid out a comb, a hairbrush, my badger, razor and curling-tongs, in short, the insignia of your noble and useful profession. You must swear to do this, or never touch a hair of my head again. You have until tomorrow to decide.[1]

Next day the nervous Coquillard was relieved to discover that his client had forgotten all about this demand.

Anyone as active in the theatre as Offenbach usually had snippets of news for reporters who called in search of copy. A regular visitor, Bourdin, asked one day for a brief biography of the composer for *L'Autographe*, an illustrated periodical that featured profiles of the famous and facsimiles of their writing. 'A short biography?' said Offenbach, 'Sit down, you can take it with you.' He then wrote, without hesitation or revision, this summary of his life and work:

Mon cher Bourdin,
You ask me for some details of my life for *L'Autographe*; here they are:

I came into the world in Cologne; the day I was born I remember perfectly being rocked to sleep with melodies.[2] I have played every instrument a little, the violoncello a great deal. I arrived in Paris at the age of thirteen. I was a student at the Conservatoire, a cellist at the Opéra-Comique, and later conductor at the Théâtre-Français.

For ten years I hammered courageously but in vain at the doors of the Opéra-Comique, to get them to accept a one-act work. Then I founded the Bouffes-Parisiens Theatre: in the course of seven years I had fifty operettas accepted, mounted and performed. I resigned as director two years ago. As a composer I began with *Les Deux Aveugles* and have just finished with *Les Géorgiennes*.

A lot will be forgiven me because my work is played a lot. I have been French for three years, thanks to the Emperor, who graciously granted me my full naturalization papers. Two years ago I was made a chevalier de la Légion d'honneur.

I shall not tell you about my *numerous* successes or my *few* failures. Success has never made me proud, nor have I been defeated by failure. Neither shall I talk about my good qualities nor my faults. However, I have one terrible, unconquerable vice: I cannot stop working. I regret this for the sake of those who do not like my music, for I shall certainly die with a melody on the tip of my pen.
Bien et toujours à vous,

Jacques Offenbach

25 March 1864

Herminie and the children always lunched in the apartment. Jacques went next door to the Café Riche or to one of his other favourite restaurants: Bignon, Noel et Peters, or La Maison Dorée. In each he had his regular table, except when he took an upstairs salon for a business lunch. He was a gourmet, but ate only tiny amounts. The menu hardly varied: three spoonfuls of boiled egg with a sippet of bread; the heart of a lamb cutlet with a mouthful of potato; a morsel of fruit. If he stayed at home the Café Riche sent up his usual meal, which he ate on his own, early, in order to be in time for rehearsals. His daughters competed for the privilege of serving him and the lucky one would get any left-over delicacies. After lunch Mathurin had the carriage waiting to take him to the Bouffes, the Palais-Royal, the Variétés, or wherever the rehearsal might be. Sometimes he rehearsed at three different theatres in the course of an afternoon.

20. A devoted family: (left to right) Marie, Berthe, Mme
Offenbach, Pepita, Offenbach, and Jacqueline
Bibliothèque nationale

With his minute appetite and burning nervous energy it is not surprising that in middle-age Offenbach was thinner than ever. His grandson said that he never weighed more than 50 kilos (7st. 12lb). In photographs of him at this time gauntness and a receding hairline emphasize his semitic features and domed head. The long blond hair of his childhood has darkened. His eyes have sunk a little, giving his expression more intensity, but humour now shows in his face as well. Something demonic about his appearance led to a rumour that he had the evil eye. Alfred de Musset, in his late drunken, syphilitic days would cross the road to avoid meeting Offenbach, his one-time collaborator. The superstition also had its jokes: one joke suggested that Offenbach's marriage took place as a result of his having been hypnotized by the reflection of his evil eye in a window.

The maestro's own humour was sometimes combined with irritability. When his friend Desalme, proprietor of the magazine *Europe Artiste*, sent a young woman to audition for him, Offenbach wrote:

My dear friend,
Your young and beautiful singer is neither young nor beautiful — so try to find me what I am asking you for, but in the name of heaven put on your spectacles; you know that in my little theatre the public is very near the artistes, and as a result the women have to be even prettier than elsewhere. Therefore do not bring me your artiste tomorrow, but try to find me another one, another day. *A toi*

J. Offenbach[3]

Offenbach was obsessively nervous of people pirating his work, and once wrote anxiously to Briguilboul, manager of the Kursaal at Ems: 'I implore you to lock up the orchestral parts and the conductor's score very carefully in a cupboard, and do not allow them to be taken out until time for the performance. You don't know the Germans [Briguilboul was a Frenchman], they are capable of copying my music for other managements, and my German rights will be down the drain.'[4] But these fits of irritability and over-caution were outweighed by generosity of temperament and a fellow-feeling for other musicians, especially less fortunate ones, like the obscure composer Rudolf Zimmer. For years Offenbach had been haunted by eight bars of a waltz his mother sang to him as a child. When he was a boy in Paris:

. . . those eight bars were a world in themselves. When they came into my head I saw my father's house and heard the voices of the friends I missed so much. At the age when other boys go into the sixth form I was on my own in Paris earning my living as a cellist. Although I admit I was happy-go-lucky and had great hopes for the future, I still had yearnings for the old days. Solitude was hard to bear, and in my eyes the waltz had taken on a new significance; it was no longer a waltz, it was almost a prayer I sang to myself from morning to night: not praying to heaven, but believing that when I sang this melody my family heard me. I could have sworn that every time the tune went through my head they were answering. . . .[5]

Jacques found out from his father that the waltz was by a once-popular composer called Zimmer. Neither Isaac nor Jacques could remember more than the opening phrase, and unfortunately the music was not to be found.

One day Offenbach's publisher said that an old composer had been trying to sell him some work. He felt he could not accept a score from an unknown composer, and would tell him so next day. 'What was his name?' asked Offenbach. 'Zimmer.' 'Do me a favour. Publish the piece, pay him ten times its value, charge it to me. Send him to me, I must see him.' But the old man never came back for his score. Some years later in Vienna, Offenbach's carriage was held up by a crowd which had surrounded an unconscious man outside a café. Offenbach got out, and found that the man on the ground was Rudolf Zimmer. Offenbach paid for medical attention, and Zimmer soon came to thank him. He told his story. After some success as a composer things had gone wrong. The girl he loved died before their wedding-day. Then he had made a living by teaching music, but was eventually reduced to a menial job in the café where Offenbach had found him. Offenbach asked him to play the waltz. Zimmer began to play, but he too could remember no more than the eight bars.

After this visit Offenbach was away from Vienna for a month. On his return he found a parcel from Zimmer, who had died during Offenbach's absence. The parcel contained a letter, the manuscript of the waltz, a sapphire engagement ring Zimmer had given to his fiancée, and a faded package. In the letter, Zimmer, explaining that the package contained some of the dead girl's hair, asked Offenbach to burn it unopened, and not to sell the ring. Offenbach told the story in a booklet, *Histoire d'une valse*.[6]. He ends, 'I burned the package which contained her hair; I did not open it. The ring shall not be sold. I have published the waltz.'

But however generous he may have been to outsiders, Offenbach's deepest affections were centred on his home and family. Family celebrations were important events, and the marriage to Charles Comte of Jacques' and Herminie's eldest daughter, Berthe, in August 1865, was an occasion for special excitement. Jacques composed a nuptial mass. More than ninety Parisian friends were invited to Étretat, where they were put up in the village for three days. Mme Offenbach had breakfast sent round to them; lunch and dinner were served in the villa Orphée, where the lofty drawing-room, billiard-room and hall became extra dining-rooms. Berthe Offenbach's marriage meant that she would now be allowed to go to the theatre, and could for the first time attend performances of the Bouffes-Parisiens in the salle Choiseul, where her husband and father had become partners ten years earlier.

In the same year as this marriage the Bouffes-Parisiens company shared a sorrow with the Offenbach family — the death of the duc de Morny. Morny's association with Offenbach had led to friendship with the family, and he was godfather to Auguste-Jacques, Offenbach's only son. But he was mourned even more deeply by Ludovic Halévy, who owed his career to Morny. The two men first met over *M. Choufleury*. Later, when Halévy's career was threatened by the closure of the Ministry for Algeria he went to see Morny, President of the Corps Législatif. Morny did not want to discuss Halévy's future. There would be no problem; a word to the Emperor would secure him a job. But, said Halévy, he only wanted to work under Morny as a secrétaire-rédacteur (writer of official reports). 'You are appointed,' said Morny; 'now leave me, I am very busy.'[7]

After Morny's death Halévy wrote, 'His house had become almost my own. My relations with M. and Mme de Morny had become part of my daily life . . . M. de Morny would have done more for me if I had wanted it, if I had asked him. But I had only one idea: to complete my career at his side, and never to leave him. Never to leave him.'[8] The friendship with Morny brought Halévy into aristocratic society. For all his amiable qualities he had the snobbery of the parvenu, and enjoyed being close to the Emperor. The connection between Offenbach, Halévy and Morny gave the Bouffes an Imperial cachet — which was all very well while there was still an Empire.

The family apartment in the rue Laffitte was destined for demolition in a changing Paris. Daniel Halévy described the scene in retrospect: 'The town is being transformed around our young men. Baron Haussmann is at work; the roads are widening, the use of gas changes the look of things at night.'[9] Théophile Gautier protested 'It's Philadelphia, it's St Petersburg; whatever you call it, it isn't Paris any more.' Until the midnineteenth century, Paris had retained, round its isolated palaces, a heritage of crowded medieval streets and bad drains. Napoleon III, however, wanted his capital city to be like London, clean and open. He loved Hyde Park and the London squares. It was Georges Haussmann's brilliance as an engineer and ruthlessness as an administrator that made Paris the tourist capital of the world. In *La Vie parisienne* (see Chapter XI) the new railways bring tourists to Paris from far and wide to be fleeced by the inhabitants.

La Vie parisienne was already running when the scaffolding was removed from Garnier's Opéra, one of the focal points of the new Paris. In the matter of the Opéra Haussmann had overstepped himself by indulging in political and financial irregularities. He had acquired the land cheaply before making known the purpose of its development, and had contrived that the cost of building, 22,000,000 francs, should be met by the state, so that the city of Paris did not have to pay a cent. Jules Ferry, later to be Minister for the Fine Arts under the Third Republic, wrote a pamphlet entitled *Les Comptes fantastiques d'Haussmann*.[10] In the course of the ensuing scandals a new minister dismissed Haussmann's architect and appointed Charles Garnier, who designed what Haussmann called 'the giant theatre in the pygmy square'.

The new building was covered in white and gilt. A critic in *Le Temps* commented:

> One might say that, not wanting to make the Opéra beautiful, they have tried to make it rich. . . .
>
> Every great city has a characteristic expression of itself. Paris herself has had many. Her monumental centre, if we may so put it, has moved with her moral centre. Originally it was round the cathedral. With the monarchy it gravitated to the Louvre, with the Revolution to the Hôtel de Ville. Must we admit that the centre of this powerful city . . . is today an opera house? Must our glory in the future consist above all in perfecting our public entertainments? Are we no longer anything more than the capital of elegance and pleasure?[11]

The writer might have added that Paris did not yet even have a genuine new Opéra, since the building was only a shell. The façade glistened at the end of the avenue de l'Opéra for eight years before a note of music was heard behind it. After only three of those years the Empire of which this building was an ironic and empty symbol disintegrated in a few weeks of pointless warfare.

CHAPTER XI

Principalities and Powers
1865–1867

·· ⚓ ··

Early in 1865 Offenbach disappeared from his Parisian haunts. The impresario Victor Koning, sharing the anxiety of friends, appealed for news through the periodical *Le Nain-Jaune*. Offenbach replied, talking of travel to Vienna, etc., and continued:

> A bout of rheumatism (between ourselves, confidentially, it was gout) was in store for me at the station; it attacked one leg. Having a few days to spare, I let it take its course.
>
> For someone undersized and quiet-living like me there is a certain *coquetterie* in admitting to an illness that normally only attacks the world's great men. I have had gout, I admit it, you may print it; it has not prevented me from ending my differences with the Bouffes in a friendly way. You know the outcome: I am taking over the direction of the theatre I founded.[1]

La Belle Hélène was doing such good business that the gala supper planned for the hundredth performance was postponed for fifty days until the Bouffes and the Variétés closed for the summer. When the day came, Schneider appeared laden with diamonds. The regular stars of the Bouffes and the cast of *La Belle Hélène* heard Offenbach and Schneider toast one another. Then, with the Paris theatres closed, Ems opened for the summer season, and Offenbach was ready with a two-act operetta, *Coscoletto ou Le Lazzarone*, a great local success that apparently never reached Paris. Its *finale ultimo*, 'Nous sommes tous empoisonnés!' (We have all been poisoned!) must have been reminiscent of the last scene in *Hamlet*, and was highly popular. In the autumn the Bouffes concocted a revue, *Le Refrain des Bouffes*, consisting of old hits, with *Bu qui s'avance* from *La Belle Hélène* thrown in for good measure; while Offenbach worked on a project he loved: *Les Bergers*.[2] Before it opened on 11 December 1865 he wrote to Villemessant, who shrewdly published the letter in *Le Figaro*:

134

The libretto of *Les Bergers* has three acts: it is a series of pastorals in the framework of a pleasing and skilful piece. That is my straightforward opinion on the work of my collaborators H. Crémieux and Ph. Gille. Moreover they told me yesterday, with the same blunt honesty, that my score was a triple masterpiece.

In the first act we are right back in antiquity, and to show that I have no prejudice against mythology I have treated it in terms of *opera seria* — it being accepted, I take it, that the music of *opera seria* does not preclude melody. You will understand me easily, my dear friend, if I tell you that the authors of the libretto have made use of the charming episode of Pyramus and Thisbe, lending that fable to their own shepherds Myriame and Daphne. I would not have dared to make the maiden mourn her lover to the air of *le roi Barbu*; I felt obliged throughout the first act to sound my shepherds' pipes in a more elevated style.

In the second act I have wallowed in Watteau, and have devoted all my efforts to recalling (how good to recall!) our masters of the eighteenth century. In the orchestra as in the vocal line I have tried as much as possible not to depart too far from the Louis XV style; the task of translating this style into musical terms fascinates me.

In the third act I have sought to represent Courbet in music. We have chosen as far as possible the pictures where the women are clothed — you will appreciate our restraint.[3]

Gustave Courbet, the unvarnished realism of whose paintings of peasant life made his work controversial during the Second Empire, was a contemporary of Offenbach.[4] *L'Atelier du peintre*, painted in 1855, the year the Bouffes opened, shows a nude female model among the clothed male Bohemians in the studio, anticipating the shock created by Manet in *Le Déjeuner sur l'herbe* (1863).

The three acts of *Les Bergers* were subtitled (1) *L'Idylle* ('The Idyll'), (2) *Le Trumeau* ('The Pier-glass'), and (3) *La Bergerie realiste* ('A Realistic Pastoral'). On 7 February 1907 the first act was presented at the Monte-Carlo Opéra under the title *Myriame et Daphné*. It preceded the première of Massenet's *Thérèse*, and was the occasion of the stage début of Maggie Teyte. Offenbach's pastiche style is exemplified in Act II of *Les Bergers* by the *Rondeau Louis XV* — a conventional rondo in A-B-A-C-A form. The key is E minor. Sections B and C are in G major and E major respectively. Ex. 28a is the opening; in Ex. 28b the end of the C section leads back into the final statement of A.

The eighteenth-century pastiche is skilfully done. Offenbach creates gavotte-like, courtly elegance with an austerely simple rhythmic accompaniment, phrases beginning in the half-bar, feminine endings, a

Ex. 28a

Ex. 28b

ont mis en bour - ri - ches Ad - mi - rez — Vé - nus en pa - niers

melody garlanded with appoggiaturas — the kind of music one might expect to have heard as an entr'acte for a Beaumarchais play or a divertimento at supper-time at Versailles.

The third act, as Offenbach indicates in his letter to Villemessant, is inspired by Courbet's peasant wenches rather than his Parisian models. Offenbach digs up dramatic devices from his past. In *La Rose de Saint-Flour* (1856) he had written a duet in dialect:

Chette marmite neuve	(Cette)
Mam'jel, est une preuve	(Mam'selle)
De mon amour pour vous.	
Elle est *cholide* et bonne;	(solide)
Ch'est moi qui vous la donne	(C'est moi)
Pour faire la *choupe* aux choux.	(soupe)

(Mademoiselle, this new pot is proof
of my love; it's good and solid,
my present to you for your cabbage
soup.)

Les Bergers had a similar dialect duet, *Ronde de la soupe aux choux*, containing the lines 'Mais c'que j'y préfère, C'est une *bounn' poumm'*de terre.'

This pet work of Offenbach's did not go down well with the Parisians: it was not funny enough. The composer was type-cast as a joker, and had disappointed his public. Vienna reacted differently: there Offenbach could do no wrong. The *Revue et Gazette Musicale* reported (4 March 1866):

We have already announced the tremendous success in Vienna of Offenbach's *Les Bergers*. The première was at the Theater an der Wien. . . . To our surprise, the act that proved most effective, contrary to what happened in Paris, was the third, with its rustic realism. . . . The orchestra, conducted by M. Offenbach, who had personally supervised the final rehearsals, acquitted itself admirably, and there was no lack of curtain-calls, encores and ovations for the maestro and his performers.

'Another management, another rumpus with Jacques', wrote Martinet.

'He now leaves the Bouffes for the second time, a separation that will last three years.' Varcollier, husband of Mme Ugalde, had taken over the Bouffes. Offenbach, having successfully litigated to compel the theatre to present more of his works, now took out an injunction to prevent them performing any at all. Varcollier took no notice, and Ugalde played the leading role in a revival of *Daphnis et Chloé*.

In spite of Offenbach's rows with the Bouffes he was on top form and soon completed a new full-length work, tailor-made for the cast of *La Belle Hélène*. Schneider was an essential ingredient. She had just had a handsome offer from the Châtelet, but blackmailed Cogniard into matching it, and stayed with Offenbach. The actors were summoned to a reading of *Barbe-bleue*, which turned out to be a story of horror and melodrama. Dupuis refused to play the title role of Bluebeard, and

21. Schneider and Dupuis in *Barbe-bleue* (Bluebeard), 1868: caricature by Gill in *L'Éclipse*

walked out of the reading of the text before he had heard the music. Offenbach, however, won him over before rehearsals started.

Dupuis's initial feelings are not hard to understand. He was to sing his principal aria — one of Offenbach's most lyrical and expansive melodies — in the tomb of his five murdered wives, just before he attempted to kill the sixth. This macabre situation was treated as comedy; the nature of the melody was ironic. The black comedy of the lyric is best felt in French, but a free translation may be helpful:

Le voilà donc, le tombeau des cinq femmes
Qui m'ont aimé d'un amour sans pareil!
Dormez en paix, dormez bien, pauvres âmes!
Je ne viens pas troubler votre sommeil.
Elles sont cinq! O destinée humaine!
Quoi! cinq déjà! cinq anges disparus!
Il en manque un pour la demi-douzaine . . .
Dans un instant il n'en manquera plus!

(See here the tomb, last home of the five beauties
Who loved me with a love beyond compare,
Sleep here in peace! — fulfilled, your wifely duties;
I have no heart to break a sleep so rare.
Five in a row! O world! O life! O time!
Already five! five angels passed away!
A round half-dozen makes a tidier crime . . .
That round half-dozen I'll achieve today!)[5]

Offenbach's knife makes a final twist in the last line with ironic *fioritura*:

Ex. 29

Dans un ins - tant, — dans un ins - tant, — dans un ins - tant, —

il n'en man - - - - - que - ra plus!

The story of *Barbe-bleue* is told against a background of court life, this time that of the neurotic King Bobèche and his entourage. The target of the satire is the obsequiousness of courtiers. The chamberlain leads an ensemble of courtiers who bend double, hoping for advancement, as they pass the king:

Ex. 30

This could as well be the court of Jupiter, the court of Menelaus, the court of Bobèche, or, soon to come, the court of the Grand Duchess of Gerolstein: court life was an obsession (and a profitable one) with Offenbach, Meilhac and Halévy, who were no republicans. These writers were accepted by the society they satirized, as court jesters would be accepted. They could parody court life (albeit in a general way) and remain close friends of the Emperor's half-brother, Morny, just as Gilbert and Sullivan could parody the House of Lords in *Iolanthe* in the year Sullivan was knighted.

It had been feared that no new show could match the success of *La Belle Hélène*, but *Barbe-bleue* took its authors, the critics and the public by surprise, perhaps because it was a change. Leaving ancient Greece behind, the writers turned again to medieval rumbustiousness, source of the burlesque comedy in *Croquefer* and *Le Pont des soupirs*. The humour was macabre, grotesque, hilarious. The music came in on the flood-tide of Offenbach's melodic invention: among the fifteen operettas he composed in 1864–6, in addition to *Barbe-bleue*, were *La Belle Hélène*, *La Vie parisienne*, *La Grande-Duchesse de Gerolstein* and *La Périchole*.

Another great Paris exhibition was planned for 1867, and theatres were preparing for the event. The director of the Palais-Royal, M. Plunkett, had a resident company of artists for whom he wanted to commission a musical show suitable for the foreign visitors who were expected to flock to Paris the following year. He approached Offenbach, Meilhac and Halévy.

In the 1855 exhibition it was a topical Parisian sketch, *Les Deux Aveugles*, that had brought immediate success to the newly opened Bouffes. Since then, however, Offenbach had avoided topicalities in favour of legend and fantasy. It was perhaps with the previous exhibition in mind that Jacques and his 'collabos' decided, in *La Vie parisienne*, to write about the Paris of the boulevards, and to bring tourists into that setting. It was a way of ensuring that as many members as possible of a mixed French and foreign audience could identify with characters in the play.

Two hard-up young *boulevardiers*, Bobinet and Gardefeu, pretend to be tourist guides to a Swedish baron and baroness. They provide a 'hotel' (Gardefeu's house) and arrange a reception where the 'guests' are Bobinet's family servants dressed in their employers' finery. The two young men procure the separate amorous requirements of the Swedish couple. *Le Ménestrel* described the piece as 'a succession of burlesque scenes written to order for, and perhaps partly by, the comics of this theatre'. Having to write for 'the comics of this theatre' was a problem. They were actors, not singers; the women sang only marginally better than the men. Offenbach made few musical compromises on this account, though he refrained from writing any of his beloved vocal cadenzas. But he made life easy for the actors by giving them plenty of lively dance tunes, the sort anyone can whistle in the bath, the kind of music people mean when they say 'Offenbach'. Waltz, bolero, polka and galop compete with each other in zest. The third act (of five) ends with a tour-de-force in which the action takes place to a series of song-dances skilfully integrated into an extended dramatic finale, which seems to culminate in the whirling —

Tout tourne, tourne, tourne,
Tout danse, danse, danse . . .

— only to top that with an even more hectic climax in the final galop. The vitality of *La Vie parisienne* bears out Ezra Pound's observation that music atrophies when it moves too far from the dance.

One outsider was admitted to the Palais-Royal cast. In order to boost the vocal strength of the company, Zulma Bouffar was given a small part. In the course of rehearsals her role increased in length and importance, till, on the opening night, 31 October 1866, she became the star of the show, and Gabrielle, the little glover, was established as one of the most famous characters in the Offenbach canon.

In January 1867 there was an amusing diversion at the Bouffes. Varcollier decided, against still more resistance from Offenbach, to bolster the theatre's takings with a revival of *Orphée*. There was a good cast available except for the part of Cupid. While a suitable singer was being sought, Varcollier received an approach from an unexpected quarter.

Cora Pearl, an English beauty whose real name was Emma Crouch, was one of the most famous of Parisian courtesans. She is said to have held a front-rank position in this field because she 'possessed such a talent for voluptuous eccentricities that Prince Gortchakoff described her as the acme of sensual delight.'[6] At the beginning of 1867 she was having an affair with Prince Napoleon,[7] the dissolute cousin of the Emperor. She was given to sudden whims, and now decided she wanted to go on the stage. Varcollier auditioned her, reckoned that she could just about manage the part of Cupid, and engaged her because he knew that such a sensational casting would fill the theatre. But Cora provided administrative problems. Because of her royal liaison, she required a dressing-room apart from the others, and with a private entrance. Prince Napoleon rented and furnished a room for her in the house next to the theatre. From there, a private staircase was built, leading to the stage.

When Cora made her first entrance she could hardly be seen for the jewels that covered her from head to foot; even her shoes were studded with diamonds. She had a tiny voice, and was petrified with stage-fright, but there were some 'bravos' from the friendly audience, which was full of wealthy aristocrats and ladies of fashion. Things went well for a few performances. Then one night a crowd of avant-garde students came to the show and started barracking. This so unnerved poor Cora that she gave up the theatre for good.

Offenbach and 'Meil et Hal' had satisfied the requirements of Plunkett at the Palais-Royal, leaving him with *La Vie parisienne* established as a success well in advance of the opening of the exhibition. The three collaborators could now concentrate on their own urgent requirement — a new show to replace *Barbe-bleue*. Work on *La Vie parisienne* had held them up, and they would have to rush to complete *La Grande-Duchesse de Gerolstein* in time for the Exposition.

The fictitious state of Gerolstein was an invention of Eugène Sue in his novel *Les Mystères de Paris*. As depicted in Offenbach's operetta, Gerolstein is not as rich in imaginative detail as Anthony Hope's Ruritania, but it is a serviceable caricature of a middle-European pocket grand-duchy. Not that such petty autocracies needed much parodying;

by the mid-nineteenth century they had become caricatures of themselves. In a typical musical-comedy story the Grand Duchess, self-willed, pretty and unmarried, keeps putting off a marriage of convenience with an unwelcome aristocratic suitor. She then falls in love with Fritz, a young fusilier, and promotes him by lightning stages to general. When he returns to his peasant girl-friend, Wanda, the Grand Duchess reduces him to the ranks again. Her behaviour infuriates the intriguing diplomats of her court, above all the demoted General Boum, an absurd character who constantly wants to go to war on any pretext in order to put his idiotic strategic plans into practice. Boum is a predecessor of Blimp, with eccentric personal mannerisms. Instead of taking snuff, he fires pistol shots into the air and sniffs the fumes from the empty cartridges. When boasting of his prowess in love and war, he confesses that the plume on his helmet, while it terrifies the enemy, gets in the way on the chaise-longue. His personality is neatly encapsulated in the onomatopoeic refrain of his personal theme-song:

Et pif, paf, pouf!
Et tara papapoum!
Je suis, moi, le général Boum! Boum!

All this amiable nonsense rides along happily on a tuneful, jolly score. There is a touching moment when the Grand Duchess sings to Fritz of her love, pretending she is giving him a message from another woman:

Ex. 31

143

This melody, which Halévy described as 'a jewel', was first played to his friends by Offenbach in the garden at Étretat.

The seemingly innocuous libretto of *La Grande-Duchesse de Gerolstein* kept running into trouble with the censors, whose trifling complaints reveal an extreme touchiness on the part of the authorities. A clue to this may be found in the nature of their objections. The operetta was originally to be called, simply, *La Grande-Duchesse*. The censors feared that, with that title, the story might be taken as a parody on the amours of Catherine II. If it seems incredible that Russia was expected to take offence at the tenuous similarity between the plot of a French operetta and the life of a Tsarina who had died more than seventy years earlier, it is less surprising when we discover that Catherine's great-grandson, Tsar Alexander II, was expected in Paris for the exhibition, and would certainly see the show. Offenbach's friend Camille Doucet came up with a good idea for the title: 'Simple,' he said, 'just add "of Gerolstein".' It was a happy solution; the operetta was given its official longer title, and everyone continued, as before, to call it *La Grande-Duchesse*.

Another complaint concerned Fritz's line, 'Madam, I have just won the war in eighteen days.' The censors saw here a reference to the eighteen-day Prussian campaign that ended in Moltke's victory over the Austrians at Sadowa. As the King of Prussia was to visit the exhibition with Bismarck and Moltke, the remark, it was thought, might give rise to the equation, Fritz = Moltke, Grande-Duchesse = King William. Fritz's 'eighteen days' had to be altered to 'four days'.

Finally, on the first night, Hortense Schneider said she would not appear, because of a last-minute dispatch from the censor forbidding her to wear on her corsage a broad ribbon with an imaginary royal Order (*un grand cordon parodique*). The authorities would not give in. Neither would the diva: no ribbon, no Schneider. But, as she related later, when she heard the overture start, she took off the *cordon* and went on stage 'like a circus horse who hears the music to which he always goes round the ring'.

When the curtain went up she was smiling. She appeased her wounded feelings by commissioning a portrait showing her in her costume as the Grand Duchess, proudly wearing the forbidden ribbon. It

22. Portrait of Hortense Schneider dressed as the Grand Duchess, and with her favourite terrier, Carlo. She is wearing the Order which the censor did not allow her to wear on the stage

Collection Viollet

hung in her salon, safely out of reach of the authorities. The veto on Schneider's sash was clearly an all-embracing safety-precaution, with so many crowned heads around. Who knew what oversensitive monarch might not detect in it a sinister insult to one of the Orders of his country?

Another reason for the anxiety of the censors was the widespread fear that war was not far off. The political commentator Prévost-Paradol — Halévy's illegitimate half-brother — expressed the opinion that in view of the spread of the Liberal movement, a war would be welcome to the Emperor. 'The idea of distracting men's minds and diverting them with the hope of territorial aggrandizement is unfortunately only too natural, and everybody knows that it is generally absolute governments which choose this way out of difficult situations.'[8] Halévy agreed with this; and transmuted the idea into comedy in the story of the Grand Duchess whose ministers planned a war as a distraction to solve their petty problems.

This exemplifies the technique by which Offenbach, Meilhac and Halévy introduced an undercurrent of seriousness into entertainment that was ostensibly frivolous (no such element was ever present in the operettas of Johann Strauss). It is unwise to read too much into it. Siegfried Kracauer, in his biography *Offenbach and the Paris of His Time*, would like to see the composer as a revolutionary *manqué*. He writes: 'At a time when the bourgeoisie were politically stagnant and the Left was impotent, the Offenbach operetta had been the most definite form of revolutionary protest. It released gusts of laughter, which shattered the compulsory silence and lured the public towards opposition, while seeming only to amuse them.'[9] In this piece of wishful politicizing Kracauer contradicts his earlier, more perceptive judgement in the same book: '. . . the emphasis lay less on the satire than on the gaiety which was the result of it . . . the critical function of the humour was only incidental.' That was nearer the truth; gentle jibes are not revolutionary protests. The distinction is crucial: we use revolutionary protest to attack our enemies, we use gentle irony to convert our friends. Offenbach's aim was certainly not to undermine the Empire under which he had flourished, but it amused him to hint that it might mend its ways — especially if he could make money by doing so. So far was Offenbach from being a revolutionary that after 1870 he suffered cruelly at the hands of the Republicans (see Chapter XIV).

The Exposition Universelle opened on 1 April 1867 and was a shop-window for the industry, arts and crafts of Europe. (Eduard Hanslick was a juror for the musical section.) England displayed a bible kiosk, a Protestant church, agricultural machines, a model farm and a school, also china by Minton, Copeland and Wedgwood. Prussia sent a 50-ton gun by Krupp and an equestrian statue of Frederick the Great. Machinery was one of the principal attractions. Halévy noted: '. . . the machine for making hats, the machine for making shoes, the machine for making soap . . . they make everything, these damned machines. I looked everywhere for the machines that turned out plays and novels. They are the only ones missing. They will be at the next Exhibition.'[10]

One of the first important social events of the occasion was the opening night of *La Grande-Duchesse de Gerolstein*. It was as much a fashion show as a theatrical event, and there was major news on the fashion front: crinolines were out! All the fashionable ladies, led by Princess Metternich, wore straight dresses. The colour of the year was brown, 'la couleur Bismarck', sometimes set off by vivid coral jewellery. Men were fashion-conscious too. The gentlemen of the Jockey Club sported side-whiskers and enormous shirt-fronts, and there was a vogue for square monocles.

Halévy's mind, however, was not on fashion:

On Friday 12 April, at half-past-eight, the curtain went up on the first act of *La Grande-Duchesse*. I promise you that at that moment a lovely shiver runs from head to foot, you're so impatient for the first reaction. The important thing is to break the ice. Once you have the public with you everything goes well, but the first burst of laughter, the first murmur of approval, the first applause, is hard to win and delicious to hear. Our suspense didn't last long. From the first words of Couder (Général Boum), and thanks, it must be admitted, to his incredible verve, the theatre was set alight, and was like that until the middle of the second act. What a beginning! Too good! It was too good to be true! We sensed that, and were both thrilled and frightened at this success. We had good reason to fear. The *Carillon de ma grand-mère* threw cold water on the enthusiasm, and the third act, with the benediction of the daggers, and the mills (that was terrible!) wasn't of a kind to put the audience back into good humour. The show finished at half-past-midnight . . . whether well or badly was hard to tell. Even great theatre pundits were perplexed. Was it a big success? a middling success? a flop? Opinions were divided, our friends didn't know what to say to us.[11]

'Che vais faire des bedides goupures.' said Jacques. Little cuts. By the third performance the daggers and the mills (a heavy-handed parody of an episode in *Les Huguenots*) had gone, and, at the suggestion of the dramatist Léon Halévy, Ludovic's father, the *Carillon* had been replaced by a new second-act finale, the conspiracy trio *Logeons-le donc, et dès ce soir*. . . . The changes were enough to overcome the initial hesitant reaction; *La Grande-Duchesse* became a success.

For Schneider it was a theatrical and social triumph. The Emperor attended and returned a few days later with the Empress Eugénie. Visitors to Schneider's dressing-room included Tsar Alexander II and his

23. The Royal visitors to the Exposition Universelle of 1867: (left to right) the Sultan of Turkey; Alexander II of Russia; Napoleon III; the Prince Imperial; Emperor Franz Josef of Austria; Don Louis, King of Portugal; Frederick William of Prussia; the Prince of Wales; Leopold II, King of the Belgians; Ismaïl Pacha, Viceroy of Egypt; the Tycoon, brother of the Emperor of Japan. All were Hortense's admirers, and at least two appear to have been her lovers as well

Collection Viollet

sons the Grand Dukes; King William of Prussia and Crown Prince Frederick; the Kings of Portugal, Sweden, Belgium, Egypt and Bavaria (the twenty-two-year-old Ludwig II, passionate admirer of Wagner). Only one monarch disappointed Schneider. The Emperor Franz Josef of Austria earned her grand-ducal displeasure by failing to attend a performance; he was in mourning for the Emperor Maximilian of Mexico, who had been shot on the orders of Juarez. When the Prince of Wales first came to the famous dressing-room Halévy was present. He recalled that Schneider, 'puffed up and putting on airs', lost no opportunity of throwing in a 'Monseigneur!' or a 'Votre Altesse Royale!' Some of the royal visitors were entertained more intimately at her house in the avenue de Versailles, activities which gave rise to the venomous comment of a female colleague, 'C'est le passage des Princes que la Schneider!'[12]

It was unfortunately impossible for Schneider to keep these visits private. She had a discarded young lover, Xavier Feuillant, who, by way of vendetta, rented an apartment opposite her house. When a royal visitor arrived thinking himself unnoticed, Feuillant would illuminate his apartment brilliantly and hang up drapes in the appropriate national colours. The Union Jack itself may even have hung there in its turn, for the Prince of Wales became a favourite. When he died, in 1910, Hortense, then nearly eighty, spoke of him to Offenbach's grandson, Jacques Brindejont-Offenbach

> Poor dear Edward: it was hardly worth the trouble of being King of England and Emperor of India, only to finish so soon. . . . What a faithful and good Prince of Wales he was! Did you know that he loved to walk my dogs in the passage des Panoramas while I was on stage. . . . In the theatre all the women had dogs. . . . I've always loved dogs. . . . They've often consoled me for the infidelity of men; I've had as many as eight at a time — no, not men, idiot, dogs (she added, on seeing my smile). . . . My Great Dane was called Gilda, my Pomeranian Miette, but my favourite was a dear little English terrier, Carlo, who weighed exactly 800 grammes; he lived in my fur muff.[13]

Other dogs were called Love, Puck, Vicky and Mimi. The pack were taken for a drive every day in the Bois de Boulogne. Mme Schneider's elegant carriages, gifts of the duc de Gramont-Caderousse, were one of the sights of the Bois. *Carrosserie* by Ehrlich was a status symbol, like owning a solid gold Cadillac. With the style of a great star, La Schneider gave as good a performance off stage as on. She behaved as if she really was a grand duchess, and on one occasion got away with it officially. Driving her carriage up to the gates of the Exposition, she demanded admittance. Only royalty were allowed to drive around inside. When challenged, she called out 'Grande-Duchesse de Gerolstein!' The gates were opened and the sentry presented arms. Hortense Schneider was identified with Offenbach's greatest triumphs. She clothed Meilhac and Halévy's heroines in flesh and blood, and composer and authors never forgot how much they owed her.

Halévy summed up the amazing years of success, and looked into the future:

> Four operettas in two-and-a-half-years, all of them successful. . . . *La Belle Hélène* performed nearly three hundred times . . . *La Vie parisienne* nearly two hundred, and now *La Grande-Duchesse*, which will be, if not the most fruitful, at least the longest and most resounding of our successes. For this is where luck comes in, and politics come to our aid; M. de Bismarck is working to double our takings. This time we are laughing at war, and war is at our gates; the Luxembourg crisis comes just in time to give topicality to our play.[14]

Prince Otto von Bismarck-Schönhausen may not have been the most glamorous of Hortense Schneider's noble visitors, but he was undoubtedly the most powerful. He came with the silent Moltke. Bismarck is reported to have been cool about Schneider's charms, but delighted with the Gerolstein parody. 'C'est ça! C'est tout à fait ça!' he said. Then: 'We are getting rid of the Gerolsteins, there will soon be none left. I am grateful to your Parisian artistes for showing the world how ridiculous they were.'

24. Bismarck: 'We are getting rid of the Gerolsteins . . .'

CHAPTER XII

War and Peace
1867–1875

···⚓···

The 'Luxembourg crisis' referred to by Halévy concerned an abortive attempt by France to annex Luxembourg by purchase. It was one of a series of futile efforts on the part of the French government to acquire new territory in order to match the increasing power of Prussia, or at least to bolster French self-respect by emulating Bismarck's example. Moltke's defeat of the Austrians at Sadowa (Königgrätz) had left Prussia stronger than ever. Austria had no alternative but to support Bismarck's unification of northern Germany in a confederation which included Schleswig-Holstein in the north and the rest of Germany as far south as the river Main. France's foreign policy was now based on her fear of German imperialism. French conservatives wanted a war, to challenge Bismarck and to strengthen the Empire.

But the threat of war is not war. There were three years to go before threat became reality, and in 1867 Halévy could still joke about Bismarck and the box-office takings, and Offenbach could safely return to Ems, now part of Bismarck's Germany, for his health, his gambling and his summer productions. King William of Prussia visited his newly acquired health resort of Bad Ems for the first time, and Offenbach prepared two operettas for the occasion. *La Leçon de chant* was a duo, improvised, according to Martinet, between rehearsals. It had already played for four weeks at the Folies-Marigny, and was now to have its first German performance. *La Permission de dix heures* (The Ten O'Clock Leave Pass') would be a world première.

On Wednesday 17 July 1867 a rowing regatta was held on the river Lahn in honour of the royal guest. This annual event normally celebrated the Duke of Nassau's birthday. This year the authorities, like the Vicar of Bray, diplomatically switched allegiance. The 1867 regatta simply had a different guest of honour. On the following Saturday, Offenbach's new operettas were performed for the King under the maestro's baton.

The theatre that is now part of the Kursaal (Assembly Rooms) at Ems is a twentieth-century addition. In Offenbach's day, performances were mounted on a stage erected in the concert hall, a lofty rectangular room known as the Marmorsaal because its high balcony is supported all round by a colonnade of marble pillars. The practical limitations of this room meant that only small-scale works could be accommodated. In the early days of the Bouffes-Parisiens, Offenbach had been limited by the French theatre licensing laws to writing short pieces for no more than three or four characters. At Ems he had to work under the same limitations for a different reason. A large amount of his output, therefore, consists of theatrical miniatures, a genre at which he became skilled as the result of a combination of inclination and necessity.

In August Offenbach returned to Paris (just missing the arrival of Bismarck in Ems) to complete his three-act comic opera *Robinson Crusoé*, due to open at the Opéra-Comique in November. His old rivals sharpened their knives, hoping for a repetition of the *Barkouf* fiasco. But it was silly of them to suppose that Offenbach had not learnt a lesson from his earlier error of judgement. Although he had described *Barkouf* as an *opéra-comique*, it was too much of an outlandish farce for the taste of the audience at the salle Favart. *Robinson Crusoé* was conventional by contrast. The opening family scene with father reading the Bible and mother at the spinning-wheel was in itself enough to wipe out painful memories of *Barkouf*, and an excellent cast gave a good account of the score.

It seems fair to suppose that anybody who was asked to identify the composer of Ex. 32a would be unlikely to guess Offenbach. Weber, Meyerbeer, Gounod, Bizet or Massenet would be more likely suggestions. The passage is part of the love duet in act two of *Robinson Crusoé*:

Ex. 32a

Compare this with a passage from Meyerbeer's *Huguenots* (originally in G flat) quoted in parody by Offenbach in *Croquefer*:

Ex. 32b

The similarity of manner is striking; the same high, passionate melody, the same slowly alternating tonic and dominant chords, sustained and endowed with excitement by the continuous 'zizz' of the accompanying tremolando. But in *Croquefer* Offenbach makes a parody of the passage from *Les Huguenots* by placing it in the middle of a farcical scene. In *Robinson*, on the other hand, we have caught him writing, in a serious context, precisely the kind of music he formerly parodied. This neither invalidates the criticism inherent in his early parodies nor diminishes the fun to be had from them, but it poses questions about the motivation of Offenbach's youthful preoccupation with parody. His distaste for the pretentious and grandiose was genuine, but was there, in his mockery of that kind of music, a secret envy? Did Offenbach's pillorying of Meyerbeer derive partly from a callow lack of confidence in his own ability to compose music on a large scale? Had he a reluctant admiration for the old master's magic? And did he now, in 1867, with the security born of years of success, feel that he could handle large-scale music without falling into the trap of pretentiousness? Some words in his 'manifesto' of 1856 (see Chapter IV) assume a new significance: 'The present demands of *opéra-comique* can easily put a young composer under a strain; one has to be a writer of experience to attempt a three-act work without tripping up. With rare exceptions no one can do it successfully until his talent has matured.' Without admitting it, he had been talking about himself. Now, eleven years later, he was to be put to the test for the second time.

Robinson Crusoé opened on 23 November 1867. *Le Figaro* reported another fashionable audience at the Opéra-Comique: Princess Metternich, the Archduke Louis Victor of Austria, the eighty-five-year-old Auber at the back of a box behind several young ladies, Alexandre Dumas *fils* in the production box, Adelina Patti, Hortense Schneider resplendent in black, and so on. But 'no ladies of the demi-monde; they had been unable to insinuate themselves'.

If there were jealous rivals hoping for Offenbach's downfall, there were also responsible critics who treated his return to the Opéra-Comique as an important event. *Robinson Crusoé* was reviewed at length on the front page of *Le Figaro*. The critic found both music and dialogue too long, but, was

25. Stewpot scene from *Robinson Crusoé*

Opera Rara Collection

still able to write, 'I am truly happy at the brilliant success of *Robinson*.' Jouvin observed, 'The success of *Robinson* heralds the return of public taste to the true genre of *opéra-comique*', and another enthusiast proclaimed 'Adam is dead! Long live Offenbach!' Jouvin was putting the cart before the horse. The success of *Robinson* proved nothing about public taste; it merely demonstrated that Offenbach, changing course a little, had written a good piece, which the public liked. It remained to be seen whether he would write more of the same. The decision was for Offenbach, not the public. He had to make up his mind whether to write more 'Helens' and 'Grand-Duchesses' or to continue looking for the road that would lead him to *Hoffmann*.

War and Peace: 1867–1875

We can learn something about Offenbach's changing objectives from the way he categorized his works (see list p. 236). In the early days, when he was striving for a hearing at the Opéra-Comique, he used the term 'opéra-comique' to describe *L'Alcôve*, *Le Trésor à Mathurin* and *Pepito*. When the Bouffes-Parisiens started in 1855, the nature of the works demanded descriptions like 'bouffonnerie', 'opéra-bouffe'. and — once he had invented the term 'opérette' for *La Rose de Saint-Flour* — 'opérette-bouffé'. Opéra-comique' appears once in 1860, to describe *Barkouf*. From 1865 onwards it shows up almost every other year: 1865, *Les Bergers*; 1867, *Robinson Crusoé*; 1869, *Vert-Vert*; (a gap for the war of 1870); 1872, *Fantasio* and *Le Corsaire noir*; 1873, *La Jolie Parfumeuse*; 1875, *La Créole*; then, with increasing frequency: 1878, *Madame Favart*; 1879, *La Marocaine* and *La Fille du Tambour-major*. For his *magnum opus*, *Les Contes d'Hoffmann*, Offenbach did not use the term 'opéra', *tout court*, but 'opéra fantastique'.

The list suggests that, for all his success with *bouffonnerie* and *opérette*, Offenbach was still hankering to be established in the Opéra-Comique theatre where he had played the cello as a youth; was still smarting under the rebuffs of Basset and Perrin, who had turned down his early work; and, with his devotion to the tradition of *opéra-comique*, was still hoping to be accepted as the keeper of its sacred flame. The words 'Adam est mort! Vive Offenbach!' were exactly what he wanted to hear. *Robinson Crusoé* was well received, but it was not the conclusive success he had hoped for, and of his eight subsequent works in this genre, four were failures. Although (or because?) his music was widening in scope and becoming more serious in intent, Offenbach's works were no longer the commercial certainties they had been at the height of the years of *bouffonnerie*. What was missing? Two things, probably: a cheerful irresponsibility that had pervaded the earlier pieces, and the pen of Ludovic Halévy, the civil servant who breathed life into librettos at the Bouffes for two decades, but whose name never appeared on the bill of an Offenbach *opéra-comique*.

In 1867 the recently opened Théâtre des Menus-Plaisirs had been having little success with its straight plays, and the director, M. Gaspari, asked Offenbach if he could provide a musical show for Christmas. There was not enough time to write a new work, and Offenbach decided to revive *Geneviève de Brabant* with a refurbished libretto. Hector Crémieux was brought in to work with Tréfeu, one of the original collaborators. The score had always worked well, and most of it was retained. A new duet was added, the *Couplets des gendarmes*. When the script was sent to the censor, the authors received a note saying, 'The duet of the gendarmes is impossible, we cannot have the gendarmerie held up to ridicule.' Crémieux and Tréfeu rushed to the censor. They went into a panegyric about military life. How could anybody think they would want to make fun of it? Moreover, they weren't talking about modern gendarmes, but *hommes d'armes*, warriors in breast-plates, chain mail and greaves:

'Yes, with tricornes!' said the censor.
'Tricornes of the Middle Ages.'
'Stop pretending! You have made Grabuge a corporal. There was no such rank in Charles Martel's[1] army.'
'Suppose we promote him to sergeant? There is no such rank in the gendarmerie.'

The censor gave in, which was just as well, for the duet was the success of the show. The French censors of course have enjoyed no monopoly in absurdity. When Sadler's Wells Opera presented *La Vie parisienne* in 1961, a script was sent to the Lord Chamberlain, who at that time fulfilled the function of censor in the British theatre. In reply came the standard letter:

Dear Sir,

LA VIE PARISIENNE

I am desired by the Lord Chamberlain to write to you about the above play. I am to say the Lord Chamberlain cannot allow those parts of the script which are set out in the appendix to the attached letter, and they must be altered and an undertaking given to that effect.

Should it be your intention to substitute any dialogue for that deleted, it will be necessary for the alterations to be submitted before they can be used.

Yours faithfully, etc.

The appendix had one item only: 'p. 5, line 30: delete "Merde!"' The word 'damn' was submitted in writing for the Lord Chamberlain's approval, and was allowed. Métella, who should have uttered the deleted expletive, would today be free to choose her language, because the power of the Lord Chamberlain to censor stage plays was abolished by the Theatres Act, 1968.

Le Château à Toto, which opened on 6 May 1868 at the Palais-Royal, was a pot-boiler. Critics agreed that Offenbach was repeating himself, and that the show was a feeble imitation of *La Dame blanche* by Boïeldieu. Jacques had a measure of revenge the following night when a revised version of *Le Pont des soupirs* succeeded at the Variétés. After the summer break the Bouffes brought in *Le Fifre enchanté*, which had already proved its worth at Ems. It was followed on the same bill by another one-acter, *L'Île de Tulipatan*.

A new theatrical and literary weekly, *Le Fouet* ('The Whip'), had started publication at the beginning of 1868. It was lively, scurrilous, and anti-Establishment. It prided itself on being hard-hitting and saw no harm in mixing metaphors. Of *Le Fifre enchanté Le Fouet* said, 'It is a very promising title, but the play is unbelievably banal and the music has no charm whatever. Offenbach has drained himself, he is scraping the bottom of the barrel.' And about *L'Île de Tulipatan*: 'Offenbach abuses his facility and wants to write too much. He pads out, drags and lengthens without satisfying. *L'Île* is put together like *Le Château à Toto*; it is the same thing all over again. It is time Offenbach pulled up on this slope; he is not working, he is wearing himself out trying too hard to coin money.'[2]

This was the most outspoken expression so far of the commonly voiced opinion that Offenbach was running out of ideas. It was not just the carping of rivals, but the legitimate conclusion of fair-minded critics who observed that he was repeating himself. But the glib accusation that he was only interested in money was unfair. Offenbach had nothing against money; but he worked continuously — his 'unconquerable vice' — irrespective of the state of his bank balance. If it is true that he lacked self-criticism, it is also true that many prolific writers of tunes do not immediately know which of their tunes are the good ones. They write them down and hope for the best, leaving the public to decide. It is the lack of inhibiting self-criticism, the lack of hesitation, that makes possible the spontaneous flow of melody. If Offenbach had been more self-critical we might have lost some of his weaker compositions, but we should also have lost some of the best: he was not the competent judge. After the astoundingly successful creativity of his recent years, it was not surprising that the voltage of his inventiveness should have dropped slightly, nor was it surprising if he failed to realize that it had. One suspects, however, that he may have had a secret germ of self-doubt.

Offenbach did not waste time replying to the critics; his continuing success with the public spoke for him. Martinet records that *Le Fifre enchanté* had an even warmer reception in Paris than at Ems, and that *L'Île de Tulipatan* was delirium all the way; people only stopped crying with laughter to clap their hands. Swept along by the enthusiasm, Berthelier, Bonnet and Victor rose to giddy heights, and the re-opening of the Bouffes was the occasion of innumerable curtain-calls.

Moreover, Offenbach was too busy for correspondence. There were only six days before the opening of *La Périchole*, and rehearsals had reached the irritable stage. One day when Hortense Schneider was 'marking' her part (not singing out), Offenbach said he couldn't hear her. She said she was tired — then decided to attack: 'Anyway, I can't sing that phrase.' 'Very well, Mlle *Schneider*,' said Offenbach, giving her name its German pronunciation, always a sign of stormy weather, 'I shall give it to one of the chorus.' Schneider, throwing her music into the stalls, declared, 'Tomorrow I leave for Italy!', swept out, and called her carriage. The rehearsal was stopped. Next day Hortense was back, as good as gold.

The incident was and still is typical of a late stage in the rehearsal of many plays. The tantrum of the 'temperamental prima donna' — an unfairly pejorative cliché — is often mistaken by the public for mere caprice. Actors know it as part of the tension and insecurity that heralds the first night. It is no more than the early symptom of stage-fright, from which Schneider suffered agonizingly all her life. A good outburst from the leading lady lets off steam for the whole company.

La Périchole, based on a one-act play by Merimée, *Le Carrosse du Saint Sacrement*, is jolly rather than witty. The complex Gilbertian plot begins with the Viceroy of Peru arriving in a provincial town in disguise. The disguise fools nobody except the one person whose immediate future it is about to affect for the worse — La Périchole, one of a duo of itinerant entertainers. La Périchole's partner, Piquillo, is her lover, and they are starving. To get money for food, she accepts a seemingly innocent invitation from the Viceroy, thereby setting in train a series of misunderstandings that takes two more acts to unravel. The lively score includes 'Il grandira, car il est espagnol!', a 'tipsy waltz' and the popular letter-song.

The reading of a letter on stage is an old device. The operatic letter song so much favoured in the nineteenth century (*Eugene Onegin*, *Werther*, *Khovanshchina*, etc.) is usually a romantic soliloquy, but is apt to feel more like a love-duet for one voice. Whether the song is sung by the sender or the recipient of the letter, we are made aware of the absent lover whose voice we do not hear. The *Périchole* letter-song has a pretty melody, but nowhere does it have the unexpected turn of phrase, the moment of surprising imagination that would raise it above the level of the Victorian drawing-room ballad. The air of the King of the Boeotians (Ex. 2) and the *Judgement of Paris* (Ex. 7) both possess greater distinction.

La Périchole had a cool reception. After certain *longueurs* were eradicated it went moderately well for several weeks, later making its way into the international repertoire, where it has survived for a century. Offenbach followed it, on 10 March 1869, with *Vert-vert*, a well-received successor to *Robinson Crusoé* at the Opéra-Comique. Two weeks later *La Diva* was a disaster at the Bouffes. A rags-to-riches fictional version of the career of Hortense Schneider, it proved again that the public does not like backstage romances. When the theatre turns a mirror on itself audiences feel excluded by private allusions, and find the product narcissistic. *La Princesse de Trébizonde* opened at Baden on 31 July 1869. An extended version came into the Bouffes in December, to be followed immediately by *Les Brigands*. These successors to *La Périchole* were the precursors of musical shows like *The Maid of the Mountains* and *The Desert Song* — naive romances in which comedy was a superimposed irrelevance. Unlike the Meilhac-Halévy pieces they were not wittily conceived. To his output in this last year of pre-war theatre Offenbach added a one-act divertissement, *La Romance de la rose*. In a mood of nostalgia he embroidered the story around the melody of *The Last Rose of Summer*, which his boyhood friend Flotow had used in *Martha*.

On 14 August 1869 Jacques and Herminie celebrated their silver wedding. Their four daughters, their son, sons-in-law, grandchildren and friends came to Étretat for the event. Jacques gave full rein to his jocularity in a poster announcing the

GRAND MARIAGE
NAUTIQUE, AQUATIQUE ET CHAMPÊTRE

which you will attend, when the *demoiselle*
HERMINIE Jacquot, femme Bach, after being a
supernumerary for twenty-five years, will marry,
for the second time, the illustrissimo, excellentissimo,
fantaisistissimo

MAESTRO
JACQUES OFFENBACH
MAGNUS

Author of a host of celebrated works, including
Berthe, the winner of hearts; *Mimi*, the devoted;
Pepita, the majestic; *Jacqueline* the lovable and
incomparable; *Auguste*, known as delight of the
eyes and nectar of the heart:

These five works in collaboration.

The programme for the day follows, full of incomprehensible family jokes. Finally:

At sunrise a salvo of artillery fired by the cannon
of the Invalides will announce the

Coucher de la mariée

(Mystery and discretion)

The firemen of Vattetot-sur-mer have sent a voluntary
deputation whose mission is to assist the bride in this
supreme moment.

IMPORTANT NOTICE

Any pretty young ladies who would like to grant
special favours to the author of this notice should
address themselves to him directly. He is ready
for anything. (Discretion guaranteed for three years.)

161

Herminie covered the passage about the bridal bed with a strip of calico bearing the words 'Rogné par la Censure' (Cut by the Censors). This, of course, only drew attention to the childish ribaldry underneath, and, at the same time, made a dig at the ever-unpopular Censorship.

The political situation remained tense. France watched nervously as Bismarck proceeded with his plans for the 'willing union' of northern and southern Germany. But there was an even greater threat — that the vacant throne of Spain might be offered to a Hohenzollern prince, thereby making Spain part of a German Empire encircling France. Secret talks in Berlin in 1869 left France with the reassurance that Prussia would discourage the Hohenzollern candidature. But Bismarck privately pressed the Spanish to make the offer, and on 2 July 1870 the French learnt that the throne of Spain had been accepted by Prince Leopold of Hohenzollern, subject to ratification by the *Cortes* in ten days' time. The French government, furious at Bismarck's duplicity, were ready for war, but there was still time for diplomacy. The situation was suddenly defused when King William of Prussia, independently of Bismarck, persuaded the young prince's father, Prince Charles Anthony of Hohenzollern, to renounce the Spanish succession on behalf of his son. Bismarck, angry at the King, took this as a bitter humiliation. His enthusiasm for a clash with France had been frustrated.

King William was at Ems — and so was Offenbach — when Gramont, the French foreign minister, made the blunder that precipitated the war. Not satisfied with the simple refusal of the throne by the Hohenzollerns, he instructed Benedetti, the French ambassador, to go to Ems and ask the King for his personal guarantee that the German candidature would *never* be renewed. This insulting demand, implying that the King could not have been trusted, met with a frosty rebuff. King William sent a telegram — the famous Ems telegram — to Bismarck. Bismarck, seeing that the French had played into his hands, edited the telegram cleverly and issued a shortened version to the press which made it appear that the King of Prussia had broken off diplomatic relations with France. Napoleon III and his government, having made the whole affair a matter of French honour, had no alternative but to declare war. On the streets of Paris people were shouting 'A Berlin!' and 'Vive la guerre!'

But the honourable, old-fashioned French army was no match for Bismarck's modern war machine. On 2 September Napoleon III capitulated at Sedan. Two days later a republic was proclaimed in Paris. The Second Empire was over. By mid-September Moltke's forces, surrounding Paris, settled down to starve the city into surrender.

The meeting at Ems between Benedetti and the King of Prussia took place on the river promenade outside the Kursaal. There, ten days earlier,

26 and 27. Two cartoonists' views of
Offenbach

BBC Hulton Picture Library

Offenbach had conducted *La Chanson de Fortunio* after a banquet given by
King William to celebrate the anniversary of Sadowa. It was normal for
Offenbach to conduct in person for the Prussian king; he could hardly
have refused. But in retrospect the association did him no good. 1870 was
no year for a man with divided loyalties. Offenbach, a German Jewish
French Catholic, was vulnerable to attack from four quarters. The Jews
and Catholics left him alone; religious feelings were not running high. But
to some Frenchmen he was a 'Prussian' (he was actually a Rhinelander,
but all Germans were 'Prussians', and Prussians were bogeymen) and to
some Germans he was a renegade. For the rest of his life he was subject to
attack from both sides.

When war broke out, and Offenbach left Ems for Étretat, his political
troubles began. In 1862 he had composed a patriotic French song, *Dieu
garde l'Empereur*. His publisher now reissued it, whereupon the German
press denounced him for betraying his fatherland. He replied in an open
letter to Villemessant, published in *Le Figaro*, 16 August 1870:

My dear friend,

Certain German journalists have slanderously stated that I have composed several anti-German songs. These assertions are accompanied by the most wretched insults.

I have a family and dear friends in Germany; for their sake I ask you to print the following:

I have been in France since I was fourteen; I have been granted papers of full naturalization; I have been appointed chevalier de la Légion d'honneur; I owe everything to France and would not think myself worthy of the name of Frenchman, which I have earned by honest toil, if I were to be guilty of dishonouring my native country.

It would deepen my love of France, if that were possible, to know that no Frenchman would accuse me of committing an action that would be infamous in the eyes of honest men of any country.

Bien à vous,
Jacques Offenbach.

But, as the war took its course, Jacques' feelings towards Germany hardened into bitterness. In March 1871 he wrote to Nuitter in German-occupied Paris:

O my poor dear friend, how I have suffered for you! I am not talking about my physical ills, I shall tell you about that in good time; I mean the mental anguish as I thought of my old friends. How relieved I was to hear finally that you had some food! I hope William Krupp and his horrible Bismarck will pay for this. What terrible people the Prussians are, and how I hate to think that I was born by the Rhine and have a connection, however slender, with these dreadful savages! Ah! my poor France, how I thank her for adopting me as one of her children! I have heard the *Trébizonde* story . . . I am sorry for my miserable little colleagues who hope to damage me by saying that I am German, when they know very well that I am French to the marrow! They will end up the losers, for their meanness.[3]

Theatres were in business again, and *La Princesse de Trébizonde* had been revived at the Bouffes in February. There was some noisy opposition to a show written by the 'Prussian' Offenbach, and the production was a failure. Much of the unpleasant nationalist pillorying of Offenbach came from jealous competitors.

In 1848 Jacques had fled from the revolution. During the war of 1870 and the revolution that followed, he again avoided personal involvement, travelling to Bordeaux, to Milan, and then to San Sebastian, where Herminie had gone with the children. His protestations of patriotism in the press were necessary as a defence against public attack, but he was no fighting patriot. As composer and entrepreneur he put his music first, and went wherever it could still be performed. He was frightened for his professional future. Charles Lecocq had predicted that Prussian shells would put an end to operetta. No one knew what kind of régime would replace the Second Empire, which provided the setting and the audience for Offenbach's operettas, and had suddenly collapsed. Anxiety aggravated Jacques' poor health, as Herminie related to Nuitter:

San Sebastian, 10 March 71

My dear friend,

I cannot tell you how much pleasure it gave us to read your letter. I heard your news from my Parisians. . . . We thought of you a lot during the long months of siege, and often tried to correspond with our poor exiles, without much success. At last it is all over. God grant that our poor country may rise up again one day, but I doubt if you and I will see that resurrection; we have been too badly hurt! It will take many years and great sacrifices before our children take part in the recovery of this unhappy country.

Jacques is in Milan, on his way round Italy. He has been terribly affected by this frightful war. His health has seriously worsened, he has not had eight good days in three months. I hope his return to surroundings he loves and needs so much will cure him completely. Can you not both come to Étretat? We sorely need to see the faces of beloved friends again.[4]

As the war against the Germans ended, the social struggle within France began. By the beginning of April Paris was held by left-wing extremists who had formed their own municipal government, the Commune. Thiers, leader of the conservative National Assembly, established his headquarters at Versailles. With a force of 130,000 he began the second siege of Paris. It lasted for seven weeks, of which the last was a 'week of blood', when terrorists burned the Tuileries and the Hôtel de Ville.

Even in the days of the Commune the theatres did well. When it was defeated social life was quick to revive. Parties of tourists arrived to see the wrecked capital. Halévy met an English family who were disappointed not to find smoke rising from the Tuileries. Marguerite Bellanger, last mistress of the Emperor, said to Arsène Houssaye, 'One can still enjoy oneself, but it's not the same.' 'It's the same', said Houssaye.

Offenbach, back in Étretat, resumed work on *Le Roi Carotte*, which he had begun before the war in collaboration with Victorien Sardou. He broke off for a brief visit to London, where he shared in the success of *Falsacappa*, the English version of *Les Brigands*, and was entertained at Chiswick by the Prince of Wales. While working on *Carotte* he persuaded

Nuitter and Tréfeu to write a new libretto to the music of *Barkouf* (see Chapter VI). The hero of *Boule-de-neige* was a bear instead of a dog, a substitution that failed to make much difference, but a strong cast steered the new piece clear of disaster.

Sardou's libretto for *Le Roi Carotte*, inspired by E. T. A. Hoffmann's story *Kleinzaches, genannt Zinnober*, was a more specific allegory of the Second Empire than any of the Meilhac-Halévy operettas: King Fridolin (Napoleon III) is deposed through the agency of a wicked fairy who brings the root vegetables (*les racines*, i.e. the radicals) to life. They are led by King Carotte, who assumes the throne. But the people find that the new king has more faults than the old one. Fridolin is restored, and Carotte is turned back into a vegetable.

Writing in 1869, Sardou made one or two predictions that were too accurate for comfort in a post-war operetta, as in a scene where King Fridolin, in council, announced his decision to declare war on the neighbouring princedom, and his minister assured him that the army was ready — shades of Napoleon III and Gramont. Sardou rewrote the script, eliminating such potentially explosive passages (Offenbach was in enough trouble already) and reset the German scenes in Hungary. The collaborators agreed to retain the ironic false prediction of the king's restoration at the end of the story. Satirical references were balanced so that monarchists and republicans came equally under fire. This non-committal attitude appealed to the censor and attracted an audience of all political complexions to *Le Roi Carotte*. Sardou's true views were revealed in his political comedy *Rabagas*, a satire on Gambetta and parliamentary government.

Le Roi Carotte had been commissioned in 1869 by Boulet, director of the huge Gaîté theatre,[5] home of melodramas and pantomimes. Boulet wanted a *féerie à grand spectacle*. A *féerie* was any piece involving supernatural characters. It was usually also a *pièce à machines*, a show with elaborate stage effects. As the Parisian theatre came to life after the war Boulet wished to outdo his rivals in lavishness of production, and he engaged 'an army of musicians, battalions of dancers'. 'We mustn't leave all these people with nothing to do', said Offenbach. Gradually *Le Roi Carotte* expanded from a normal-scale operetta to a show with four acts and twenty-two[6] scenes, and was described as an 'opéra bouffe-féerie'. An insect ballet alone had dancers portraying beetles, midges, crickets, gnats, xylophagans, maybugs, cicadas, butterflies, Spanish flies, ladybirds, dragonflies, grasshoppers, moths, hornets, wasps and bees. Illustrations of this and other lavish productions at the Gaîté (e.g. the third, *féerie* version of *Geneviève de Brabant*) show the principal characters standing about in the background while a mammoth ballet takes place downstage. As rehearsals began it was calculated that the production of *Le*

Roi Carotte would cost 6,000 francs a night to run. The brilliant success of the opening justified the extravagance. As André Martinet reported: 'When the lights went up on Pompeii, with its sun-drenched décor, its teeming merchants, gladiators, patricians and courtesans, all to exquisite music, there were cries of admiration from the audience.'

The success of *Carotte*, followed three nights later by the failure of his opéra-comique *Fantasio*, combined to determine the direction of Offenbach's career for the next four years. In *Fantasio* Paul de Musset had made a boring libretto out of his brother Alfred's play, and the music could not save it. It was withdrawn in February. Though it was immediately successful in Vienna, it was the last of the four Offenbach works (the others were *Barkouf*, *Robinson Crusoé* and *Vert-Vert*) to be presented at the Opéra-Comique in the composer's lifetime.

Since 1867, after *La Grande-Duchesse*, the public had been confused by Offenbach's uncertainty of style. He was not sure how to satisfy changing tastes. The critics' approval of *Robinson Crusoé* and *Vert-Vert* was welcome, but was not enough to satisfy the entrepreneur in Offenbach, to whom commercial success was a *sine qua non*. *Le Roi Carotte* seemed to provide the answer to his problems: he would become the impresario of the spectacular. He began a campaign to take over control of the Gaîté from Boulet, but met with stubborn resistance; Boulet turned down every offer. On the principle of *reculer pour mieux sauter* Jacques gave up the fight temporarily and amused himself with a new experiment — writing both words and music of an operetta. *Le Corsaire noir* was to appear at the Variétés, but was dropped, apparently from lack of enthusiasm, and Jacques found a home for it at the Theater an der Wien. In September 1872 he left for Vienna with a party of friends including Villemessant, Albert Wolff, his boyhood friend from Cologne, the librettist Philippe Gille, Gaston Mitchell and others. Several French critics also went to Vienna for the opening.

The libretto, however, was universally condemned. Louis Schneider, in his biography of Offenbach, suggests that the composer's name was used to conceal the identity of another writer; then switches to the conclusion that the libretto was bad enough to have been the work of a musician trying to make his début as a playwright. The matter was settled when Jacques Brindejont-Offenbach found some pages of the script in his grandfather's handwriting, and a letter about the contract, saying 'poème et musique de moi'.

In Vienna Jacques received a letter from Chivot and Duru, his collaborators on a new project, *Les Braconniers* ('The Poachers'). They wanted assurances that he was not putting their work in second place to *Le Corsaire noir*. Jacques wrote, on the eve of his Vienna première, promising that *Les Braconniers* would have the earlier Parisian production. Had he waited forty-eight hours, he could have told them that *Les Braconniers* would be the only candidate; *Le Corsaire noir* never reached Paris, and the score has disappeared, though it must be remembered that, if Offenbach was running true to form, the music was probably used piecemeal in later works, while some of it, equally, might have been served up before.

Jacques had not lost hope of taking over the Gaîté. He is said to have had an agreement with Adelina Patti and the distinguished tenor Capoul that they would appear at the opening in Massé's *Paul et Virginie*.[7] After a period of silence surrounding his affairs it was announced that he was to take over management of the Gaîté on 1 June 1873.

In January 1873 *Les Braconniers* was in rehearsal at the Variétés. Jacques, aware of an increasing tendency to lose his temper at rehearsals, wrote to his collaborators:

> Wishing always to preserve excellent relations with MM. Chivot and Duru, I, the undersigned Jacques Offenbach, composer of music, residing in Paris, rue Laffitte, hereby make formal written apologies in advance. MM. Chivot and Duru may make use of these on any occasion when they are offended, without, however, having claim to profit or pecuniary advantage of any kind; these advance apologies are strictly personal.
>
> Jacques Offenbach[8]

Les Braconniers opened on 29 January. It was regarded as a pale imitation of *Les Brigands*, and achieved a run of only two months.

Offenbach planned a double company for the Gaîté — one troupe for plays, and one for opera and operetta. He immediately met with opposition from the Society of Authors (which included both composers and authors) who had a ruling that directors of theatres must not present their own works. Offenbach wanted to put on *Orphée aux Enfers* and *Geneviève de Brabant*, both of which had already been accepted by Boulet, plus one new work of his own per year. Two meetings of the society were held with its president, Alexandre Dumas *fils*, in the chair. Offenbach made the point that to ban his work was to ban that of his collaborators. Dumas, an old friend, was sympathetic, but the society's ruling was upheld by 109 votes to 22. Offenbach, deciding on a test of strength, said that they would in future have to do without his subscription, left the meeting, signed his contract at the Gaîté, and went ahead with his plans unchanged and subsequently unchallenged. A few days after the authors' meeting Boulet died. Offenbach, once again finding a theatre under his control, began spending in the grand manner, as in the old days at the Bouffes. The auditorium was re-painted, re-carpeted, and re-upholstered. Offices and dressing-rooms were replanned. Having spent 316,000 francs for his lease, Jacques ran up another bill for 154,000 before performances began.

War and Peace: 1867–1875

On 2 September 1873 the Gaîté reopened with *Le Gascon*, a play by Théodore Barrière and Louis Davyl. It contained a duet, *Légende béarnaise*, set by Offenbach; Vizentini contributed a ballet. As it was only moderately successful Offenbach brought forward the opening date of *Jeanne d'Arc*, by Barbier, with incidental music by Gounod. This settled down to a good run, leaving Offenbach free to concentrate on composition. The Renaissance Theatre, in addition to reviving some earlier Offenbach works, had recently put on a one-act piece, *Pomme d'api* ('Lady-apple') in which Offenbach's latest discovery, Louise Théo, won all hearts. Jacques approached Crémieux and Blum: 'I think Théo is ready for three acts.' In seven weeks *La Jolie Parfumeuse* was written, composed and produced. Théo and her co-star Rose Michon were likened to a pair of Galateas created by Pygmalion/Offenbach.

The size and scenic facilities of the Gaîté now began to affect Offenbach with *folie de grandeur*. He decided to lengthen *Orphée aux Enfers* into four acts and to mount a spectacular production in his new theatre. In the first days of February 1874 a large negro stood on guard at the door of the Gaîté. He was thought to be a cannibal, and it had been put about that M. Offenbach had given orders for him to be starved for two days in order to render him fiercer. His job was to keep out the curious hangers-on of the theatre who were trying to sneak in to the final rehearsals of the new production of *Orphée aux Enfers*, which had become a legend before it opened. Offenbach had inherited the negro from Boulet, who had brought him back from central Africa after a trip in search of coal-mines. His menacing presence made him an effective guardian, but with the numbers involved in the present operation it was impossible to keep the rehearsals completely secret.

Offenbach had engaged 120 choristers, 60 orchestral musicians, a military band of 40, 8 principal female dancers and a corps de ballet of 60. He wrote a pastoral ballet, a ballet of dreams and hours, and a ballet of flies. The *Duo de la mouche*, sometimes cut in the past, was restored. There were additions to the plot, including a court-room scene for the trial of Pluto and a scene in Pluto's study where Cupid promises to help Jupiter find Eurydice, and summons twenty little (female) 'agents de police de l'amour' who join Cupid in a kissing song (the sound of kissing is the bait to attract Eurydice). *L'Opinion publique* again became a male character (see Chapter V) now played by Mlle Gilbert, *travestie*.

The censors demanded that the costumes of the fauns and shepherd-esses in the pastoral ballet should be lengthened, but the *ballet des mouches* must have escaped them. Arnold Mortier,[9] praising the costume designer, Grévin, wrote, 'No one in Paris shows more taste and wit in the art of uncovering a dancer: they are naked but decent.' Kracauer, the sociologist, writing seventy years later, looked at things from a different

169

point of view. Recalling that many of the extras were midinettes, seam-stresses in local clothing factories, who were given one large store-room to change in, he commented, 'They were only too glad to earn another twenty or thirty sous, and when their naked limbs were exposed on the stage their proletarian origins could not possibly be detected.'

The end of the second act, when the gods leave Mount Olympus to go down to Hades, was 'one of the most astonishing processions ever seen in the theatre'. Arnold Mortier described it:

> The characters are so numerous that I shall not attempt a fully detailed list of the never-ending cortège — a whole walking dictionary of comic mythology; there is the Olympus Conservatory of Music, with a complete brass band, kettledrums and bass drums; then the organs of the press with the banners of the contemporary newspapers — *Le Phigaros*, *Les Débatés*, etc. After that Pluto's suite, the court of Jupiter, the different celestial ministers; Literature and the Fine Arts, represented by Apollo and the Muses; War, Industry and Commerce, Finance and Agri-culture; Love and his retinue, including the Vestal Virgins — followed by the Navy, a nice juxtaposition; Crémieux has no respect for any-thing. Then the menagerie, that is to say, Juno's peacock, Minerva's owl, the hindquarters of the centaurs, etc. After them the wine-growers of Burgundy, with Bacchus astride a barrel and Silenus riding an ass. Finally the minor gods and goddesses, and, to end the cavalcade, the omnibus reserved for aged and infirm divinities.
>
> As the procession ends, the back of the set opens up, and the chariot of Phoebus rises into a sunlit sky, the white horses standing out against the dazzling light.

Mortier ends his account of the evening with a shrewd observation:

> A man — whom no one has named — has helped Offenbach with advice, and supervised the magnificent production, the unprecedented splendours, the unending brilliance.
>
> His name is Billion![10]

The remark was not entirely flippant. Mortier, who knew Offenbach, and was to be his collaborator on *Le Docteur Ox*, perceived that he was using extravagance as a substitute for invention; it was a symptom of his uncertainty of purpose. The old style of operetta was out of date. Meilhac and Halévy now refused to write in the genre, which put Offenbach at a disadvantage. Charles Lecocq, who owed his professional début to Offenbach — having been the co-winner with Bizet of the operetta com-petition at the Bouffes in 1856 — was writing comic operas; his *La Fille de Madame Angot* was the success of the day. Offenbach would not have admitted to being jealous of his talented junior, though he later let bitterness show in his letters; but in *La Jolie Parfumeuse* and its immediate successors *Bagatelle* and *Madame l'Archiduc* he followed half-heartedly in Lecocq's footsteps. *Whittington*, written hastily for London at the end of 1874, was another conventional comic opera. Although these pieces were successful, Offenbach the originator was now Offenbach the imitator — never plagiarizing, but no longer a leader.

The spectacular 1874 production of *Orphée aux Enfers* gave him an illusion of success. To the public he was a big name. Though crippled with gout he conducted the hundredth performance himself, and parents who remembered *Orphée* in 1858 brought their children to see the great star of the Second Empire. But what these children saw on stage bore no relation to the tightly knit satire once played in the intimacy of the salle Choiseul, where if the lanky Bache lifted his arms, he touched the proscenium fringe. The *féerie* had now made 1,800,000 francs. When Jacques heard that some of the company had not come to the celebrations for the centennial performance because they had no decent clothes, he raised their salaries by thirty per cent. He was rich again and could afford big gestures. But this did not solve his real problem: what sort of music should he now write, for what theatre and with what collaborators?

To make matters worse, the success of *Orphée* deceived Offenbach into thinking that any kind of theatrical material would benefit from spectacular presentation. It did not occur to him that *Orphée* might have succeeded in spite of the spectacle rather than because of it, or that, whereas a lively musical romp like *Orphée* at least provided some excuse for showy presentation, the same was not true of Sardou's prose tragedy *La Haine*, which he now intended to mount on a scale approaching madness. His growing admiration for Sardou had led to a close friendship, and nothing was to be spared that might make *La Haine* a success. The casualty in the process was Sardou's better judgement, which he allowed to be swamped by Jacques' enthusiasm. Where Sardou wanted twenty armed men, he was given a hundred. Where he wanted the audience to imagine a procession off-stage with distant sound effects, Offenbach insisted on parading hoards of extras in front of the footlights.

The result was disastrous. It destroyed Sardou's play and ruined Offenbach. Childishly sure of success, he had mounted the production without adequate capital. After three weeks he brought back *Orphée*, 'the eternal life-buoy', but even that old faithful could not make enough to pay more than a fraction of his debts. The *opéra-féerie* version of *Geneviève de Brabant*, with a mass of new music, including three ballets, did nothing for the company's finances. Summoning his actors and staff, Offenbach promised to pay everyone in full. With no hope of doing this out of his savings, he sold his interest in the Gaîté to Vizentini and mortgaged his royalties for three years. Once his debts were discharged, Offenbach went back to the straightforward business of writing music for a living.

He had three projects for 1875: *Le Voyage dans la lune*, from Jules Verne's novel, designed to be a science-fiction spectacular for the Gaîté (with Vizentini now taking the financial risks), *La Créole*, later to be successful in London as *The Commodore*, and *La Boulangère à des écus* (The Wealthy Bakerwoman), a new vehicle for Hortense Schneider. As an economy, Offenbach had let the villa Orphée, but he went briefly to a hotel in Étretat to start the year's work. Friends already in residence arranged an elaborate practical joke in the form of an absurd reception party for the composer. A group of twelve, in halberdiers' costumes with bits and pieces of armour dug out of attics and store-rooms, lined the road outside the station. Albert Wolff's nephew sat astride a donkey waving a tricolour flag borrowed from the casino. Midday fireworks were set off from the hotel balcony, and Wolff presented Jacques with his room key on a galvanized tin tray. The maestro took it all as a serious gesture of affection. Moist-eyed, he said, 'It's too much, it's too much!'

After the war Hortense Schneider visited St Petersburg, where she was treated royally. Tsar Alexander II, with memories of the great exhibition and the *Grande-Duchesse*, sent a special train to meet her at the border. Her appearances were triumphant. On her return to France she went into semi-retirement. In 1874 Bertrand lured her back to the Variétés with a revival of *La Périchole*. Unlike Offenbach, Schneider did not need the money. She lived in style between her mansion in the avenue du Bois and her villa near Étretat. But she could not resist the opportunity of proving that she was still a star in Paris. Although she was running to *embonpoint* and breathlessness, necessitating a dressing-room at stage level, her singing of the letter song could still enchant an audience, and people were mesmerized by her display of diamonds. Bons mots were exchanged: 'She must have discovered a mine!' 'Yes — and miners!'

But Jacques wanted something better for Hortense than a mere revival, and longed to re-unite the team that had created his greatest successes. He persuaded a reluctant 'Meil' and 'Hal' to work with him on *La Boulangère à des écus*. When Schneider received the script she was dissatisfied with her role. A series of discussions and revisions culminated in a bitter row between the star and Halévy. When she arrived next day to start rehearsals, Schneider learned that her part had been given to her rival Marie Aimée. With a neat dig at Bertrand, manager of the Variétés — 'Il lui sera beaucoup pardonné . . . parcequ'il a Aimée!' — she went off to her lawyer and started proceedings that eventually won her damages of 5,000 francs. But Marie Aimée continued to play the role.

A week after the opening of *La Boulangère* in October 1875 Halévy entered in his diary a private epitaph on a collaboration:

Offenbach, Meilhac and I are exhausted, that is the truth; we have done too much. We have said all there is to say about choruses, entrances, exits, processions, partings, verses for bridesmaids and rondos for pages. We are no longer twenty or even forty. Bold and imaginative ideas disappear as we get older, and our genre, more than any other, needs daring and fantasy. I think we now know our medium very well, but that has its disadvantages. It makes us timid and careful. We have lost the boldness of inexperience. Instead of plunging in at the deep end without asking the depth, we want to ease into the water down a ladder. We explore the ground; is it firm? yes . . . all right. So we risk it and write *La Boulangère*, a dull, banal piece which can neither succeed nor fail. That is what has happened.[11]

La Boulangère was the last collaboration of the three 'collabos'.

CHAPTER XIII

Maiden Voyage
1875–1877

······☩······

In the summer of 1875 Offenbach rented accommodation for the family in the Pavillon Henri IV on the terrace at Saint-Germain-en-Laye. This former palace looks towards Paris, twelve miles away, from an escarpment above the Seine. Tenants had the use of the royal gardens. Here Jacques worked with only his family around him, refusing to receive visitors, although once, when Hortense Schneider was announced unexpectedly, he lacked the courage to send her away. While they chatted in the garden, a stranger arrived, insisting on an interview, and Offenbach resigned himself to listening.

The man was Lino Bacquero, a South American. He and a colleague, Maurice Grau, wanted Offenbach to conduct a concert tour in the United States the following year — 1876,[1] centenary year of the Declaration of Independence. Bacquero left the composer to think it over. The family were distressed, and pleaded with Jacques to say no. It was a hazardous venture for someone in his state of health, they said, and the separation would be long and painful. But when Bacquero returned next day with an offer of $30,000 payable in advance into the Bank of France, Jacques felt he 'had no right to refuse'. Although that phrase, in his memoir of the incident, sounds disingenuous, he goes on to tell how he kept hoping that something would happen to release him from his obligation; the money might not be paid, civil war might break out in the States. But the money arrived, and there was no war.

On 21 April 1876 Offenbach left Paris, accompanied, as far as Le Havre, by his two sons-in-law, Charles Comte and Achille Tournal; his two brothers-in-law, Robert and Gaston Mitchell; several friends including Albert Wolff; and his thirteen-year-old son Auguste-Jacques. Next day he boarded the *Canada*, newest vessel of the French line, about to make her maiden trip to New York. The sending-off party stood on the quay, and Jacques' parting memory was of the sunlight glinting off the buttons of his son's school uniform.

Plymouth was the only port of call. Here, with the ship at anchor, Jacques had a good night's sleep, his last on the voyage. Twenty-four hours later the *Canada* developed intermittent propeller trouble and kept stopping. Soon she ran into a storm that lasted three days and four nights. Jacques refused to stay in his cabin (he had already nervously taken to sleeping in his clothes). A bed was made for him in the saloon, and the captain and crew kept him company for part of the night. He later wrote to

28. Offenbach sets off to the New World in the attempt to bolster his dwindling resources

Collection Viollet

Halévy, 'Don't laugh, I seriously thought I would never see you again.' Learning that the young ship's doctor, Flamant, was seasick, and unable to cure himself with his own medicine, Jacques took malicious pleasure each morning in asking how he was.

The captain, M. Franguel, inspired confidence, and was friendly and witty. The purser, M. Betsellère, having 'had the good fortune to have been shipwrecked before' — and to have survived — no longer feared anything. Among the passengers noted by Offenbach were: Mlle Marie Aimée, star of *La Boulangère*, who was on her way to New York after a

175

29. Marie Aimée, Schneider's great rival, in *Barbe-bleue*

Opera Rara Collection

triumphant season in Moscow; M. Boulard, accompanying Offenbach as leader of the orchestra and assistant conductor, and his young wife; Mr Bacquero, 'who succeeded by the power of the dollar in getting me to make this little artistic journey', and M. Arigotti, once a fine tenor who was now Bacquero's secretary.[2]

When the *Canada* reached New York in the early morning of 5 May there was the customary festive reception for a liner completing her first trans-atlantic voyage. A fleet of small boats, dressed with flags, hooted their welcome. On one boat there was a military band. When this vessel struck rough water the musicians began to disappear 'as in that droll Haydn symphony [No. 94] where the musicians leave one after the other, putting out the lights. Our musicians here had nothing to put out, but instead of pouring out sounds, they poured out . . . their souls into the sea.'[3] Jacques assumed, typically, that the whole thing was a personal reception. When the New York reporters came on board he quickly made friends with them, and they noted in the papers that M. Offenbach came ashore in the company of Mlle Aimée.

On the day of his arrival Offenbach visited the theatre twice. After the evening performance (*Henry V* at the Booth Theatre) he returned to the Fifth Avenue Hotel, where there was a genuine personal reception for him. At midnight a large band played a serenade that included music from *Orphée aux Enfers* and *La Grande-Duchesse*. A crowd of three or four thousand outside the hotel called for the composer. 'I was forced to appear on the balcony, just like Gambetta. There I shouted a terrific "Thank you, sir!", a polite expression that no one could call subversive.'

The New York Times, however, was less enthusiastic than the public. Its leader-writer, while acknowledging Offenbach's importance, saw cause for concern. Under the heading 'A DISTINGUISHED FOREIGNER' he wrote:

M. OFFENBACH long ago found that to use his gift of melody in the service of immorality was a sure path to fortune. . . .

The opéra-bouffe [*La Belle Hélène*] is simply the sexual instinct expressed in melody. . . .

Priapism is put on a level with music, and composers who have devoted their lives to the composition of works which no man can hear under-standingly without being lifted out of the grossness of his earthly nature, are virtually asked to take notice that they have made a grave mistake in not wedding their music to indecency.[4]

Offenbach's reaction to these observations is not recorded, but no impresario of his astuteness could have failed to realise the immense

30 and 31. Formal elegance in America Cartoon of Offenbach by Ferdinand Bac
Collection Jean Vincent-Bréchignac

box-office value of that kind of publicity. Readers of the article, after a little seemly tut-tutting, would certainly buy tickets. And the composer had more pressing things on his mind; his first concern was to visit the Gilmore Garden, where his concerts were to take place.

A station of the Harlem railway had been converted into a covered stadium to hold eight or nine thousand people. It had recently drawn crowds to the revivalist meetings of Moody and Sankey. A century later, rebuilt as Madison Square Garden, it was to be the scene of title fights between Cassius Clay (Muhammad Ali) and Joe Frazier. On the ground was a garden with grass and flower beds.

A platform to hold an orchestra of over a hundred was surrounded by tropical foliage. There was a waterfall designed to simulate Niagara in the intervals of the concerts. Round the perimeter of the stadium were chalets for seven or eight people, taking the place of boxes in a theatre. The upper levels had ordinary boxes and tiers of seats. Coloured lighting created rainbow effects.

Grau had hired New York's best musicians, and Offenbach got on well with them from the start. He had heard from Boulard that no musician here could play in an orchestra unless he joined their musicians' organization. Boulard, who conducted some of the rehearsals, had been compelled to join. When Boulard was on the podium the orchestra was led by John Philip Sousa, soon to become the world's most famous composer of marches.

Offenbach began his first rehearsal with the overture to *Vert-Vert*. After sixteen bars he stopped the orchestra to point out that they were failing in their duty by allowing him, a non-member of their assocation, to conduct them. There was laughter. Then Offenbach spoke seriously, saying that he approved of such an association, and would like the honour of being made a member. This gesture was loudly applauded. Throughout the season the orchestra regarded their maestro with affection and respect.

For the first concert the Gilmore Garden doubled its prices. General admission was $1.00, a box $5.00. An audience of five thousand turned up and gave the composer an ovation on his first appearance. But the evening was a failure. Offenbach only conducted four items; Boulard, conducting the others, was dull. There were no cancans, no dancers, no singers. Some of the audience left after the first number, more drifted away during the evening.

The critics agreed with each other: a programme confined to the works of one composer resulted in monotony, especially as the music was all from *opéra-bouffe*, and was all instrumental, lacking a Schneider, a Tostée or an Aimée to interpret Offenbach's famous melodies. But the composer was warmly applauded. 'He has, personally,' wrote one critic, 'a great deal of magnetism, and reflects much of the spirit of the delightful, yet naughty, school of music which he so ably represents.'

Another moral judgement; strange that the reviewer of a purely orchestral concert could not rid himself of the connotations of 'naughtiness' in the words of the operettas. Or did he think that the music was *in itself* 'naughty'? If so, he was in famous company. George Bernard Shaw, at his most governessy, wrote, 'I warn . . . solemnly, that Offenbach's music is wicked. It is abandoned stuff; every accent is a snap of the fingers in the face of moral responsibility.'[5] Even if Shaw had, perhaps, his tongue in his cheek, this was the voice of English puritanism, the hypocrisy that allowed the English to condemn the French for naughtiness, and then go to Paris to enjoy it.

Offenbach was to run into more puritanism in Philadelphia, but for the moment that did not concern him. He was mortified by the failure of his concert, and offered to release Grau from his contract. But Grau was a fighter. Following up the hints from reviewers, he introduced works by other composers — Weber, Strauss, Gounod, Berlioz, Vieuxtemps (at that time highly popular as a composer of violin music). He engaged well-known soloists and a much-liked second conductor, Max Maretzek. Offenbach composed *The American Eagle Waltz* for the virtuoso cornettist Jules Levy. Prices were halved. The recipe worked, and the crowds returned. Grau immediately exploited the success with a hastily mounted production of *La Vie parisienne* at the Booth Theatre, with Marie Aimée as Gabrielle, and Offenbach conducting. This was what New Yorkers had expected all along — including the 'naughtiness'. It brought in $20,000, making Offenbach's American tour a financial success. He left for Philadelphia, accompanied by sixty musicians, to perform at the Centennial Exhibition.

Before leaving New York he wrote some impressions of the city in a letter to Bertrand, director of the Variétés:

> New York, a splendid city, beautiful streets, beautiful houses, beautiful women etc., but what a strange country. Liberty, indeed! Everyone is free, but free in a way you could not imagine in France. So free that on Sundays you are absolutely forbidden to take a glass of beer or a little glass of cognac in a café or anywhere else. Last Sunday thirty waiters were trotted off to prison because they thought, in view of the great liberty that obtains here, that they would be allowed to serve their customers. (Quite right too, why should these people be given all this freedom?!)[6]

The first morning in Philadelphia Jacques took breakfast in the hotel, then went out to see the exhibition. He was disappointed:

> I had forgotten it was Sunday. The exhibition is closed on Sunday, the shops and restaurants are closed, everything is closed in this joyous town. And what gaiety! The few people you meet are coming out of church with bibles and funereal faces. If you are unlucky enough to smile, they look at you with blazing eyes, if you were unlucky enough to laugh, they would have you arrested.[7]

However, professional matters went well. A new covered garden had been erected, modelled on the Gilmore Garden, but smaller. The management asked the composer's permission to call it the Offenbach Garden. 'I could not refuse', he wrote, disingenuous as ever. 'Offenbach Garden was as favourable to me as Gilmore Garden. The same enthusiasm, the same encores, the same brilliant concerts. The day after each performance, the press showered praises on me.'[8]

The director of the Offenbach Garden wanted to put on a Sunday concert. Concerts were not allowed in Philadelphia on Sundays, but a concert of sacred music might just be permitted. A poster was put up (see facing page).

For a week my *Grand Sacred Concert* was billed on posters all over the

OFFENBACH GARDEN

COR BROAD ANT CHERRY STS

SUNDAY EVENING, JUNE 25 TH

AT 8 O'CLOCK P. M.,

GRAND

SACRED

CONCERT

BY

M. OFFENBACH

AND THE

GRAND ORCHESTRA

IN A CHOICE SELECTION OF

SACRED ET CLASSICAL MUSIC

ADMISSION,   50 CENTS

LEDGER JOB PRINT. PH LAD'

32. The programme was neither as sacred
nor as classical as the poster suggests;
when this was discovered, the guardians
of local morality insisted on the concert
being cancelled.

town. During that time I had prepared my programme, a really nice
programme:

Deo gratias, from Le Domino noir;
Ave Maria, by Gounod;
Marche religieuse, from La Haine;
Ave Maria, by Schubert;
Litanie from La Belle Hélène: dis-moi, Vénus;
Hymne, from Orphée aux Enfers;
Prière, from La Grande-Duchesse (dites-lui);
Danse séraphique: polka burlesque;
Angélus, from Le Mariage aux lanternes.

Unfortunately permission was withdrawn at the last minute. I am sorry they did not follow up this project; for I am convinced that my Sacred Concert that evening would have been a big success.[9]

Offenbach had promised Marie Aimée that he would conduct a performance of *La Jolie Parfumeuse* in a town which he refused to name in his memoir because the occasion was a disaster. The town he calls 'X' was on the way from New York to Chicago. It has been tentatively identified as Buffalo, a possibility if he travelled via Lake Erie. No one had told Offenbach that his score had been reorchestrated. When the rehearsal began he found that the music 'bore only a distant family resemblance to my operetta'. He tried to get out of conducting the performance, but was held to his contract. The orchestra was 'small, but execrable'. The worst moment of the evening was when a player who had to give the singer her note gave the wrong one, and she started singing in a key a fifth above the orchestra. Offenbach, desperate but inspired, signalled to the drummer to play a loud roll. 'The public certainly did not understand why, in the middle of the night in a scene full of mystery, the drummer suddenly burst out with such strength and persistence. . . . I was expecting a flood of insults in such newspapers as reviewed the performance. Quite the reverse: praise, nothing but praise, for the masterly way in which I had conducted!'[10]

On his return to New York he conducted at his own suggestion a farewell concert in aid of the Association of New York Musicians, of which he was now a member. On 8 July 1876 he embarked for France on the *Canada*. This time the weather was magnificent, and the voyage was marked by only three incidents of note. As the ship cast off it crashed into the *America*, another French boat, which had the worst of the encounter; the *Canada* proceeded unharmed. One evening a Brazilian passenger swallowed a whole 'basket' of rum, and came into the saloon 'dressed, or rather, undressed, like a baker at work'. There was a moment of embarrassment because of the ladies present. 'The third episode', wrote Offenbach, 'is so sad and so ridiculous that I am omitting it. Perhaps I will tell it later. . . .' He had no need later to tell it himself; it was, as we shall soon see, to be the subject of a bitter *cause célèbre*.

When the *Canada* docked at Le Havre Jacques' whole family and some of his friends were on the pier. He cried with happiness. After the embraces they all set off on the ten miles to Étretat, where the villa Orphée was waiting to welcome him home.

Although the Third Republic was not formally established until 1875, the republican mood was strong from 1870 onwards. The left-wing press was sensitive and aggressive, on the look-out for scapegoats among the 'men of the Empire'. These included Offenbach, who stood for everything they hated. He was labelled 'le grand responsable', (one of the chief culprits). Bewildered and embittered by ill-defined accusations, and harassed by financial problems, he found relief on both counts in his visit to America, but the hostility of the Republicans was resumed when he came back. On 11 February 1877 the newspaper *Le Siècle* published an article entitled 'Offenbach in America'. It alleged that while dining on the *Canada* on his return voyage he had made fun of France 'to a degree that enraged the captain and the passengers, whatever nationality they were, and drove a friend of ours, a Republican senator who was making the crossing with "le sieur Offenbach", to remind him forcefully of the ribbon he wore and the naturalization papers he had acquired.'[11]

Offenbach was stunned by the attack. It referred to the incident he had mentioned but omitted to describe in his account of the voyage home: an argument in the course of which he had been caustic about the Republicans. The account in *Le Siècle* was, in his view, such an absurd distortion that he decided not even to comment. Unfortunately, a week later, the senator for the Loire, Lucien Arbel, wrote to *Le Siècle*, 'I was the senator concerned, and I confirm that you have given the most scrupulously accurate account of the details.'

The affair became serious, and the left-wing press started referring to 'Herr Offenbach'. Luckily for Offenbach an authoritative witness of the incident, a left-wing deputy, Théophile Roussel, intervened on his behalf. Roussel recalled that one day on board ship Offenbach said to him laughingly, 'How about talking politics?' 'With pleasure, if it's as entertaining as in Gerolstein.' Roussel's account continued:

> This was the tone in which you spoke about the Republicans, in terms that were joking rather than offensive, at which none of those who heard the beginning of the conversation would have dreamed of taking offence. Unluckily, one of our fellow-passengers came in, who, not knowing the situation, gave way to a burst of anger, and enjoined you to show respect for our French form of government. I immediately tried to explain that your quarrel was due to a misunderstanding. Everybody seemed to acknowledge this, and I was sure no one would give it another thought.

Public argument became so intense that the police were involved. There was an inquiry and a report: 'There is no truth in the *affaire Offenbach*. He has written a signed letter to his friends denying the allegations of senator Arbel. R. Mittchell [sic] strongly defends Offenbach and says that the Republicans attacked him because they knew his Bonapartist opinions.'[12] Robert Mitchell was Offenbach's brother-in-law, a respected journalist who had supported the liberal Émile Ollivier in Empire days. Lest he could be accused of family bias, there were other witnesses on

Offenbach's side. The purser of the *Canada*, M. Betsellère, attested, 'Your words on board the *Canada* <u>offended nobody</u>, and I can state with complete honesty that several passengers were upset when the epithet <u>Prussian</u> was applied to you during this unfortunate discussion.'

But the acrimony lingered on. Finally Jacques decided to speak. He wrote to the editor-in-chief of *Le Rappel*:

> Permit me to draw a conclusion from the letter printed by *Le Rappel* concerning an accusation levelled at me. From M. Arbel's second letter, and the testimonies of the three people who made the crossing on the *Canada* (MM. Roussel, deputy of the Left, Betsellère, purser of the ship, and de la Forest, consul-general of France in New York) it emerges that I never made any statement <u>about France</u>, my country, that could possibly bring my patriotism into question: that is all I wish to establish. The story can still have an excellent outcome, which depends on M. Arbel. Let a jury of honour examine the parties, and, according to whether they find in favour of M. Arbel's allegations or my denials, let a sum of 25,000 francs be paid by him or me to the funds of the workers of Lyon.

M. Arbel did not take up the challenge. There was one more abortive outburst from the Left, described by Arnold Mortier after he attended the first night of a revival of *La Périchole*. As he entered the theatre people were saying that when the overture started in a few minutes there would be whistling:

> 'Whistling! why?'
> 'A demonstration against Offenbach.'
> 'Impossible!'
> 'Well, they claim at the desk that at least forty people are here specially for that.'
> 'Forty! You'd never find forty people so stupid!'
> 'You'll see.'
> And, in fact, we saw. Never did such a grotesque demonstration fail so pitifully. When the curtain went up whistling came from the upper balconies, from which we usually hear the applause of the *claque*. This was greeted with an immense burst of laughter. No one got angry, no one protested. Why protest? Everyone laughed, that was all. The whistlers, who had expected heavy opposition, shamefacedly pocketed their key-whistles, and the show continued without interruption.
> It is a week since we forgot the Arbel-Offenbach incident, in which the composer of *La Belle Hélène* had the last, and winning, word. Yet someone actually thought that an audience — the Variétés audience, moreover — would associate itself with a demonstration organized by

who knows who, in aid of who knows what! Really a massive error of judgement![13]

Offenbach was exonerated from the charge of being unpatriotic. That was fair; to suggest that he was pro-German was a silly smear. On the contrary, he had become progressively more anti-Prussian over the years. He loved France, loved being French. Even a cynic would have seen it to be against the interest of Offenbach, the opportunist, to express anti-French sentiments to a Republican senator in the political climate of 1876. But was there more to the story? Offenbach's public supporters were his brother-in-law Mitchell, his friend and collaborator Mortier, the officers of the *Canada*, with whom he had made friends on the outward journey, and Roussel, a new-found shipboard companion. All these would naturally support him.

The scene in the saloon can be imagined. The celebrated Jacques Offenbach, witty, charming, is enjoying the adulation of his fellow-passengers. There is a half-serious political conversation. Enter a Republican senator, worthy, idealistic, humourless, the perfect butt for Offenbach's waspish tongue. The senator demands to be taken seriously; Offenbach becomes sarcastic, offensive. He has all the cards on his side; in the present company he can only win. The atmosphere turns sour. The senator leaves, frustrated and furious. Offenbach, politically naive, unused to being disliked, fails to understand what he has done wrong. For once he is at a loss, upset enough not to want to write about the incident. One small mystery remains: why did the senator wait eight months before attacking Offenbach in the press?

Halévy, in a diary entry, laughs at his friend's political pretensions: 'Offenbach has suddenly gone mad on politics . . . proud as anything at having Mitchell for a brother-in-law, he fancies sticking his nose, his great goblin's nose, into politics. You should hear him, it's unbelievable.' Anyone could see that Jacques was a child in politics. Did his friends observe that he was naive in other matters too — in business, for example, and with women? And did they perceive that an element of childlike naivety was present in his music as both a weakness and a strength?

CHAPTER XIV

Meno mosso
1878–1880

······

In October 1875 the façade of the Gaîté was obscured by a model of the moon in relief, advertising *Le Voyage dans la lune,* based on Jules Verne's novel, with music by Offenbach. Scenes in the show included a re-production of the interior of the Paris Observatory, and a foundry where an enormous cannon was forged, which later stood in a valley with its barrel resting on the mountains. Effects of this kind are more entertaining in the theatre than in the cinema. The cinema can cheat; however effective the result, we know that the film has been through months of optical processing. The live theatre has to achieve its miracles in the presence of the audience. An element of the excitement of theatrical effects is the possibility of failure; cinematic effects are weakened by the certainty of success. Live theatre does not make the mistake of aiming at realism, but entertains us with the cleverly artificial; ingenious machines become stars in the show.

In science-fiction Offenbach found another substitute for satire. The success of *Le Voyage dans la lune* made up for some of his losses at the Gaîté, but meant that the theatre was not available for *Don Quichotte,* on which he was working with Sardou, the two of them quarrelling away about the treatment of Cervantes' novel, scale of production, etc. The project was finally abandoned.

When *La Créole* opened at the Bouffes on 3 November 1875 it was Offenbach's third première within a month. The Bouffes, the Gaîté and the Variétés were all showing Offenbach successes. Mortier called them his 'trilogy'. Later, when four more works came out in quick succession, the description 'tetralogy' was inevitable. These words were com-pliments; they referred, not to any artistic unity in either group, but merely to the amazing speed at which Offenbach, now living in constant pain, could produce three or four works in a row.

Saint-Saëns looked down his nose:

Offenbach's facility and speed of execution were unheard-of. He literally improvised. His scores are covered with little flies' feet, microscopic notes. He had a system of abbreviations which he pushed to its extreme limits; and the simplicity of his method of composition allowed him to use it frequently. Nevertheless, great fecundity, the gift of melody, some harmonic distinction, plenty of wit and invention, high theatrical skill — that was all he needed to succeed.[1]

Abbreviations in musical notation are standard throughout the world, as Saint-Saëns well knew, though Offenbach did invent one time-saver of his own. In orchestral scores, if he had to write, for example, seventeen E major key-signatures on the left of the page, he would indicate sharps by the sign + instead of #, thereby saving himself 136 strokes of the pen, and at least half a minute per page. The reference to 'the simplicity of his method of composition' must refer to his use of repetition (as a master of repetition himself Saint-Saëns was on rather shaky ground) and certain musical formulas. But there is nothing wrong in that; the inspired use of the formula is fundamental to popular music, and unites the Strausses and Irving Berlin, Offenbach and George Gershwin, Sullivan and the Beatles.

Maître Péronilla,[2] the last work in the 'tetralogy' was the subject of bitterness on Jacques' part towards his friends Meil and Hal. The Republican government, not wishing to be less showy than its predecessors, was planning another great Paris exhibition for 1878. Offenbach took it as an omen; the exhibition of 1855 had seen the founding of the Bouffes, that of 1867 had marked the peak of his success, with *La Grande-Duchesse*. He wrote to Halévy: 'My dear Ludo, for the first time in my life I am superstitious. We had all the biggest successes of the last exhibition; I would love it if the piece was by *us three*, nobody but *us three*, Meilhac, Halévy, Offenbach. So look round, search, work. . . .'[3] Another letter went to Meilhac:

> Think about it seriously, it would be a great idea for the exhibition. In 1867, the year of the last exhibition, we had *La Vie parisienne* and *La Grande-Duchesse* on the bills in Paris. It's absolutely essential that we have our three names together again with a big new success for the 1877 [sic] exhibition. We could then rest for ten years and start all over again for the exhibition of 1887. I'm sure that's what you think, so will Ludo; in any case it's what *I* think. . . .[4]

His two friends reluctantly started to sketch something out, then gave up. They preferred working with Charles Lecocq, whose work was fresher than Offenbach's. Jacques turned to Nuitter and Ferrier, who helped him with *Maître Péronilla*, but he wrote most of the libretto himself (Nuitter and Ferrier did not even want acknowledgement for their small contribution); the programme gave the librettist as 'Monsieur X'. Bitterly, Jacques wrote to Halévy telling him of the 'successful' first night of *Maître Péronilla* (which proved to be a failure): 'My dear *friend*, you know that *friend* Péronilla went very well, and that it will be a real financial success if Comte does a quarter of the publicity that your *friend* Koning is so good at. I'm telling you this because I know how much interest you take in the work of your *friend*.   Ch. Lecocq'.[5] The childish sarcasm of the false signature reveals the extent to which Offenbach felt threatened by Lecocq's success.

By the beginning of 1877 Jacques and his family were living in a large apartment in the boulevard des Capucines, at the corner of the place de l'Opéra. Jacques spent every morning indoors, no longer going out to the Café Riche for luncheon. From his room he could look out on the boulevard, or down the rue de la Paix past the Vendôme column to the gardens of the Tuileries. Wolff describes him lying back in a great armchair, his feet up higher than his head to relieve the pain. Through the fur collar of his silk dressing-gown one did not so much see as guess his presence. Family sorrows aggravated his physical suffering. His brother Jules, prematurely senile at sixty-three, had been admitted permanently to a nursing-home in Bordeaux; and the doctors were seriously worried about the health of the sixteen-year-old Auguste, who had a chronic cough and was losing weight.

Towards lunchtime Jacques would call his valet and dress with scrupulous care. After a tiny lunch and a large strong cigar he put on a topcoat edged with tawny fur, which mingled with his side-whiskers and the long hair that fell over his nape. He was helped into a hermetically sealed coupé, where more furs were thrown over his knees, and went off to his theatre. The vehicle was hired by the month; it had a writing-desk installed so that he could get on with his work. If he was only going to the Bouffes, three hundred yards round the corner, it was hardly worth getting out his pen, but a trip to a more remote theatre could mean two pages of orchestration, and the journey to Saint-Germain-en-Laye was worth half an act.

In 1877 Offenbach began work on *Les Contes d'Hoffmann*. For the first time in his life he wrote slowly, not because of ill-health — he broke off five times to write other pieces at normal speed — but because his attitude to *Hoffmann* was different. He had too often been seduced by his own facility into writing in a way that did not fully extend his powers; and knew that, now or never, he must put his imagination to harder work, if he was to make the more serious musical statement of which he felt himself capable. It was as if he had written everything else for the Second Empire, but intended *Hoffmann* for posterity. We should be grateful, both that he now felt this, for it resulted in *Hoffmann*; and that he had not

33. The most famous of all Offenbach portraits, a photograph by Nadar. In his later days the composer wore a fur coat indoors and out

Bibliothèque nationale

worried about it early in his career. The facility of which he was now suspicious, and which drew a sneer from Saint-Saëns, was born of spontaneity, which was the quintessence of the Offenbach operetta. It was because he had never despised facility nor regarded light music with condescension that Offenbach's music carried conviction.

But it was a long time since he had had a triumph. His next works were damp squibs, the kind of material 'that can neither succeed nor fail', such as had caused Halévy to break away from the collaboration. *Madame*

Meno mosso: 1878–1880

Favart, delayed in production, was beaten to the post by two similar shows on back-stage subjects. *La Marocaine*, at the Bouffes, was a poor man's Gaîté spectacular, though a scene in a Moroccan harem brought a few monocles to the alert. It depressed Offenbach, too, that managers, instead of commissioning new pieces, preferred to play safe and revive *La Grande-Duchesse* and, yet again, *Orphée aux Enfers*. These revivals were uncomfortably like exhumations, but it must have been a moving moment when, at the première of *Orphée*, on 4 August 1878, Offenbach conducted the second act, which was all his strength would allow; and the thousandth performance of *Orphée* was a theatrical landmark.

In the spring of 1879 Offenbach retreated to Saint-Germain-en-Laye to work. There were friends about when he needed them; Halévy was in another apartment in the Pavillon Henri IV. Jacques wrote to Herminie:

> It's 8 o'clock in the evening. I am alone. Absolutely alone. Halévy is dining in Paris. I have been working all day on my *Contes*. Barbier came to work with me part of the time. I let him hear various bits of the score. He cried and kissed me. He was in raptures. I'm happy myself, and happy with the work. I am going to write to Roques, of the Bouffes, to arrange for you to hear three or four completed numbers before dinner on Friday. Members of *the family* who would like to be in on the audition have only to turn up a little early. You can tell them. I think you will be very pleased, and I hope my son will approve of my work.

There follows the mild expostulation of a hard-working father whose children are too lazy to write to him. He concedes that his wife has an excuse for not writing, because her feet are hurting. Then, in a postscript, he says: 'I have been thinking: I shall let only *you and Auguste* hear the passages from the *Contes*. My daughters will be kept out of this little audition, which has really nothing to do with them.'[6]

Ever since they were married, Jacques had enlisted Herminie as a critic; he now set great store by the opinions of Auguste, who had grown up knowing every note of his father's music. It would be Auguste, who, after Offenbach's death, made decisions on behalf of the family about the handling of his father's compositions — such as the choice of Guiraud to finish the orchestration of *Les Contes d'Hoffmann*. But on 18 May 1879 the completed sections of the opera were eventually performed to a sizeable group of family and professional friends, who were taken by surprise at a new depth they found in Offenbach's music. Two impresarios made offers — Jauner of the Ringtheater in Vienna, and Carvalho, director at the Opéra-Comique. Though he knew he would get a better performance in Vienna, Offenbach had no hesitation. For thirty years it had been his obsession to have an incontestable success at the Opéra-Comique. He knew the time had come.

Meno mosso: 1878–1880

In 1879 he was just fit enough to travel. After working on *Les Contes* at Saint-Germain-en-Laye during the spring, he took the waters at Wildbad in Germany, then paid a sentimental visit to Cologne, to find that his parents' house was no longer there, and that most of his friends were dead. He spent the summer with his family in Étretat before returning to Paris. He never saw the villa Orphée again.

Progress on *Les Contes d'Hoffmann* was interrupted by spells of work on *La Fille du Tambour-major*. It is tempting to suppose that there was a touch of mischief in this choice of subject. It glorified the first Napoleon's invasion of northern Italy and the French conquest of Milan. Offenbach assumed the role of a tricolour-waving patriot. He must have enjoyed cocking a snook at the po-faced Republicans who had given him all the trouble over the *Canada* incident. The show opened in unfavourable conditions. The winter of 1879–80 was bitterly cold. The temperature in Paris dropped to minus fifteen degrees centigrade, and the streets were deep in snow. Most theatres closed, including the Folies-Dramatiques, where *La Fille* was to appear. Offenbach used the closure as an excuse for extra rehearsals, but as soon as he thought the actors were ready he insisted on opening the show before they became stale.

La Fille du Tambour-major was Offenbach's hundredth[7] work; it received a standing ovation, and was the last of his premières that he lived to attend. The hundred-and-first performance was given in honour of the Paris Garrison, whose soldiers applauded their predecessors-in-arms. At a supper after the show the orchestra played an Offenbach quadrille (a selection of melodies arranged for dancing). Jacques recognized his own music, but had to offer a reward to anyone who would tell him which of his operettas the tunes came from — he could not remember.

La Fille became an international hit. After Vienna came Brussels, where, according to a contemporary account, 'when the maestro conducted the fifty-ninth performance, it rained flowers. The house was transformed into a garden; on stage the Harlequin curtain disappeared behind the roses; chaplets were thrown at Offenbach and his leading lady, Mme Lucy Abel. Offenbach's triumph was complete, down to the serenade organized beneath his window.'

The success prompted Koning, director of the Renaissance theatre, to commission a three-act work. This offer meant more to Offenbach than any other for years, not only because the Renaissance was now the most important Parisian musical theatre apart from the opera houses, but because it had recently devoted itself solely to the works of Charles Lecocq. With acid pride Offenbach remarked to Koning that he would now have real music in his theatre; the intensity of Jacques' jealousy of Lecocq was in the open. He knew that he had not long to live, and wanted desperately to survive for the first night of *Hoffmann*. But he was prepared to postpone completion of *Hoffmann* in order to compose *Belle Lurette*, an *opéra-comique* that would effect his triumph over his rival. If Offenbach had not been so intent upon this rivalry *Les Contes d'Hoffmann* might have been orchestrated by its own composer.

In the summer of 1880 Offenbach, forbidden by his doctor to go to the sea, and wanting peace and quiet to complete *Hoffmann* and *Belle Lurette*, went again to Saint-Germain-en-Laye. Herminie took some of the family to Étretat, leaving her daughter Mimi, now Mme Tournal, to visit Jacques regularly. On Sundays Auguste came over from school and played through the new sections of his father's scores. Albert Wolff, Halévy and Henri Meilhac took the first-floor apartment above that of their friend. Jacques' friendship with Meil and Hal had survived the bitterness of their row over Lecocq; in any case, Lecocq had now been put in his place.

However warm the weather, Jacques stayed in his room for fear of draughts. When he stopped work at four o'clock his friends came down to play whist. Occasionally they were worried to find him lying almost motionless. The room was a hothouse. Bushes outside obscured the view of the terrace and the forest. When Wolff and Meilhac went for their evening drive, after going through the formality of inviting Jacques to join them, they sometimes wondered if he would be alive on their return. Once or twice it was possible to carry him to a restaurant to spend an evening with a larger circle of friends. The doctor said, 'It's shocking, there's nothing left in his body; it's destroyed and exhausted.' But early every morning Meilhac would hear the piano in the room below, as Offenbach forced himself to continue his fight against time.

Although he was used to living and working in pain, this summer lowered his spirits. He would refer to his death, and kept urging Carvalho to speed the preparations for *Les Contes d'Hoffmann*. ('Je suis pressé, pressé. . . .') He was heard saying to his borzoi Kleinzach, 'I would give everything I have to be at the première.' But Offenbach preserved his wit, and when colleagues came out to work with him, he seemed lively and cheerful. One day he handed Vizentini an old musical sketchbook full of melodic ideas. 'Here, take this,' he said; 'give it to Saint-Saëns when I'm dead.'

At the end of July he began to worry about money. He wrote to his daughter Pepita:

Mademoiselle Pepita Offenbach
'Maid'
Villa Orphée

Étretat   Seine-Inférieure

My dear Pepita,
I enclose the list of our expenses for the month of July, so that your

mother can have a look at it. I know, and understand, that economies at your end are difficult. I intend therefore to move back into the Capucines-House, which will be cheaper. . . .

I have just a month to write the third act of *Belle Lurette,* orchestrate the three acts, and compose the finale and the whole fifth act of *Les Contes d'Hoffmann.* (I am not even talking of the orchestration, which will come later), and I have to write the one-acter[8] for the Variétés. Will I make it? Let's hope so. In Paris I can work just as well as here. It's not too hot with the windows closed. . . .[9]

Jacques was becoming increasingly frail when the family came back in mid-September. They took him to one rehearsal of his beloved *Contes.* Before long he was too feeble to stand, and for ten days could take nothing but grog made with brandy. Old Mathurin worried: 'It won't do; Monsieur has not yet called me "Imbécile!" today.' Jacques was reflective, but not without humour. Musing one day on the size of his musical output, he said to Herminie, 'Our grandchildren will be rich.' On 4 October he was working on the last act of *Les Contes d'Hoffmann* when he fainted. When he came round he was in great pain, and said, 'I think tonight will be the end.' His doctor came, then another doctor, and finally a priest. At 3.30 on the morning of 5 October 1880 Offenbach died, surrounded by his family.

Next day *Le Figaro* devoted its entire front page and most of its second to the death of Offenbach. In the summer at Saint-Germain Jacques had often said with childlike pleasure, 'What a fine article Wolff will write about me when I'm gone!' Albert Wolff's leading article in that day's *Figaro* would have pleased his friend all the more in that it was not just an encomium. Wolff spoke perceptively of the borderline between vanity and the self-confidence needed for creative work:

The excessive affection the composer had for his own talent, with which he has so often been reproached, kept him going in his struggles . . . The man who approaches his task without the conviction that he will succeed better than others loses the best of his talent in self-doubt. Offenbach would never have written a hundred operettas if he had wasted time debating with himself. . . . His vanity was a little more naive than that of the others; *voilà tout!*[10]

On the morning of 7 October the 31st Regiment of the Line formed a guard of honour in the crowded rue Royale. Offenbach's funeral procession appeared, escorted by a contingent of the Garde républicaine (police), and led by a master of ceremonies who carried a cushion bearing the composer's cross of the Legion of Honour, the plaque of Franz Josef of Austria, and the *grand-cordon* of Charles III. The coffin bore flowers from the Bouffes, the Variétés, the Opéra, the Folies-Dramatiques; from Vienna, Brussels, London. Walking by the funeral-carriage were Victorien Sardou and M. Perrin. Behind Offenbach's children and sons-in-law were Meilhac, Halévy, Musard, Strauss, Ambroise Thomas, Massenet, Lecocq, Planquette, Camille Doucet. The actor Berthelier escorted Hortense Schneider, who had been his mistress when he introduced her to Offenbach a quarter of a century earlier.

The Madeleine was so full of Parisians and English tourists that many of the funeral guests could not get through the crowd; Halévy, Crémieux and Tréfeu listened from the porch as the organ played the *Chanson de Fortunio*. Famous opera singers — Taskin, Talazac, Faure — sang a requiem, in which the Dies Irae and Agnus Dei were set to music from *Les Contes d'Hoffmann*, music as yet known only to Jacques' close friends and the future cast of the opera, who were present at the service. (It was common practice to adapt a composer's music for his funeral; at Bizet's funeral the Pie Jesu was set to the melody of the duet from *Les Pêcheurs de perles*.)

After the ceremony the cortège, instead of going direct to the Montmartre cemetery, took a lengthy detour along the boulevards past Offenbach's theatres. In the Paris police archives there is a series of reports from the police chiefs of each arrondissement through which the procession passed. They all tell the same story: quiet crowds filled the street to watch, and there were no incidents. It was raining. When the cortège turned off the boulevard Montmartre the funeral-followers thinned out. But Hortense Schneider walked the full two miles. Sardou was too moved to give his graveside oration. Maquet and Joncières spoke briefly, and Offenbach was buried. At the Alhambra Theatre in London that night the cast of *La Fille du Tambour-major* wore black crêpe arm-bands.

A telegram had been sent to Jacques' brother Jules in the nursing-home at Bordeaux. It was forty-seven years since the two boys had accompanied their father from Cologne to Paris, and Jules had spent that time, without resentment, in the shadow of his younger brother's success. They told him of Jacques' death, and he died three days later.

The day after the composer's funeral Delibes went to the Renaissance Theatre to supervise *Belle Lurette*. He rehearsed the piece with assiduous affection, and arranged the overture and an entr'acte. Koning provided stylishly imaginative sets and costumes. At the première, three weeks after Offenbach's death, the gaiety of the music overcame the sadness of the occasion. There was a joke about a love affair by the Blue Danube with an Offenbachian quotation from Strauss's waltz. There was a scare when a lantern took fire. The fireman who came on stage to put it out was a great success, though he was the only artist in *Belle Lurette* who was not encored.

194

Meantime, someone had to be chosen to complete the last act of *Les Contes*, and to do most of the orchestration, on which Offenbach had made a start. The opinion of the composer's son carried weight. Auguste-Jacques Offenbach — now known simply as Jacques — was eighteen, and an acknowledged authority on his father's music. The family, in consultation with Carvalho, decided to approach Ernest Guiraud, who demurred at first, but changed his mind when the young Jacques appealed to him in person. He made one condition: that he should see only the score of *Les Contes*, and should not have access to Offenbach's other manuscripts. There was a curious reason for this. Years earlier Fromental Halévy and Adolphe Adam had shared the task of orchestrating Hérold's opera *Ludovic*, and had been given access to the late composer's papers. Both of them were subsequently accused in current gossip of stealing ideas from Hérold's unpublished work.

If Bizet had been alive the young Offenbach would certainly have asked him to orchestrate *Les Contes d'Hoffmann*. He was not only an old friend of the family, but the boy's teacher, mentor and idol, and he had brought new exotic colour into French orchestration, paving the way for Ravel (who was born in 1875, the year Bizet died). No one disputes the craftsmanship of Guiraud's work; but Bizet would have orchestrated *Les Contes d'Hoffmann* better than Guiraud, and perhaps even better than Offenbach.

What mattered when the opera went into rehearsal was not so much the loss of Offenbach the orchestrator as the absence of Offenbach the impresario and director. The complicated structure of the work gave rise to many musical and dramatic problems, and the attempts to solve these without Offenbach's guidance produced a result radically different from the composer's intentions. The alterations made before the first night and the subsequent search for an authentic version of the opera are discussed in the next chapter. It says much for the strength of *Les Contes d'Hoffmann* that the work survived the bumbling good intentions of the people responsible for its first production.

CHAPTER XV

Les Contes d'Hoffmann

··☙··

In 1851 Michel Carré and Jules Barbier wrote a play based on the grotesque tales of E. T. A. Hoffmann. 'Hoffmann', wrote Théophile Gautier, 'is more popular in France than in Germany. Everybody reads his stories; they appeal to the concierge and the great lady, to the artist and the grocer.'[1] The play was a success. Offenbach conducted the stage music, and observed to the authors that the piece would make a good *opéra-comique*.

The audiences who saw this early dramatization of Hoffmann's work knew his stories. They were accustomed to his use of autobiographical elements, literal and symbolic, and they did not have to be told why Carré and Barbier employed the unifying device of putting Hoffmann on stage as the principal character in his own tales. Carré died before Offenbach composed the opera; but Barbier, writing the libretto twenty-five years after the play, was able to retain the original structure. Modern audiences, especially those outside France, unfamiliar with the tales and knowing nothing about Hoffmann, miss much of the significance of the work. To appreciate the opera we have to know something about E. T. A Hoffmann, a writer admired in France by Baudelaire, Gérard de Nerval, Villiers de l'Isle-Adam and the symbolists; and in Russia by Gogol, Pushkin and Lermontov. His influence is seen in the work of Edgar Allan Poe and Jules Verne; and had it not been for Hoffmann we should never have had *Dr. Jekyll and Mr. Hyde*.

Hoffmann's parents belonged to the respectable upper middle class of Königsberg in Prussia. Theirs was an arranged marriage, and an unfortunate one; they were an ill-matched pair. Christoph Ludwig Hoffmann was more interested in poetry and music than in his legal duties. Louise-Albertine Dörffer was delicate and of a nervous disposition. They quarrelled frequently. Ernst Theodor Wilhelm, their third son, was born on 24 January 1776. Two years later his parents separated. Of their two surviving sons, the elder went away with Christoph Ludwig, while

Ernst was left in the care of his mother. She took him back to her family home, where, neurotic and bitter, she kept to her room, nursing the shame of her divorce.

The household was ruled over by a devout matriarch of a grandmother. Louise-Albertine, capable neither of standing up to her mother nor of coping with the upbringing of her son, left the boy's education in the hands of her brother Otto-Wilhelm, Ernst's 'Onkel O Weh' (a pun on the initials O-W and 'O weh!' meaning 'Oh dear!'). This weak, narrow-minded, self-important, timorously conventional middle-aged bachelor had retired from his position as an official advocate after, it was maliciously said, making a mess of his only case. He lived in fear of his mother and took it out on Ernst, over whom he exercised the discipline of a tyrannical and pedantic schoolmaster. Punctuality was an obsession. All signs of imagination were suppresssed.

Otto-Wilhelm Dörffer's control over his nephew was maintained until, at twenty, Ernst was given his first appointment as an 'Auskultator' — a young lawyer attending court. As a child Ernst slept in the same room as Uncle O Weh, and did his homework in the next room under constant supervision. At school he was ill-at-ease with the other children; his scholastic performance was only fair. To encourage him to work, his uncle chose a study companion for him — Theodor Hippel, son of the local pastor. This healthy, well-balanced boy became Hoffmann's lifelong friend and confidant, and the recipient of hundreds of his letters, his equable temperament acting as a safety-valve for his friend's emotional pressures. Many of Hoffmann's early letters to Hippel include passionate expressions of affection.

Ernst adored his mother, but she was not much help to him. He was deeply affected by the absence of his father and the ever-presence of his terrible uncle. His character Johannes Kreisler was to say, 'I now think that even a bad father is better than the best tutor.' Kreisler was to Hoffmann what David Copperfield was to Dickens; a means of trans-muting autobiography into a work of imaginative fiction. In his recent biography of Hoffmann, Marcel Schneider lists the similarities of cir-cumstance in the lives of the fictional Kreisler and the real Hoffmann: the divorce of his parents, the lack of a father, the tutelage of a tyrannical and narrow uncle, with his absurd ideas of education, the importance of his aunt Sophie in his musical vocation, the premature deaths of his mother and aunt, the child without defence against the family edicts, the pressure put on him by his uncles to forego art in favour of a career in the law, the portrait of his first music teacher, the love of singing, and of a woman who sings — a voice rather than a woman — the passion for Julia, his eventual self-knowledge and blossoming as an artist.

If we are to understand Offenbach's opera *Les Contes d'Hoffmann*, we have to realize that in *Kreisleriana* and many other works Hoffmann's heroes or anti-heroes represent different aspects of himself. This helps to justify the device adopted in the opera of presenting Hoffmann as the principal character in his own stories. It is doubtful whether Hoffmann would have approved of this procedure. Not only does it drain the three characters for whom Hoffmann is substituted of much of their significance, but it results in a grotesquely misleading portrait of Hoffmann himself. We shall discuss later whether these things matter, if we consider the opera in its own terms; but it is a fair guess that Hoffmann, who died nearly sixty years before the work was written, would have been wittily sarcastic about it, though he might have admired Offenbach's music.

If, like David Copperfield, the young Hoffmann was surrounded by monstrous adults, like Copperfield he also had allies. When Uncle O Weh was out, Aunt Sophie eased up on the iron discipline and even liked to spoil Ernst and Theodor. But this sensitive woman unwittingly did the young Hoffmann a greater service. In the Calvinist Dörffer household, emotional self-expression was unknown, with one exception — when Aunt Sophie sang at family musical evenings. Ernst learnt the piano and the mechanics of music from Uncle O Weh, but it was his aunt's voice that first revealed to him the power of musical expression. Once, when Sophie Dörffer sang, Ernst started crying. His tears were misunderstood, and he was sent out for being an 'anti-musical dog'. The female voice came to represent kindness, love, passion, freedom of expression, emotional release from the stifling limitations of his upbringing. The three great loves of Hoffmann's life were all singers. Johanna Eunike, a professional opera singer, played the leading role in his opera *Undine*. In this respect Carré and Barbier were faithful to Hoffmann's character. In three of the four Hoffmann stories that they used in their play a woman's voice is an instrument of the plot. 'Der Sandmann' (The Sandman) gives us Olympia, 'Rat Crespel' (Councillor Crespel) has Antonia and the voice of her mother, 'Don Juan' provides the Stella of the prologue and epilogue.

Though the young Hoffmann loved music, during his schooldays he showed more talent for art, particularly drawing. (His skill in caricature was later to get him into trouble.) At sixteen, he entered Königsberg University to study law, the career chosen for him by his family. He worked as hard as the examinations required, attending, among other lectures, those of Immanuel Kant (in whose philosophy he found nothing to interest him), and he devoted the rest of his time to art. In 1794 a new influence, reawakening the inspiration of his aunt Sophie, directed his talents back to music. Johannes Hatt, a middle-aged wine merchant, and his young wife Dora took an apartment in the Dörffer house. Ernst taught Dora music, and they fell in love. It was an up-and-down affair, not helped by the propinquity of the husband, but it lasted for three years, continuing after the Hatts moved out.

Inspired by 'Cora', as he called her, Hoffmann took to composing. His first major work was a setting of part of Goethe's *Faust*. He obtained a copy of Mozart's *Don Giovanni* and studied it minutely, acquiring a passion for Mozart that eventually led him to abandon his third Christian name 'Wilhelm' and substitute 'Amadeus' in honour of his idol (who, of course, was Offenbach's too). He wrote to Hippel, 'I should like to study *Don Giovanni* for another six weeks and then play it to you on an English grand piano. . . . You would sense its beauty even more than in the theatre, where one is too distracted to perceive anything properly.'[2]

Before he was twenty Hoffmann wrote two novels and other literary pieces, and was given his first legal appointment. He had displayed precocious ability in all four vocations — lawyer, artist, composer and author — in which he was to achieve success during the remaining twenty-six years of his life. Hoffmann's legal career took him first to Glogau, where he lived with a more congenial branch of the family, and became engaged to his cousin Wilhelmine (Minna); then to Berlin where, though he enjoyed the musical and artistic life, he spent most of his spare time at home, working for advancement in his career and composing. His hard work resulted in his promotion from Auskultator to be 'Assessor' in Posen. It was in this culturally sterile town, recently acquired from Poland by the Germans, that the hard-drinking, womanizing Hoffmann pictured in the opera, first emerged. As he wrote to Hippel in 1803: 'A battle of emotions, of resolutions, and so forth, many of them in mutual conflict, had already raged within me for a couple of months. I wanted to an-aesthetize myself, and I became what school principals, preachers, uncles and aunts call dissolute. You know that debauchery always reaches its highest goal when indulged in on principle, and that was the case with me.'[3]

Early in 1802 Ernst and Minna ended their engagement. Soon after that Hoffmann, hoping for promotion to Berlin, wrecked his chances by circulating malicious caricatures of senior officials and army officers in Posen, and was posted to Plock, a desolate border town. He decided to take a wife with him, and in July 1802 married Maria-Thekla-Michailowna Trzcinski (in German, 'Michaëlina Rohrer'), or 'Mischa' for short — a big, pretty, blue-eyed Polish brunette. She travelled everywhere with her husband, tolerated his excesses, and bore him a daughter, Caecilia, who died at two. This happy marriage is of significance in Hoffmann's tales, in many of which, set against the woman who is the object of his passionate desire, we find a 'good' woman, creating a conflict that strengthens the stories, but is missing in the opera (perhaps an unavoidable simplifi-cation). In 'Der Sandmann' the hysterical Nathanael has his cool-headed, if priggish and prosaic fiancée, Clara. In 'Die Geschichte vom verlornen Spiegelbilde' (The Story of the Lost Reflection) the naive Erasmus Spikker's love for his devout wife tears him away from Giulietta.

During a two-year appointment in Warsaw Hoffmann helped to found a musical society, for which he conducted and composed operas, a symphony and many other works. When the French invaded Warsaw he was forced to take his wife and child to Berlin, where his daughter died, Mischa became seriously ill, and he could make no money. He took a post in Bamberg as Musikdirektor at the theatre. His only performance was a fiasco (it was not entirely his fault, the conditions were appalling), but he stayed to compose for the theatre and made a success as its set designer. His literary career began here, when the *Allgemeine Musikalische Zeitung* accepted his story *Ritter Gluck*, and invited him to write regular reviews. In Bamberg Hoffmann augmented his income by teaching singing, and again fell in love, this time with his thirteen-year-old pupil Julia Marc. The affair was not consummated; it is doubtful if Hoffmann wanted that (though Julia's mother, suspicious of his intentions, quickly arranged her daughter's betrothal to a Hamburg banker). Hoffmann was in love with a voice and a romantic ideal of youthful beauty, and sublimated this passion in his writing.

Marcel Schneider compares Julia to Alice Liddell, the child who inspired Lewis Carroll's Wonderland; but to Carroll Alice remained a child, whereas Hoffmann's Julia was a woman. She is recognizable in a score of his tales; often he does not even disguise her name. In 'Don Juan' (a title referring to strange events during a performance of Mozart's *Don Giovanni*), which he wrote in 1812 at the height of his infatuation, Julia is the young Italian who sings Donna Anna, as Hoffmann listens from the private box that leads to the inn. This identifies her as the Stella of *Les Contes*. In 'The Lost Reflection' she appears by name with her husband, of whom Hoffmann was pathologically jealous; the pair are symbolic counterparts of Giulietta and Dapertutto. There is possibly also something of Julia Marc in Antonia and Olympia; Julia's father, like Rat Crespel, was a councillor. But the women in the stories must have had in them elements of Hoffmann's other loves, Cora Hatt and Johanna Eunike. Attempts at precise identification are misleading, particularly as the point of the play and the opera is that three women fuse into one — the 'ideal' Stella, who deserts Hoffmann in the end, leaving him with only his Muse for a mistress. The play ends with the Muse's lines:

Cesse d'être homme, Hoffmann! je t'aime!
sois poète!

In 1812 Hoffmann, who had been composing prolifically, started work on his opera *Undine*, to a libretto by la Motte-Fouqué, author of the fairy-tales. He was always short of money, but early in 1813 a small legacy from his uncle Otto Dörffer enabled him to pay off his debts and move to Dresden, to join Seconda's opera company as a conductor. After a row with Seconda, Hoffmann appealed to his old friend Hippel for assistance in getting back into the legal profession, and on 10 October 1814 he resumed his career in Berlin as a judge of the Supreme Court. He was in great demand as a writer, and found difficulty in keeping pace, partly because he was finishing *Undine*, partly because of his hectic social life. With a group of well-known artistic and literary friends — Fouqué, Chamisso (author of *Peter Schlemihl*), the author and painter Contessa, Doctor Koreff, the actor Devrient and others — he formed a club, Die Serapionsbrüder ('The Serapion Brethren'), and they drank, smoked and talked in the wine-cellars of Manderlee, or of Lutter and Wegener. When Hoffmann died Lutter was his principal creditor, but cancelled the debt. Hoffmann had made his cellar famous. Offenbach subsequently immortalized it as Luther's Tavern. *Undine* was produced in Berlin on 3 August 1816. It was highly praised by Weber, admired by Beethoven, and received more than a dozen performances before the Royal Theatre burnt down the following year. The orchestral parts were destroyed, but the score survives.

In 1818 Hoffmann was appointed a member of a commission set up by King Frederick William III to investigate left-wing activities. The commission so far overstepped the mark in carrying out its duties, going beyond the law in the impetus of its witch-hunt, that Hoffmann began to attack its members in his writings. In 1821 his 'Meister Floh' would have landed him in serious political trouble had he not by then become too ill to answer charges. He was suffering from *tabes dorsalis*, a syphilitic spinal condition. An operation in which he was burned on each side of the spine with red-hot irons was, not surprisingly, a failure. As he gradually became totally paralysed he continued to dictate to an amanuensis. He thought at one time that the Minister of Police was 'having him leaded, lest he should slip out as contraband'. An hour before he died, on 25 June 1822, he asked his amanuensis to read back some dictation, then turned his face to the wall.

Théophile Gautier, reviewing the play *Les Contes d'Hoffmann*, praised Carré and Barbier for introducing verse into a prose drama, a practice then common in England but unusual in France. The verse, mostly in hexameters, now seems stilted, and the play would be in danger of being laughed off the stage. The subtlety with which Hoffmann introduced a sense of disquiet into apparently mundane situations (cf. the films of Alfred Hitchcock) was replaced by the conventional trappings of Victorian melodrama. Complex Hoffmann characters — Spikker, Nathanael, Clara

34. Offenbach working in his study with his borzoi, Kleinzach: from a watercolour by Edouard Détaille

Bibliothèque nationale

— were abandoned or reduced to ciphers. Peter Schlemihl, cast as the devil's evil accomplice instead of his foolish victim, lost the point of his surname; the Yiddish word *schlemihl* means a born loser or 'fall guy'. At the end of Hoffmann's story 'The Lost Reflection', Erasmus Spikker meets Peter Schlemihl. They have both sold their souls to the devil, Schlemihl by surrendering his shadow, Spikker by sacrificing his reflection. They try to make an arrangement whereby they take it in turns, one to borrow a reflection, the other a shadow. But with the irony that imbues all Hoffmann's writing, the two human beings cannot come to terms: the devil wins. This kind of nuance went missing in Carré and Barbier's play, which is no more than tangential to Hoffmann's world. Offenbach used music — and no medium could be more apposite to Hoffmann's genius — to touch its very heart.

Because of its composer's premature death there can never be a definitive version of *Les Contes d'Hoffmann*. Until recently it was thought that Offenbach had completed the vocal score. We now know that he did not do so. But even if he had reached the last note of the opera, we must remember that Offenbach did not think of a work as complete until it had been performed before an audience, after which he would revise and finalize it. When he wrote a new operetta he regarded the version performed on the first night as a basis for negotiation with public opinion; his assessment of audience reaction was a factor in his method of composition. Since he did not live to attend the première of *Les Contes d'Hoffmann* we cannot tell what final form he would have chosen for the work.

It was first presented at the Opéra-Comique on 10 February 1881, four months after Offenbach's death, in a form far removed from the composer's intentions. Research has now revealed what those intentions were. Manuscripts discovered since the Second World War by Antonio de Almeida include rough drafts, outlines and fair copies completed by Offenbach's hand, as well as vocal parts made by his copyists. These manuscripts enabled Fritz Oeser to compile a critical edition of the work,[5] in which he revoked alterations made in the score for the early productions of the opera, and restored missing passages, using the newly found material. In the absence of Offenbach there can be no such thing as a perfect reconstruction, but Dr Oeser's edition has a greater claim to authenticity than any of its predecessors. He tells us why, when and how Offenbach's original conception of the opera was either modified by the composer or distorted by other people.

The diagram illustrates the original scheme of the opera and outlines the mechanics of the plot.

Offenbach arranged with Vizentini that the work would be put on at the Gaîté — by then known as the Théâtre de la Gaîté-Lyrique. It was to be a

ORIGINAL STRUCTURE OF *LES CONTES D'HOFFMANN*

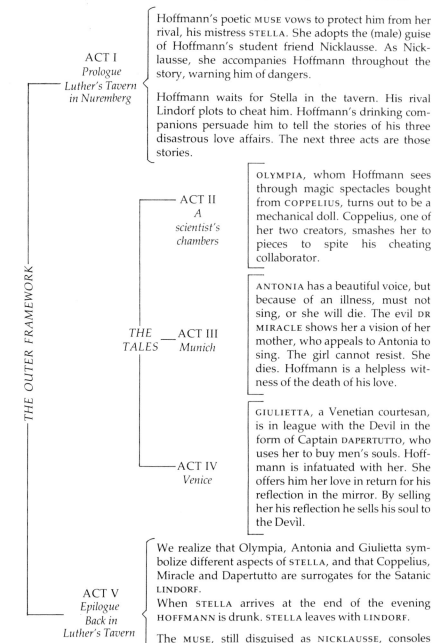

ACT I
Prologue
Luther's Tavern
in Nuremberg

Hoffmann's poetic MUSE vows to protect him from her rival, his mistress STELLA. She adopts the (male) guise of Hoffmann's student friend Nicklausse. As Nicklausse, she accompanies Hoffmann throughout the story, warning him of dangers.

Hoffmann waits for Stella in the tavern. His rival Lindorf plots to cheat him. Hoffmann's drinking companions persuade him to tell the stories of his three disastrous love affairs. The next three acts are those stories.

ACT II
A
scientist's
chambers

OLYMPIA, whom Hoffmann sees through magic spectacles bought from COPPELIUS, turns out to be a mechanical doll. Coppelius, one of her two creators, smashes her to pieces to spite his cheating collaborator.

THE
TALES

ACT III
Munich

ANTONIA has a beautiful voice, but because of an illness, must not sing, or she will die. The evil DR MIRACLE shows her a vision of her mother, who appeals to Antonia to sing. The girl cannot resist. She dies. Hoffmann is a helpless witness of the death of his love.

ACT IV
Venice

GIULIETTA, a Venetian courtesan, is in league with the Devil in the form of Captain DAPERTUTTO, who uses her to buy men's souls. Hoffmann is infatuated with her. She offers him her love in return for his reflection in the mirror. By selling her his reflection he sells his soul to the Devil.

THE OUTER FRAMEWORK

ACT V
Epilogue
Back in
Luther's Tavern

We realize that Olympia, Antonia and Giulietta symbolize different aspects of STELLA, and that Coppelius, Miracle and Dapertutto are surrogates for the Satanic LINDORF.

When STELLA arrives at the end of the evening HOFFMANN is drunk. STELLA leaves with LINDORF.

The MUSE, still disguised as NICKLAUSSE, consoles HOFFMANN. Calling on him to give up his dreams of love, she reveals herself as his MUSE, his only true friend and mentor.

grand opera without spoken dialogue. The character of Hoffmann was a baritone, the quadruple female role of Stella/Olympia/Antonia/Giulietta was a lyric soprano. Some of the parts were already cast, when Vizentini went bankrupt. The artists dispersed. When Carvalho accepted the work for the Opéra-Comique changes had to be made to accommodate the singers available in the new company. The tenor Talazac and the lyric coloratura Adèle Isaac had recently made successes in the title roles of Gounod's *Roméo et Juliette*. Offenbach transposed Hoffmann's part into higher keys for Talazac. Isaac, who visited the composer at Saint-Germain, persuaded him to exploit her coloratura with a new 'doll song' for Olympia. The original F-major setting of 'Les Oiseaux dans la charmille' was in a gently lilting 6/8, with this refrain:

Ex. 33a

Offenbach re-set the same words to the melody that became famous, including passages that gave Mlle Isaac full scope for her skill:

Ex. 33b

The new version was in G, but Isaac finally sang it in A♭, which became its traditional key.

It was essential for the symbolism of the work that the roles of Stella, Olympia, Antonia and Giulietta should be played by the same woman. Offenbach therefore set about making the music consistently suitable for Adèle Isaac throughout the opera. He had written a simple dance-song in F for Giulietta, and was in the process of re-writing it in A♭ with coloratura passages, when he suddenly died. This left Giulietta without an adequate solo, and was one reason why the Giulietta act was omitted from the first production, and was not published in early editions of the work.

The drastic decision to cut the act was made by Carvalho in the face of violent protest from Barbier. The official story was that the opera was too long, but there is now evidence that in rehearsal the Giulietta act seemed 'obscure and ineffective', which was probably true. Guiraud either had not obtained (because of his own stipulations about the MS?) or did not use material that would have both clarified the action and helped to achieve Offenbach's intention of making the Giulietta act the climax of the opera. As it was, Giulietta's role became little more than a costume part.

The fact was that Offenbach, far from having completed the opera 'to the last chord', as Martinet reports,[7] had left only fragments of the Giulietta act. Subsequent attempts to complete it sometimes included the insertion of music not written by Offenbach. For example: Dapertutto's jewel song 'Scintille, diamant!', included in most later editions, consists of a 16-bar phrase from the overture of Offenbach's *Le Voyage dans la lune*, altered slightly and developed into an aria by an unknown hand. For that moment in the opera Offenbach had given Dapertutto the following melody:

Ex. 34

Tour - ne,   tour - ne, mi – roir__ où se prend_l'a - lou - et . . . . te,

We are used to hearing this sung by Coppelius, to the words 'J'ai des yeux'. Oeser reassigned it to Dapertutto. He also restored newly found Offenbach music such as Giulietta's dance-song. But there were still gaps to fill. Knowing that Offenbach, at the time of his death, was making use of material from *Die Rheinnixen* to complete *Les Contes*, Oeser continued the process. In the new edition, the gaps are filled only with music by Offenbach, set to new text based on notes left by Barbier.

The decision to cut the troublesome act created more problems than it solved. It meant losing two of the best numbers in the opera — the Barcarolle and the Hoffmann/Giulietta duet. To get over this, Carvalho and company set the Antonia act in Venice instead of Munich (which did not matter, since the location of Antonia's problems was irrelevant). But after Antonia sang 'Elle a fui, la tourterelle!', the chorus, for no discernible reason, sang the Barcarolle outside the window, led by two anonymous female voices (replacing Giulietta and Nicklausse). The great B♭ melody in the duet, where Hoffmann declares his passion for Giulietta, was transferred to the Epilogue. Hoffmann addressed the words to the Muse, with the result that those lines that are explicitly physical became ridiculous. ('Et je sens, O ma Muse aimée, ton haleine embaumée/sur mes lèvres et sur mes yeux!') Not surprisingly, in the 1930 English edition of the work this passage is marked 'Usually Cut'. (From 1885 onwards, the melody, demoted yet again, was played by a solo violin as a 'Hearts and Flowers' background to the Muse's speech. The opera ended in kitsch.)

The role of the Muse was decimated. She did not appear in the opening, a change that weakened the character of Nicklausse and his relationship with Hoffmann. If we do not know that Nicklausse is the Muse in mortal disguise, he emerges as no more than Hoffmann's priggish companion. But if we see him as Hoffmann's poetic *alter ego*, we are reminded, every time Nicklausse appears, that Hoffmann is in conflict with himself. In the first production the Muse appeared only in the Epilogue, as an unconvincing *deus ex machina*.

One major departure from the original conception of the opera was sanctioned by Offenbach before he died. He abandoned for the time being such recitative as he had written, and agreed that the scenes between the set numbers should be played in dialogue. This was common practice at the Opéra-Comique. (The term *opéra-comique* does not mean comic opera, but opera that employs spoken dialogue instead of recitative. *Carmen* and Gounod's *Faust* in their original form were both in this genre.) With the opera already in rehearsal, the decision to drop the recitative gave Offenbach more time for his rewriting. Guiraud, in completing and re-storing the recitative at a later stage, was being faithful to Offenbach's first intentions; there is therefore a case for performing the opera with either recitative or dialogue.

Ernest Reyer wrote, 'M. Offenbach n'est peut-être pas sans défaut; mais il a une précieuse qualité, c'est d'être original et de boire constamment dans son verre.' He drank only from his own glass — he knew his limitations. There was a range of subjects Offenbach would never have tackled: the heroics of *Il Trovatore*, the idealism of *Fidelio*, the mixture of religion and the erotic that was found in *Samson et Dalila* and *Faust*. The reason it took him so long to find a text that stretched his powers beyond the idiom of operetta was that he was too much of an ironist to write a romantic grand opera. *Die Rheinnixen* had proved it; he had flung that commissioned work together with more than a touch of irresponsibility, in order to seize an opportunity in Vienna that was too good to miss. If he was to compose seriously he required an anti-heroic subject; and finally chose a story in which the protagonist, three times a loser with women, ends up dead drunk while his 'ideal woman' leaves him to prostitute herself with an elderly rival. If Offenbach did E. T. A. Hoffmann a service by reanimating the ingenious but not entirely satisfactory play that Barbier and Carré had made out of his life and writings, the composer in turn was in debt to

Hoffmann, inheriting from him theatrical material which, because of its irony, was never conventionally romantic. Hoffmann's tales, grotesque, fantastic, hovering between reality and the supernatural, and rich in symbolism, gave Offenbach the opportunity he needed.

What distinguishes the music of *Les Contes d'Hoffmann* from that of the operettas is that Offenbach finally believes in himself as a serious composer. There is no parody. The dramatic passages are no longer pseudo-Meyerbeer, pseudo-Bellini, pseudo-anybody; they are Offenbach. It is not that the thematic material is of higher quality than hitherto. The tunes are no better than Offenbach's previous best (some of them *are* his previous best), but he now exploits them to greater advantage. If, for instance, *The Legend of Kleinzach* had occurred in an operetta, the verses would have been sung — one, two, three — without interruption. Offenbach would have regarded an interruption as an adulteration of 'le genre primitif et vrai' of French operetta. But he is now free of such restraints. When he allows Hoffmann to float off into his mystifying musings about a woman, Offenbach achieves a minor *coup de théâtre*. The sudden unexpected lyricism of the passage creates a feeling of unease: something is not quite what it seems. Offenbach has begun to delineate Hoffmann's character, and in doing so has recaptured the disquieting flavour of E.T.A.'s work (for it was by his initials that he was popularly known in France).

The set pieces in *Les Contes* are more successful than the linking passages, though they vary in effectiveness. This is not always Offenbach's fault. In Lindorf's first song, 'Dans les rôles d'amoureux', the exaggerated stage villainy of the lyrics is unhappily reminiscent of the Sorcerer and Sir Rupert Murgatroyd of Ruddigore: 'My eyes flash with lightning, my whole being has a Satanic aspect that affects the nerves like an electric shock! I reach a woman's heart through her nerves; I triumph by fear!' The opening phrases of the melody could come straight out of Sullivan (that is not to belittle Sullivan, who was writing comedy) —

Ex. 35

Dans les rô-les d'a-mou-reux lan - gou-reux,　Je　sais que je suis pi - to - ya - ble

— but Offenbach continues with a full-blooded vocal line leading to a strong climax. Nevertheless, Lindorf has to be a good actor to make such lyrics convincing so early in the play. They have to supply the first hint of the supernatural in his character.

Coloratura singing is so obviously a display of vocal technique that, when used indiscriminately, it becomes dramatically meaningless, conveying no message other than that of the singer's ability to perform it. But three composers, Mozart, Donizetti and Offenbach, realized that coloratura can be used to dehumanize a character; the Queen of the Night is evil, Lucia di Lammermoor is mad, Olympia is an automaton. Olympia's *Doll Song*, out of context, would amount to little more than a pretty showpiece for a good coloratura, a suitable flipside to 'Caro nome'. But it is tailor-made for its function in the opera. Faced with the question, 'How would a doll sing?' (bearing in mind that she has to accompany herself on the harp, an instruction often ignored in production), what composer would have come up with a better way of satisfying the vocal demands of his leading lady? The musical-box quality of the song and its accompaniment, while reminding us that Olympia is only a piece of clockwork, endows her with a fairy-tale charm. Ex. 36 is given in G, Offenbach's original key, though it is no sacrilege to perform the piece in A♭. If Offenbach had lived to discover that A♭ was the best key for Adèle Isaac, he would certainly have agreed to the transposition:

Ex. 36

The refrain of the waltz in the finale of Act II is pure gold Offenbach, and a lesson to music students not to change their harmony too often. The first seven bars work because the harmony does not change, the eighth bar works because the harmony did not change in the first seven (Ex. 37). The company sings the melody in unison. Offenbach is keeping to his normal practice of concentrating the ear on the melody, directing the attention of the audience to the stage, without distraction from the orchestra pit.

Ex. 37

Before examining the more cultivated accompaniments that we find elsewhere in *Les Contes*, let us consider Offenbach's attitude to the art of composing theatrical accompaniments. The picture is not, as might be expected, one of steady development over the years from the simple vamp to a complex orchestral texture. Some of Offenbach's most imaginative accompaniments occur in his early work. Their style varies according to their function and context. At his simplest Offenbach provides the standard functional light opera orchestration (Ex. 38). A vamp establishes the rhythm and harmony (*a*), the voice part or snatches of it, are doubled in the orchestra (*b*), with orchestral fills between the

Ex. 38

Allegretto

Que pour te faire ai - mer tu n'o - ses Te mon-trer tel que l'on t'a

fait! Ah! ah! ah! ah! ah! ah!

phrases (*c*). Here and there the vamp abandons its regular pattern to emphasize a cadence (*d*) or duplicate the rhythm of the vocal parts (*e*). Sometimes the vamp is given a special character of its own as in Ex. 2 (page 30). There the accompaniment, instead of merely supporting the melody, complements it with a second musical idea which enhances the mood of the number. Both the examples mentioned above are from *Orphée aux Enfers*. In the same work we find something quite different:

Ex. 39

Here Offenbach allows himself a countermelody in the orchestra, shared between a solo clarinet and the pizzicato basses. It is one of his most beautiful accompaniments. (If *Orphée* had been a flop, we might have expected this song to turn up with new words in *Les Contes*.) The fact that, in 1858, Offenbach uses counterpoint so successfully in the orchestra, indicates that his habitual reluctance to write contrapuntal accompaniments in operetta was a matter of deliberate restraint, not of haste or lack of imagination. He stubbornly refuses to complicate the accompaniment if he thinks it will be inappropriate or distracting.

In his article on *opéra-comique*, written in 1856, Offenbach refers to simplicity of melodic form and restraint in instrumentation as 'the distinguishing merits of the early works'. Nevertheless, in his own *opéras-comiques*, as opposed to his earlier operettas, *opéra-bouffes*, etc., he gives the orchestra a more important role than hitherto. Counter-melody reappears:

Ex. 40a

Les Contes d'Hoffmann

The motif of the above counter-melody foreshadows the *ostinato* and opening vocal motif of the Romance that Hoffmann sings to Olympia in *Les Contes*:

Ex. 40b

The orchestral part cannot here be described as accompaniment. Offenbach has written a contrapuntal trio. The double *ostinato* is an organic part of the music. The way the *ostinato* binds the music together allows Offenbach to fragment the melody with a rhythmic subtlety that has never before appeared in his writing. The single 2/4 bar gives the passage still more freedom, which he uses to vary the emotional colour of the music from moment to moment. The successive snatches of melody — six of them with feminine endings — are by turns passionate, tentative, tender, confident. Unfortunately Offenbach fails to follow his idea through. He makes a promising attempt to develop the *ostinato*, then opts for the security of a conventional French operatic build-up:

Ex. 41

Even if this homophonic passage is seen as a deliberate contrast to the contrapuntal opening of the song, it is too like others of its species. In the Flower Song in *Carmen* Bizet accompanies an almost identical vocal line with stronger harmony. Offenbach, after judiciously breaking up the tonality with the sequential chromatic harmony of bars 1 to 3 of Ex. 41, reaches the dominant seventh of F major in fine style, only to end abruptly. His perfunctory perfect cadence is not enough to re-establish the tonality while the chromaticism of the previous bars is still in our ears.

Nevertheless, in the opening of this song Offenbach achieves a sensitivity of expression that has hitherto eluded him. The reflectiveness of the writing bears witness to, and justifies, the slower pace at which he composed *Les Contes d'Hoffmann*. In Antonia's Romance, *Elle a fui, la tourterelle* — perhaps the only sad song Offenbach ever wrote — the same depth of feeling reminds us that, when he was writing *Les Contes*, Offenbach liked to be alone, whereas in the past he would happily have composed with a party going on around him.

In the operettas, when Offenbach uses simple song forms with repeated verses, the music normally maintains the same mood, not only within the verses, but throughout the song. There is no musical development, no variation in dramatic intensity. The endings are satisfactory but not climactic. In *Les Contes*, on the other hand, even when employing a simple A-B-A form, Offenbach develops and dramatizes. *Elle a fui* starts wistfully —

Ex. 42a

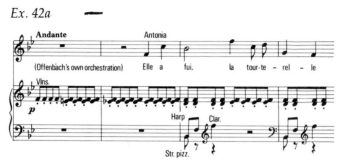

—then achieves a climax of some intensity at the end of the central section before returning, with its simple but beguiling enharmonic modulation, at (*a*) to the wistfulness of the opening:

Ex. 42b

This is true dramatic writing: Offenbach has moved a long way from the popular song. In the extended finale of Act III he creates a dramatic scene of steadily increasing tension between Dr Miracle, Antonia and her mother, controlling a mixture of arioso, recitative and ensemble with a sure hand. If he too often resorts to the use of sequence in the orchestra, it is a hallmark of the period:

Ex. 43

But all is forgiven Offenbach for the moment at the end of this moving scene when Hoffmann and Crespel, Antonia's father, find the girl dead, and the music in E minor, fortissimo, changes to E major, pianissimo, for the expression of the father's grief:

Ex. 44

Inferior verse sometimes makes for a good opera libretto; and in the play *Les Contes d'Hoffmann* there was no shortage of it. Its overblown staginess must have been acceptable at the time, or Gautier would hardly have admired it. Lines that were transferred to the opera text would not have survived anywhere else without Offenbach's music:

Ex. 45

The beginning of Hoffmann's phrase is unusual, possibly unique. Anyone who questions the individuality of Offenbach's melodic writing
should try to find another (tonal) vocal melody that begins with an
upward leap of a fourth followed by a further leap of a sixth; or that

contains the notes  in that order. But the passage flows
with ease. The confident simplicity of the tonic/dominant harmony makes
possible the wide-ranging leaps that give the tune its generosity and
passion; the gently falling chromatic resolutions at (*a*) and (*b*) relax the
tension. It may seem absurd to suggest that there is no other melody in
opera, oratorio or lieder that begins this way; but I have failed to find one.

For the most part the collaboration between Offenbach and Barbier
followed the usual procedure: Barbier wrote the words, Offenbach set
them to music. But in five instances music was lifted from earlier sources,
and words had to be supplied. It is hard to dissociate the Barcarolle from
the Grand Canal, and realize that it was originally written to depict the

Rhine. But its theme provided the overture, a central chorus of elves, and the finale of *Die Rheinnixen*. A peasants' chorus in the same opera became Hoffman's drinking-song (*Couplets bachiques*) in the Giulietta act; and Offenbach had completed a new scene, from music out of *Rheinnixen*, to insert in that act. The scene, restored by Oeser, helps to make sense of the story. Two earlier instrumental themes, developed for voices, supply the material for the end of the Antonia act. Dr Miracle is given a motif from the ballet *Le Papillon*:

Ex. 46

A passage from the overture to *Fantasio* becomes the motif for Antonia's Mother, and the basis of the final trio:

Ex. 47

We see, therefore, that in two of the strongest passages of this powerful opera the themes were not *inspired by*, but were, rather, *applied to* the dramatic situations in which they occur. Ex. 46 was originally a dance-theme in a ballet, Ex. 47 was a motif briefly stated towards the end of an overture. In *Les Contes d'Hoffmann* Offenbach took these two ideas and developed them dramatically according to the requirements of the action on stage. It was unusual for him to work this way, and it was his new-found ability to exploit the potential of his thematic material that endowed *Les Contes d'Hoffmann* with the dramatic intensity that makes it stand out from his other works.

But was it really a new-found ability? Or was it a new-found willingness to use skills that he had neglected? It is tempting for a natural melodist to avoid this process; it is always easier for him to invent a new melody than to develop the one he has already written. He will tend to write in song forms, short self-contained entities which not only demand no extension, but preclude the possibility of extension. A song-writer can easily write an operetta or a musical comedy where the score is to consist of separate short items. If he wants to write an opera requiring extended dramatic passages, he must emulate Mozart, who employs song forms where they are appropriate, but bases the extended passages on motifs (as opposed to complete melodies) that allow him all the possibilities of development.

Offenbach, of course, had learned from his beloved Mozart, and it is no coincidence that the musical ideas in Exs. 46 and 47 were not song-tunes, but short motifs from orchestral passages. We have no reason for supposing that, if Offenbach could write in this manner at the age of sixty, he could not have done so when he was fifty or forty. The sources of the above examples, dating from 1860 (*Le Papillon*) and 1872 (*Fantasio*) respectively, confirm that he had long been capable of dramatic inventiveness.

Why then did he wait so long before writing a serious work? It is true that in *Robinson Crusoé* he devoted more thought than usual to the development of his ideas; but even *Crusoé* was written in comparative haste, in the course of thirteen months in which he produced two other full-length works and two single-act pieces. It was not until Offenbach realized that he could not have long to live that he gave himself wholeheartedly to the task that he at once dreaded and valued above all others. Knowing instinctively that *Les Contes* was to be his final testament, he once again went off to work alone at St Germain.

In the role of devil's advocate, we could be hard on Offenbach. We could portray him as a type commonly found in all fields of endeavour, the man who forever puts off doing his best, in case his best should fall short of his own expectations. We could suggest that he often allowed his gift of melody to seduce him. We could point out that in his early days he indulged in parody to an extent that delayed the development of a serious style of his own. We could suggest that there eventually came a time when each new operetta he wrote was an evasion of his responsibility to himself, a means of postponing the moment when he would have to discover the truth, good or bad, about the nature and extent of his talent, and display the result to the world. But in reply to such an attack Offenbach would be entitled to ask: 'If I offered to write a second *Contes d'Hoffmann* in return for the deletion of *La Belle Hélène*, would you accept the bargain?'

Les Contes d'Hoffmann opened at the Opéra-Comique on 10 February 1881. Arnold Mortier wrote: 'It is the sad privilege of dead composers to have no enemies at their premières. To be sure, the recent works of Offenbach were performed to sympathetic houses, but none was awarded anything like tonight's universal acclamation.' Mortier gave a general account of the occasion in *Le Figaro*. Composers of all schools were there, and every music publisher in Paris. The presence of Jules Ferry, the (Republican) Minister for the Fine Arts, indicated that Offenbach was now held to be above politics, no longer 'le grand corrupteur'. The critics joined the public in praise of Offenbach's music, but there were reservations about the play, with its false portrait of E. T. A. Hoffmann and its distortion of his work. Auguste Vitu found the identification of the author with the characters in his tales not only unjustifiable from a literary point of view, but confusing in the theatre, a criticism which is still voiced by people seeing this complex opera for the first time.

But the evening had one clear outcome: Offenbach rose in everyone's estimation. In 1881 *Les Contes d'Hoffmann* was performed at the Opéra-Comique 101 times — a high percentage of the total number of performances for the year in any opera repertory company. But in the decades following Offenbach's death the work suffered a decline in popularity and critical esteem. Debussy, referring in 1903 to the success of Offenbach's parodies, wrote, 'But serious music, the kind that cannot take a joke, took its revenge: it made sure that the one work in which he tried to be serious met with no success. I mean, of course, *Les Contes d'Hoffmann*.'

For some time after Offenbach's death nobody really knew what to make of him as a composer. In the puritanical atmosphere of the Third Republic his operettas were at first dismissed as irrelevant and meretricious souvenirs of a discredited Empire. If there had been no more to it than that, he would have been easy to categorize. But he had confused matters by composing, in his dying months, a work that quickly began to look uncommonly like a masterpiece, and it would have been uncomfortable for anyone to have been the first to acknowledge it as such.

Like *Carmen*, *Les Contes d'Hoffmann* had to fight for its place among the classics. In December 1881 it was presented in Vienna at the Ringtheater, which, on the second night, was the scene of one of the worst fires in theatre history. Hanslick records that this event planted a superstitious fear of the opera in the minds of German theatre directors, as a result of which it did not reach Berlin until 1905, when Hans Gregor restored the

35. Kevin Miller, Anna Pollak and Eric Stannard in the Sadler's Wells Opera production of *Orpheus in the Underworld*, 1960. This production, which started a recent Offenbach revival in England, was directed by Wendy Toye, the designer was Malcolm Pride, and the author conducted.

English National Opera Archives

Giulietta act, but placed it before the Antonia act. Gregor's edition formed the basis for productions of the opera for half a century. London finally saw *The Tales of Hoffmann* in 1907, and Thomas Beecham's production of 1910 established it in the popular repertory. After the Second World War, thanks to the research of Arthur Hammond and others (prior to the work of Dr Oeser), productions of the work began to come closer to the composer's intentions.

Offenbach's major comedies remained fairly popular in France, Germany and Austria; less so in England, where there was no tradition of operetta-houses like the Vienna Volksoper. But in 1960 the Sadler's Wells Opera, now the English National Opera, stimulated a new interest in the composer with a successful revival of *Orpheus in the Underworld*, followed by *La Vie Parisienne*, *La Belle Hélène* and *Bluebeard*. In the 1970s London saw two productions[8] of *Robinson Crusoe*. In the United States the pattern has been similar. The New York première of *The Tales of Hoffmann* took place in 1913. In 1956 it was possible in the same week to see *La Périchole* at the Metropolitan Opera and *Orpheus in the Underworld* at the New York City Center. But though Offenbach's music is now established in the international repertory, the works performed constitute less than one-tenth of his output. Amateur companies and colleges of music have shown enterprise in promoting lesser-known Offenbach pieces. Now it is up to the professionals.

Auguste-Jacques Offenbach died at 21 in 1883; Herminie four years later. Jacques and Herminie had many descendants; in 1979, ninety-nine years after Offenbach's death, the first of his English great-great-granddaughters was married in the Catholic church of St Peter's, Winchester. Meilhac died in 1897. Ludovic Halévy lived to see a little of the twentieth century, and sometimes dropped in to rehearsals at the Variétés to talk to young actresses about old times. Hortense Schneider, after marrying and divorcing an Italian adventurer, who posed as a French count and cheated her out of a lot of money (she had plenty left), watched across the Channel from Étretat while the reign of her precious Edward came and went; then became a religious recluse, devoting herself to good works until her death in 1920.

French music changed. In the continuity that is inherent in all change, teachers are important links. Ernest Guiraud, orchestrator of *Les Contes d'Hoffmann*, became the teacher of Debussy, who rebelled against Guiraud's traditional theorizing, but respected him, and never lost touch. Debussy loved the painting of the Impressionists, and gave France her Impressionist music; but he never rejected the music of the past if it gave pleasure, and when he was homesick in Rome in 1885 his greatest longing was to go back to Paris — 'to see Manet and hear Offenbach'.

Notes

·· ⚖ ··

Biographers of Offenbach are dependent for much valuable material on the work of André Martinet, friend of the family and the composer's earliest biographer, to whom Mme Offenbach related memories of her husband and showed letters written by him which can no longer be traced. In Martinet's excellent, concise and personal memoir he often quotes from Offenbach's letters without naming a date or an addressee. These quotations are too illuminating to omit from a new book, and where their origins cannot be fully identified I give the source as *Martinet*.

Date and place of publication are given only for sources not included in the Bibliography. The page numbers to which the notes refer are indicated in the headings to the following pages.

CHAPTER I

1. A photograph of a passport of Isaac Juda Eberst's, dated 1799, is published in Hans Kristeller, *Der Aufstieg des Kölners Jacques Offenbach: Ein Musikerleben in Bildern*. See Bibliography.

2. *From the Register of Births of the City of Cologne, 1819, No. 997:*

   In the year one thousand eight hundred and nineteen, on the twenty-first day of the month of June, at ten o'clock in the morning, I, Franz Rudolph von Monschaw, representative of the Mayor of Cologne, in my capacity as Registrar of Births, received Isaac Offenbach, teacher, resident in Cologne, Government District of Cologne, who brought before me a male child and declared to me that the child was born on the twentieth day of the month of June in the year one thousand eight hundred and nineteen, at three o'clock in the morning, to him, Isaac Offenbach, and Marianne Rindskopf his wife, unemployed, residing in Cologne in the house No. 1 on the Grosser Griechenmarkt; and further declared that the child was to be given the first name Jacob.

   This presentation of the child and declaration took place in the presence of Arnold Schneider, forty-nine years of age, shoemaker, and Joseph Hamacher, forty-one years of age, by profession servant to [*illegible*], resident in Cologne, and both the above-named attestant and the two witnesses have signed the certificate in my presence after it was read to them.

[Signed]   Isaac Offenbach
                    Joseph Hamacher
                    Arnold Schneider
[Countersigned]   Fr. R. von Monschaw

3. André Martinet, *Offenbach, sa vie et son oeuvre*, p. 2.
4. Anton Henseler, *Jakob Offenbach*, p. 68.
5. From the register of pupils at the Paris Conservatoire, 1833:

30 Novembre No. 1138	Mr. [*sic*] Offenbach (Jacob) né à Cologne, (Prusse), le 21 juin 1819. (14.3). — (Violoncelle) Élève étranger, admis chez M. Vaslin, le 30 Novembre.	rayé le 2 xmbre 1834 a quitté volontair- ement.

6. *L'Artiste*, 25 March 1855, in Offenbach's column 'Causeries musicales'.
7. Quoted by Flotow's widow in *Friedrich von Flotows Leben, von seiner Wittwe*, pp. 67–70.
8. 'Eberscht' was, at a guess, Flotow's way of spelling 'Eberst', a name he had heard but had never seen written down. Since his personal memoirs of Offenbach were used by many biographers, it is understandable that this version of the name turned up from time to time before the passport mentioned above (note 1) was unearthed by Hans Kristeller.
9. Martinet, op. cit., p. 6.
10. Henseler, op. cit., p. 90.

CHAPTER II

1. Julien Tiersot (Ed.), *Lettres françaises de Richard Wagner*, p. 393.
2. Since Mitchell was to become Offenbach's father-in-law, we must be precise about his identity, which has been the subject of error in previous biographies. It is commonly stated that the composer's father-in-law was John Mitchell, a well-known London impresario; but the register of marriages in Bayonne records the wedding on 16 September 1835 of *Michael George* Mitchell and Jeanne-Anaïs-Céleste d'Alcain (née Sénez), widow of General Joseph-Marie-Xavier d'Alcain. It is likely, though as yet unproven, that the two Mitchells were related, because it was very soon after Offenbach met the Paris Mitchells that he was introduced to London audiences and presented to Queen Victoria by John Mitchell, who was the Queen's concert agent.
3. Jacques Brindejont-Offenbach, *Offenbach, Mon Grand-Père*, p. 173.
4. The salle du Cirque, boulevard du Temple.
5. Adolphe Adam, *Souvenirs d'un musicien* 'Notes biographiques', p. xxxvii.
6. Alfred Cobban, *A History of Modern France*, vol. ii, p. 148.

CHAPTER III

1. André Maurois, *A History of France*, p. 394.
2. Arsène Houssaye, *Les Confessions*.
3. Ibid., vol. ii, book xii, p. 403.

4. Martinet, op. cit., p. 13.
5. Houssaye, op. cit., vol. iii, book xviii, p. 172.
6. Brindejont-Offenbach, op. cit., Preface ('Avertissement amical'), p. ii.
7. Martinet, op. cit., p. 13.
8. Ibid., p. 14.
9. It was originally to be called *Vertigo*.
10. Henseler, op. cit., p. 158.
11. Martinet, op. cit., p. 16.
12. Archives nationales (Paris), Folio 21.1136.
13. Ibid.

CHAPTER IV

1. *Le Ménestrel*, November 1855.
2. M. Rouff and T. Casevitz, *Vie de fête sous le Second Empire*, p. 48.
3. As note 1.
4. *Le Ménestrel*, 27 July 1856.
5. *Revue et Gazette Musicale de Paris*, 20 July 1856.
6. Henseler, misquoting the original article, which was published twice (see notes 4 and 5), gives 'gai' instead of 'vrai'. This error has frequently reappeared in biographies, dictionary entries and programme notes, including one (long ago) by the present author — *mea culpa*.
7. *Revue des Deux Mondes*, 1 June 1856.
8. Not to be confused with Offenbach's opéra-comique *Les Bergers* (1865).
9. Martinet, op. cit., p. 44.
10. *Le Ménestrel*, 31 May 1857.
11. Barry Duncan, *The St James's Theatre*, pp. 102, 103.
12. Brindejont-Offenbach, op. cit., p. 177.
13. Martinet, op. cit., p. 40.

CHAPTER V

1. The anniversary of the opening of the Bouffes-Parisiens, 5 July 1855.
2. Brindejont-Offenbach, op. cit., p. 14.
3. *L'Autographe*, No. 9, 1 April 1864. For the context of this quotation see Chapter X, p. 128
4. See Alain Decaux, *Offenbach, roi du Second Empire*, p. 103.
5. Ibid., p. 114.
6. *Journal des Débats*, 6 December 1858.
7. Martinet, op. cit., p. 54.

CHAPTER VI

1. *Journal des Débats*, 9 February 1860.
2. Ibid., 22 February 1860.
3. In his biography *Offenbach* (1923) Louis Schneider states that *Le Musicien de l'avenir* was first performed, in the presence of the Emperor, at a gala performance for which he gives two contradictory dates: '5 June 1859' (p. 80) and 'May 1859' (p. 86). Both dates are impossible: not only was 5 June 1859 the day of the last (228th) performance of the original run of *Orphée aux Enfers* at the Bouffes, but Napoleon III was in Italy, having won the battle of Magenta on the previous day. Moreover, the Wagner concerts of which *Le Musicien de l'avenir*

was a parody did not take place until early in 1860. Martinet identifies the date of the gala performance as 27 April 1860, more than two months after the opening of *Le Carnaval des revues*. Schneider also mentions a *separate* occasional piece called *La Symphonie*, with words by Grangé and Gille. In the absence of any evidence for the existence of such a work it may be assumed that he is confusing this with *La Symphonie de l'avenir* by the same librettists.

4. For the complete dialogue of this sketch see Schneider, op. cit., pp. 87–9. The full score of *La Symphonie de l'avenir* is in the Bibliothèque nationale. It consists of 113 bars, scored for flute, piccolo, oboe, 2 clarinets, 2 cornets, trombone, bass drum, cymbals, and strings.
5. Richard Wagner, *Gesammelte Schriften und Dichtungen* (E. W. Fritzsch, Leipzig, 1898), vol. ix, pp. 34–6.
6. Martinet, op. cit., p. 65.
7. *Journal des Débats*, 3 January 1861.
8. Maurois, op. cit., p. 402.
9. Ludovic Halévy, *Carnets*, p. 39.
10. Martinet, op. cit., p. 71.
11. Ibid., p. 72.
12. Brindejont-Offenbach, op. cit., p. 122.
13. Ibid., p. 143.
14. Archives de l'Opéra (Fonds Nuitter-Beaumont).
15. Brindejont-Offenbach, op. cit., p. 113.

CHAPTER VII

1. According to Schneider it was Laurent de Rillé, composer of several operettas.
2. Martinet, op. cit., p. 81.
3. Archives nationales, Folio 21.1136.

CHAPTER VIII

1. *Les Géorgiennes* was not completed in time for the reopening of the Bouffes (see p. 100).
2. Brindejont-Offenbach, op. cit., p. 161.
3. Probably Karl Binder (Vienna, 1816–1860).
4. Wagner, op. cit., vol. vi, p. 271. N.B.: The article from which this quotation is taken does not appear in all editions of the *Ges. Schr.*
5. Peter Gay, *Freud, Jews and Other Germans*, pp. 262–4.
6. Friedrich Nietzsche, *The Will to Power* (Ed. Walter Kaufmann), p. 439.

CHAPTER IX

1. Martinet, op. cit., p. 91.
2. Ibid., p. 92.
3. Brindejont-Offenbach, op. cit., p. 29.
4. Camille Saint-Saëns, *Harmonie et Mélodie*
5. Rouff and Casevitz, op. cit., p. 26.
6. E. J. Dent liked to think that London's Swiss Cottage was an 'operatic railway station' inspired by Adam's opera, and he also claimed to have discovered that there was another such station in Budapest, the Szép Ilona, which had been named after *La Belle Hélène* (see Dent's book *Opera*, Pelican edn., 1945, p. 38).

7. Martinet, op. cit., p. 97.
8. The original (1928) version of *Die Dreigroschenoper* did not end this way, but a later version, prepared by Weill for a proposed film, did.
9. Martinet, op. cit., p. 101.

CHAPTER X

1. Brindejont-Offenbach, op. cit., p. 155.
2. *L'Autographe*, No. 9, 1 April 1864. The second paragraph is punctuated as follows: 'Je suis venu au monde à Cologne le jour de ma naissance; je me rappelle parfaitement qu'on me berçait avec des mélodies.' This may have been one of Offenbach's whimsical jokes, but I have followed the practice of previous biographers in regarding it as an error in punctuation.
3. Henseler, op. cit., p. 465.
4. Ibid., p. 473.
5. Decaux, op. cit., p. 33.
6. Translated as 'The Story of a Waltz' in *The Theatre*, 1 October 1878.
7. Halévy, op. cit., vol. i, p. 40.
8. Ibid., vol. i, p. 56.
9. Ibid., vol. i, p. 19.
10. J. M. and Brian Chapman, *The Life and Times of Baron Haussmann*.

CHAPTER XI

1. Martinet, op. cit., p. 104.
2. Not to be confused with the tableau vivant *Les Bergers de Watteau* (1856).
3. *Le Figaro*, 3 December 1865.
4. See Joanna Richardson, *La Vie Parisienne*, p. 186.
5. Author's translation.
6. Siegfried Kracauer, *Offenbach and the Paris of His Time*, p. 207.
7. Kracauer refers to him (see note 6) as 'the young Prince Napoleon', thereby adding to the confusion that often surrounds the ramifications of the Bonaparte family. Cora Pearl's lover, 'Plonplon', (Prince Napoleon Joseph Charles Paul Bonaparte) was forty-four. In 1866 the only 'young' Prince Napoleon was the Emperor's son Napoleon Louis, the Prince Imperial, who was ten.
8. Quoted in Kracauer, op. cit., p. 260.
9. Kracauer, op. cit., p. 273.
10. Halévy, op. cit., vol. i, p. 158.
11. Ibid., vol. i, p. 153.
12. 'Passage' has a sexual connotation. 'Le passage des Princes' is an alley near the Théâtre des Variétés.
13. Brindejont-Offenbach, op. cit., p. 64.
14. Trans. Joanna Richardson, op. cit., p. 273.

CHAPTER XII

1. 'Charles Martel reigned *de facto* over Austrasia and Neustria for twenty-six years. He had shaped a body of rugged Frankish infantry with which, near Poitiers, he stopped in its tracks a raiding-party sent out by the Arab Governor of Spain.' (AD 732) (A. Maurois, op. cit., p. 36.)

2. *Le Fouet*, 4 October 1868.
3. Brindejont-Offenbach, op. cit., p. 207.
4. Ibid., p. 205.
5. The Gaîté was in the square des Arts et Métiers, where the Centre Georges Pompidou now stands. It is not to be confused with the Gaîté-Montparnasse.
6. Or eighteen, or seventeen scenes; accounts vary according to the state of the production at the time different writers made their counts.
7. If this plan existed it was never realized. *Paul et Virginie* opened at the Opéra on 15 November 1876.
8. Martinet, op. cit., p. 180.
9. From 1874 to 1885 Arnold Mortier wrote a weekly theatre diary in *Le Figaro*, headed 'Les Soirées parisiennes', and signed 'Un Monsieur de l'orchestre' (A gentleman in the stalls). In these articles Mortier not only described anything that took his fancy about the performance (he had a particular interest in scenery and costumes), but gave a general account of the occasion, chatting about the audience and supplying current theatrical gossip. The articles were collected and published annually for eleven years. Each volume has a preface by a celebrity, as follows: 1874, Jacques Offenbach; 1875, Théodore Barrière; 1876, Alphonse Daudet; 1877, Edmond Gondinet; 1878, Édouard Pailleron; 1879, Adolphe-Philippe d'Ennery; 1880, Émile Zola; 1881, Ludovic Halévy; 1882, Henri Becque; 1883, Charles Gounod; 1884, Albert Wolff.

   Mortier also collaborated on the librettos of *Le Voyage dans la lune* and *Le Docteur Ox*.
10. Mortier, *Les Soirées parisiennes*, op. cit., February 1874.
11. Unpublished diary entry, 18 October 1875.

CHAPTER XIII

1. The Centennial Exhibition in Philadelphia celebrated the centenary of the Declaration of Independence, 1776.
2. Jacques Offenbach, *Notes d'un musicien en voyage*, p. 16.
3. Ibid., p. 22.
4. *New York Times*, 8 May 1876.
5. Quoted in Fantel, Hans, *Johann Strauss, Father and Son and Their Era*.
6. Brindejont-Offenbach, op. cit., p. 225.
7. Offenbach, op. cit., p. 169.
8. Ibid., p. 174.
9. Ibid., p. 177.
10. Ibid., pp. 205–13.
11. *Le Siècle*, 10 February 1877.
12. This comment, and the relevant letters to the press, are in the archives of the Prefecture of Police in Paris.
13. Mortier, op. cit., March 1877.

CHAPTER XIV

1. Saint-Saëns, op. cit., p. 224.
2. It was originally to be called *Le Moustique*.
3. From letter quoted in Decaux, op. cit., p. 239.
4. Ibid., p. 239.
5. Brindejont-Offenbach, op. cit., p. 248.
6. Ibid., p. 254.

7. It depends how you count. *La Fille du Tambour-major* was publicized as Offenbach's hundredth work.
8. *Le Cabaret des lilas*, libretto by Blum and Toché.
9. Brindejont-Offenbach, op. cit., p. 258.
10. *Le Figaro*, 6 October 1880.

CHAPTER XV

1. Marcel Schneider, *Ernest Théodore Amadeus Hoffmann*, p. 14.
2. Johanna C. Sahlin (Ed. and trans.) *Selected Letters of E. T. A. Hoffmann*, p. 35. The English piano was no doubt a Broadwood, whose makers had developed an instrument with a fuller tone than that of the Viennese pianos of the day, which had a different type of action.
3. Ibid., p. 94.
4. The brothers Joseph and Franz Seconda ran an opera company which divided its activities between Dresden and Leipzig. Hoffmann was engaged and dismissed by Joseph Seconda.
5. *Hoffmanns Erzählungen,* Quellenkritische Neuausgabe von Fritz Oeser.
6. The character Dr Miracle does not appear in E. T. A. Hoffmann's stories. He was invented by Barbier and Carré for the sake of symmetry in the stage work.
7. Martinet, op. cit., p. 273.
8. By Opera Rara, in the Camden Festival, at the Collegiate Theatre, 1973; and by the London Opera Centre at Sadler's Wells Theatre, 1976.

APPENDIX A

The *Orpheus* Claimants

·····

1. Carl Cramer

In 1869 a Cologne editor, Wilhelm Kaulen, hinted in his humorous magazine *Rheinische Funken* that Offenbach had taken the idea of *Orphée aux Enfers* from a farce in the Cologne carnival. J. J. Merlo, a contemporary historian of the arts, recorded that Offenbach knew and was influenced by Carl Cramer, a left-wing poet who wrote satirical sketches for the carnival. In 1877 Kaulen published in *Frankfurter Feuilleton-Correspondenz* an article entitled 'A Theatrical Secret', which, though it contains many errors, cannot be disregarded. Without giving a source for his information Kaulen alleges:

a) that Offenbach was a school friend of Cramer's (doubtful);
b) that in 1849 Cramer gave Offenbach the libretto of an *Orpheus* parody to set to music (possible — in Cramer's review of *Marielle* he had praised Offenbach's music);
c) that Offenbach, hearing later that Cramer had died, gave the script to Crémieux and Halévy, who used it as the basis for their libretto.

Here Kaulen is in error; Cramer did not die until 1860. *Orphée aux Enfers* was first performed in Paris in 1858, then in Breslau and Berlin in 1859. There is no evidence that Cramer made any claim between 1858 and 1860 to have been the originator of the work. But this does not demolish Kaulen's case; Offenbach could have given the libretto to his collaborators before Cramer died, just as he gave that of *L'Alcôve* (*Marielle*) to Inkermann (see Chapter II). And Cramer, who died, destitute, in a Cologne hospital, may never have heard of the success of the operetta.

The tone of Kaulen's article is sentimental, his final sentence revealing a local patriotic bias: 'The French librettists subsequently continued the work — with plenty of frivolity, but without the healthy German humour of the carnival poet from Cologne.'

A letter from Liszt to an unknown addressee (it opens with the bald 'Geehrter Herr') refers to an *Orpheus* 'manuscript' (score? libretto?). If, as has been guessed but not confirmed, Offenbach was the recipient, he must have had a version of *Orpheus* by May 1855, the date of the letter; this could have come from Cramer. Julie Offenbach, Jacques' sister, tells that Liszt was in and out of the family house. In 1848 Liszt and Offenbach appeared on the same concert bill in Cologne.

Appendix A: The Orpheus Claimants

2. Derval and Tacova

From *L'Éclipse* VII, No. 279, 1 March 1874:

> The two *Orphées*. At the beginning of the year 1858 two young men, Henri Derval — son, I think, of the unpleasant director of the Gymnase — and Henri Tacova, a lawyer, since dead, brought M. Offenbach the libretto of an operetta in three acts, entitled *Orphée*. This operetta was performed the following October in the Bouffes-Parisiens theatre. But in the interval it had changed its title, its style and its signatories; it now ran to four acts and was called *Orphée . . . aux Enfers*. The posters gave MM. Hector Crémieux and Ludovic Halévy as the authors. The two Henris, dispossessed, made quite a fuss in the papers at the time. But the noise of their protests was drowned by the enthusiastic bravos that greeted the illustrious maestro's score.

These mutually exclusive claims suggest (1) that parodies of the Orpheus story were fashionable, (2) that various writers made their own versions and invited Offenbach, an obvious choice, to set them to music, and (3) that Offenbach liked the idea but preferred to work on it with his own librettists. Cramer made no accusation of plagiarism; Derval and Tacova did, but no one paid any attention.

Cause of Offenbach's Death — A Medical Comment
by Dr Harriet Rhys-Davies

······

In the nineteenth century the diagnosis of gout was common and often erroneous. There were no reliable diagnostic procedures for differentiating between tuberculous arthritis and the crippling inactivation of the joints caused by gout. X-rays were not known until 1895, fifteen years after Offenbach's death. Nevertheless, Offenbach's doctors were undoubtedly correct in their diagnosis.

Gout is caused by the patient's inability to metabolize purines, forms of protein found in high concentration in some foods and drinks, e.g. sweetbreads, anchovies, peas, beans, strawberries and port. The disease causes deposits of urates, known as *tophi*, which appear as white swellings in the ear and in certain joints. A late photograph of Offenbach (in the archives of the Prefecture of Police in Paris), where, for once, the long hair of which he was so proud was brushed back, shows tophaceous swelling of the right ear.

The cause of gout was not understood until after the Second World War. The disease is now easily treated; but in Offenbach's time acute attacks of gout were common. The classic description of the symptoms given by the great seventeenth-century physician Dr Thomas Sydenham still appears in modern medical text-books: he describes how the sufferer would wake in the night with such exquisite pain in, say, a toe or an ankle, that he could not bear the weight of the bedclothes or the jar of a person walking across the room. Fever, restlessness, dyspepsia and irritability would follow. In the absence, over a long period, of anything other than palliative treatment, the condition of the patient would deteriorate, resulting in death from renal failure, or, as in Offenbach's case, heart failure.

Offenbach's initial reluctance to admit that he had gout is typical of his time. The disease then carried a mild moral stigma, as it was mistakenly supposed to indicate that the patient habitually over-indulged in good living. It is now thought that the benefit (minimal) of trips to watering-places such as Bad Ems was due not so much to the quality of the waters as to the amount of water drunk, and the fact that the restricted diet excluded many of the noxious ingredients.

Offenbach's long-standing bad cough may indicate that he also had a low-grade tuberculous condition of the lungs. But the doctors of the time, used to this highly prevalent affliction, would have been in no doubt had it been the primary cause of death, just as they were in no doubt when Offenbach's son Auguste died of pulmonary tuberculosis three years later.

List of Works

Details of the stage works have been compiled from the vocal scores, and, where no score exists, from contemporary press records. This list is, I hope, complete. The catalogue of other works, not fully comprehensive, is based on that of Jacques Brindejont-Offenbach and the catalogues of the Bibliothèque nationale and the British Library. For a complete list of Offenbach's works we must await Antonio de Almeida's forthcoming thematic catalogue, the product of his prolonged world-wide research.

There have been many stage productions based on compilations of Offenbach's music; some of the more important of these are listed on p. 256.

Year	Title	Description	No. of Acts	Librettist(s)
1839	Pascal et Chambord	Vaudeville	1	Bourgeois & Brisebarre
1847	L'Alcôve	Opéra-comique	1	De Forges & De Leuven
1853	Le Trésor à Mathurin	Opéra-comique	1	Battu
	Pepito	Opéra-comique	1	Moinaux & Battu
1855	Oyayaye ou la Reine des Îles	Anthropophagie musicale	1	Moinaux
	Entrez, Messieurs, Mesdames	Prologue for Opening for Bouffes	1	Méry & Servières (Halévy)
	Les Deux Aveugles	Bouffonnerie musicale	1	Moinaux
	Une Nuit blanche	Opéra-comique	1	Plouvier
	Arlequin barbier	Pantomime Music arr. after Rossini by Lange (Offenbach)	1	Lange (Offenbach) after Rossini
1855	Le Rêve d'une nuit d'été	Saynète	1	Tréfeu
1855	Pierrot Clown	Pantomime	1	Jackson
1855	Le Violoneux	Légende bretonne	1	Mestépès & Chevalet
1855	Polichinelle dans le monde	Pantomime	1	Busnach
1855	Madame Papillon	Bouffonnerie	1	Serviéres (Halévy)
1855	Paimpol et Périnette	Saynète lyrique	1	De Forges
1855	Ba-ta-clan	Chinoiserie musicale	1	Halévy
1856	Le Postillon en gage	Bouffonnerie	1	Plouvier & Adenis
1856	Tromb-al-ca-zar ou Les Criminels dramatiques	Bouffonnerie musicale	1	Dupeuty & Bourget

OPENING NIGHT OF LES BOUFFES-PARISIENS

Theatre	Date of Production	German Title	English Title
Palais-Royal	2 March		
Concert Hall of La Tour d'Auvergne	24 April	Marielle oder Sergeant und Commandant	
Salle Herz	May		
Variétés	28 October	Das Mädchen von Elizondo	
		2 Versions. Viennese version was in 2 acts	
Folies-Nouvelles	26 June		
Bouffes-Parisiens	5 July		
Bouffes-Parisiens	5th July	Die beiden Blinden	The Blind Beggars
Bouffes-Parisiens	5 July		
Bouffes-Parisiens	5 July		
Bouffes-Parisiens	30 July		
Bouffes-Parisiens	30 July		
Bouffes-Parisiens	31 August	Die Zaubergeige	
Bouffes-Parisiens	31 August		
Bouffes-Parisiens	31 August		
Bouffes-Parisiens	29 October		
Bouffes-Parisiens Salle Choiseul	29 December	Tschin-Tschin	
Bouffes-Parisiens	9 February		
Bouffes-Parisiens	3 April		

Year	Title	Description	No. of Acts	Librettist(s)
1856	La Rose de Saint-Flour	Opérette (Offenbach's first use of this term)	1	Carré (& Truinet* anonymously) *Pseudonym Nuitter adopted later
1856	Les Dragées du baptême		1	Dupeuty & Bourget
1856	Les Bergers de Watteau	Tableau vivant, music 'Lange' (Offenbach)	1	Mathieu & Placet
1856	Le "66"	Opérette	1	De Forges & Laurencin
1856	Le Savetier et le Financier	Opérette bouffe	1	Crémieux
1856	La Bonne d'enfants	Opérette bouffe	1	Bercioux
1857	Les Trois Baisers du diable	Opérette fantastique	1	Mestépès
1857	Croquefer ou Le Dernier des paladins	Opérette bouffe	1	Jaime & Tréfeu
1857	Dragonnette	Opérette bouffe	1	Jaime & Mestépès
1857	Vent du soir ou L'Horrible Festin	Opérette bouffe	1	Gille & Battu
1857	Une Demoiselle en loterie	Opérette bouffe	1	Jaime & Crémieux
1857	Le Mariage aux lanternes (from Le Trésor à Mathurin)	Opérette	1	Carré & Battu
1857	Les Deux Pêcheurs	Bouffonnerie musicale	1	Dupeuty & Bourget
1858	Mesdames de la Halle	Opérette bouffe	1	Lapointe
1858	La Chatte métamorphosée en femme	Opérette	1	Scribe & Mélesville

List of Works

Theatre	Date of Production	German Title	English Title
Bouffes-Parisiens Salle Marigny	12 June		The Rose of Auvergne, or 'Spoiling The Broth'
Bouffes-Parisiens Salle Marigny	12 June		
Bouffes-Parisiens Salle Marigny	1 (24?) June		
Bouffes-Parisiens Salle Marigny	31 July	Die beiden Savoyarden	
Bouffes-Parisiens Salle Choiseul	23 September	Schuhflicker and Millionär	
Bouffes-Parisiens Salle Choiseul	23 September		
Bouffes-Parisiens Salle Choiseul	15 January		
Bouffes-Parisiens Salle Choiseul	12 February	Ritter Eisenfrass	
Bouffes-Parisiens Salle Choiseul	30 April		
Bouffes-Parisiens Salle Choiseul	16 May		
Bouffes-Parisiens Salle Choiseul	27 July	Die Kunstreiterin (Longer version, Vienna, 1864)	
Bouffes-Parisiens Salle Choiseul	10 October	Die Verlobung bei Laternenschein or Die Verlobung bei der Laterne	Treasure Trove
Bouffes-Parisiens Salle Choiseul	16 November		
Bouffes-Parisiens Salle Choiseul	3 March	Die Damen der Halle	
Bouffes-Parisiens Salle Choiseul	19 April		

List of Works

Year	Title	Description	No. of Acts	Librettist(s)
1858	Orphée aux Enfers	Opéra bouffon	2	Crémieux & Halévy, anonymously)
1859	Un Mari à la porte	Opérette	1	Delacour & Morand
1859	Les Vivandières de la Grande Armée		1	Jaime & De Forges
1859	Geneviève de Brabant	Opéra bouffon	2 (7 scenes)	Jaime & Tréfeu
1860	Le Carnaval des revues	Revue	—	Grangé, Gille & Halévy
1860	Daphnis et Chloé	Opérette	1	Clairville & Cordier
1860	Le Papillon	Ballet	2 (4 scenes)	Taglioni & Saint-Georges
1860	Barkouf	Opéra-comique	3	Scribe & Boisseau
1861	La Chanson de Fortunio	Opérette	1	Crémieux & Halévy
1861	Le Pont des soupirs	Opéra bouffe	2 (4 scenes)	Crémieux & Halévy
1861	Monsieur Choufleury restera chez lui le . . .	Opéra bouffe	1	St. Rémy (Morny) Halévy, Crémieux & Lépine
1861	Apothicaire et Perruquier (Un Mariage par les cheveux)	Opérette	1	Frébault
1861	Le Roman comique	Opéra bouffe	3	Crémieux & Halévy
1862	Monsieur et Madame Denis	Opérette	1	Delaporte & Laurencin
1862	Le Voyage de MM. Dunanan, père et fils	Opéra bouffe	3	Siraudin & Moinaux
1862	Jacqueline	Opérette	1	Pol d'Arcy (Crémieux & Halévy)

List of Works

Theatre	Date of Production	German Title	English Title
Bouffes-Parisiens Salle Choiseul	21 October	Orpheus in der Unterwelt	Orpheus in the Underworld *or* Underground
Bouffes-Parisiens Salle Choiseul	22 June	Ein Ehemann vor der Tür	
Bouffes-Parisiens Salle Choiseul	6 July		
Bouffes-Parisiens Salle Choiseul	19 November	Genovefa	
Bouffes-Parisiens Salle Choiseul	10 February		
Bouffes-Parisiens Salle Choiseul	27 March	Daphnis und Cloë	
Opéra	26 November		
Opéra-Comique	24 December		
Bouffes-Parisiens	5 January	Fortunios Lied	The Magic Melody
Bouffes-Parisiens	23 March	Die Seufzerbrücke	The Bridge of Sighs
Bouffes-Parisiens	14 September	Vienna: Salon Pitzelberger Berlin: Salon Jäschke	
Bouffes-Parisiens	17 October		The Barber of Bath
Bouffes-Parisiens	10 December		
Bouffes-Parisiens	11 January		
Bouffes-Parisiens	23 March	Herr von Zuckerl Vater und Sohn	
Bouffes-Parisiens	14 October	Dorothea	

List of Works

Year	Title	Description	No. of Acts	Librettist(s)
1862	Bavard et Barvarde later	Opéra bouffe	2	Nuitter (Truinet)
1863	Les Bavards	Opéra bouffe	2	Nuitter (Truinet)
1863	Le Brésilien (a straight play: Offenbach composed the only number)	Comédie	1	Meilhac & Halévy
1863	Lieschen und Fritzchen oder Französische Schwaben later	Conversation alsacienne	1	Boisselot
1864	Lischen et Fritzchen	Conversation alsacienne	1	Boisselot
1863	Il Signor Fagotto	Opéra bouffe	1	Nuitter (Truinet) & Tréfeu
1864	Il Signor Fagotto	Opéra bouffe	1	Nuitter (Truinet) & Tréfeu
1864	L'Amour chanteur	Opérette	1	Nuitter (Truinet) & Lépine
1864	Die Rheinnixen	Opéra	3	Wolzogen, from French of Nuitter (Truinet)
1864	Les Géorgiennes (orig. title: *Feroza*)	Opéra bouffe	3	Moinaux
1864	Jeanne qui pleure et Jean qui rit	Opérette	1	Crémieux & Gille
1865	Jeanne qui pleure et Jean qui rit	Opérette	1	Crémieux & Gille
1864	Le Fifre enchanté *ou* Le Soldat magicien	Opérette	1	Nuitter (Truinet) & Tréfeu
1864	La Belle Hélène	Opéra bouffe	3	Meilhac & Halévy
1865	Coscoletto *ou* Le Lazzarone	Opéra-comique	2	Nuitter (Truinet) & Tréfeu

List of Works

Theatre	Date of Production	German Title	English Title
Ems: Kursaal	11 July	Die Schwätzerin von Saragossa	Beatrice the Chattering Wife
Bouffes-Parisiens	20 February	Die Schwätzerin von Saragossa	Beatrice the Chattering Wife
Palais-Royal	9 May	Fürst Acapulco	
Ems: Kursaal	18 July		
Bouffes-Parisiens (new theatre)	5 January	Lieschen und Fritzchen	
Ems: Kursaal	11 July		
Bouffes-Parisiens	13 January		
Bouffes-Parisiens	5 January		
Vienna: Hofoper	4 (8?) February		
Bouffes-Parisiens	16 March	Die schönen Weiber von Georgien	
Ems: Kursaal	July	Die Hanni weint, der Hansi lacht	
Bouffes-Parisiens	3 November		
Ems: Kursaal see also, Paris 1868, Le Fifre enchanté	9 July	Der Regiments-zauberer	
Variétés	17 December	Die schöne Helena	La Belle Hélène Fair Helen
Ems: Kursaal	24 July		

List of Works

Year	Title	Description	No. of Acts	Librettist(s)
1865	Les Refrains des Bouffes	Revue	1	(Various)
1865	Les Bergers	Opéra-comique	3	Crémieux & Gille
1866	Barbe-bleue	Opéra bouffe	3	Meilhac & Halévy
1866	La Vie parisienne	Pièce en cinq actes mêlée de chant	Orig. 5 red. to 4	Meilhac & Halévy
1867	La Grande-Duchesse de Gerolstein	Opéra bouffe	3	Meilhac & Halévy
1867	La Leçon de chant électromagnétique	Bouffonnerie	1	Bourget
1867	La Permission de dix heures	Opérette	1	Mélesville & Carmouche
1867	Robinson Crusoé	Opéra-comique	3 (5 scenes)	Cormon & Crémieux
1867	Geneviève de Brabant (2nd version) see also Feb. 1875	Opéra bouffe	3 (9 scenes)	Crémieux & Tréfeu
1868	Le Château à Toto	Opéra bouffe	3	Meilhac & Halévy
1868	Le Pont des soupirs (2nd version)	Opéra bouffe	4	Crémieux & Halévy
1868	Le Fifre enchanté *ou* Le Soldat magicien see also Ems 1864	Opérette	1	Nuitter (Truinet) & Tréfeu
1868	L'Île de Tulipatan	Bouffonnerie	1	Chivot & Duru
1868	La Périchole	Opéra bouffe	2	Meilhac & Halévy
1869	Vert-Vert	Opéra-comique	3	Meilhac & Nuitter (Truinet)
1869	La Diva	Opéra bouffe	3	Meilhac & Halévy
1869	La Princesse de Trébizonde	Opéra bouffe	2	Nuitter (Truinet) & Tréfeu

List of Works

Theatre	Date of Production	German Title	English Title
Bouffes-Parisiens	21 September		
Bouffes-Parisiens	11 December		
Variétés	5 February	Blaubart	Bluebeard
Palais-Royal	31 October	Pariser Leben	
Variétés	12 April	Die Grossherzogin von Gerolstein	The Grand Duchess of Gerolstein
Ems: Kursaal see also Paris 1873	20 July		
Ems: Kursaal	20 July	Urlaub nach dem Zapfenstreich	
Opéra-Comique	23 November	Robinson *or* Robinsonade	
Menus-Plaisirs	26 December	Genovefa	
Palais-Royal	6 May		
Variétés	7 May	Die Seufzerbrücke	The Bridge of Sighs
Bouffes-Parisiens	30 September	Der Regiments-zauberer	
Bouffes-Parisiens	30 September	Die Insel Tulipatan	
Variétés	6 October		
Opéra-Comique	10 March	Kakadu	
Bouffes-Parisiens	22 March	Die Theater-prinzessin	
Baden: theatre unknown	31 July	Die Prinzessin von Trapezunt	The Lawful Wife of Rustifum

Year	Title	Description	No. of Acts	Librettist(s)
1869	La Princesse de Trébizonde	Opéra bouffe	3	Nuitter (Truinet) & Tréfeu
1869	Les Brigands	Opéra bouffe	3	Meilhac & Halévy
1869	La Romance de la rose	Opérette	1	Tréfeu & Prével
1871	Boule de Neige (music of Barkouf re-used)	Opéra bouffe	3	Nuitter (Truinet) & Tréfeu
1872	Le Roi Carotte	Opéra bouffe-féerie	4 (See note 6, Ch. XII page 228	Sardou
1872	Fantasio	Opéra-comique	3	after A. de Musset
1872	Fleurette	Opérette	1	De Forges & Laurencin
1872	Le Corsaire noir	Opéra-comique	3	Offenbach
1873	Les Braconniers	Opéra bouffe	3	Chivot & Duru
1873	La Leçon de chant	Bouffonnerie	1	Bourget
1873	La Permission de dix heures	Opérette	1	Mélesville & Carmouche
1873	Pomme d'Api	Opérette	1	Halévy & Busnach
1873	La Vie Parisienne (New version)	Pièce mêlée de chant	4	Meilhac & Halévy
1873	La Jolie Parfumeuse	Opéra-comique	3	Crémieux & Blum
1874	Orphée aux Enfers (New version)	Opéra-féerie	4	Crémieux (& Halévy, anon.)
1874	La Périchole (New version)	Opéra bouffe	3	Meilhac & Halévy
1874	Bagatelle	Opérette	1	Crémieux & Blum

List of Works

Theatre	Date of Production	German Title	English Title
Bouffes-Parisiens	7 December		
Variétés	10 December	Die Banditen	Falsa cappa
Bouffes-Parisiens	11 December		
Bouffes-Parisiens	14 December		
Gaîté	15 January		
Opéra-Comique	18 January		
Vienna: Karltheater	8 March	Fleurette oder Näherin und Trompeter (Viennese version by Julius Hopp & Zell)	
Vienna: Theater an der Wien	21 September	Der schwarze Korsar	
Variétés	29 January	Die Wilddiebe *or* Die Wilderer	
Folies-Marigny	17 June		
Renaissance	4 September	Urlaub nach dem Zapfenstreich	
Renaissance	4 September	Onkel hat's gesagt	
Variétés	25 September	Pariser Leben	
Variétés	29 November	Schönröschen, *or* Pariser Parfüm	
Gaîté	7 February	Orpheus in der Unterwelt	Orpheus in the Underworld *or* Underground
Variétés	25 April		
Bouffes-Parisiens	21 May		

Year	Title	Description	No. of Acts	Librettist(s)
1874	Madame L'Archiduc	Opéra bouffe	3	Millaud & Halévy (who was not billed)
1874	La Haine	Drama	5	Sardou
1875	Whittington	Féerie	4	Nuitter (Truinet) & Tréfeu trans. Farnie
1875	Geneviève de Brabant 3rd version	Opéra-féerie	5	Crémieux & Tréfeu
1875	Les Hannetons	Revue	3	Grangé & Millaud
1875	La Boulangère à des écus	Opéra bouffe	3	Meilhac & Halévy
1875	Le Voyage dans la Lune	Opéra-féerie	4	Vanloo, Leterrier, Mortier
1875	La Créole	Opéra-comique	3	Millaud & Meilhac
1875	Tarte à la crème	Play for which Offenbach composed one number, a waltz	1	Millaud
1876	Pierrette et Jacquot	Opérette	1	Noriac & Gille
1876	La Boite au lait	Opérette	4	Grangé & Noriac
1877	Le Docteur Ox	Opéra bouffe	3 (6 scenes)	Mortier & Gille after J. Verne
1877	La Foire Saint-Laurent	Opéra bouffe	3	Crémieux & Saint-Albin
1878	Maître Péronilla	Opéra bouffe	3	M. 'X'. (Offenbach, with Nuitter & Ferrier, who were not billed)

List of Works

Theatre	Date of Production	German Title	English Title
Bouffes-Parisiens	31 October		Marietta
Gaîté	5 December		
London: Alhambra	2 January		
Gaîté	25 February		
Bouffes-Parisiens	22 April		
Variétés	10 October	Die Millionenbäckerin	
Gaîté	26 October	Die Reise in den Mond	
Bouffes-Parisiens	3 November		The Commodore
Bouffes-Parisiens	14 December		
Bouffes-Parisiens	14 October		
Bouffes-Parisiens	3 November		
Variétés	26 January		
Folies-Dramatiques	10 February	Der Jahrmarkt von St Laurent	
Bouffes-Parisiens	13 March		

List of Works

Year	Title	Description	No. of Acts	Librettist(s)
1878	Madame Favart	Opéra-comique	3	Chivot & Duru
1879	La Marocaine (orig. title: *Fatime*)	Opéra-comique	3	Blum, Blau & Toché
1879	La Fille du Tambour-Major	Opéra-comique	3 (4 scenes)	Chivot & Duru
1880	Belle Lurette (composed after *Hoffmann*, produced first)	Opéra bouffe	3	Ferrier & Halévy
1881	Les Contes d'Hoffmann	Opéra fantastique	4	Barbier
1881	Mam'zelle Moucheron	Opérette	1	Leterrier & Vanloo

UNFULFILLED THEATRE PROJECTS

1848	La Duchesse d'Albe (Blanche?)	Opéra-comique
1860	Le Testament de Sganarelle (Nérée-Désarbres and Nuitter)	Opéretta
1862	Fédia (Meilhac and Halévy) Original title: La Baguette	Opéra-comique
1863	La Belle Aurore (Fee Rosa) (for the Viktoria-Theater, Berlin)	Opérette
1863	Friquette (one act, for the Theater an der Wien)	
1865	Le Bourgeois Gentilhomme (for the Porte Saint-Martin theatre)	
1866	Le Jockey	
1877	Le Zéphir (Nuitter)	Opérette
1875	Don Quichotte (Sardou and Nuitter, after Sardou's play)	Opéra-bouffe-féerie
1880	Le Cabaret des lilas (Blum and Toché, for the Variétés)	

UNDATED FRAGMENTS

Phénice
Léonard

Theatre	Date of Production	German Title	English Title
Folies-Dramatiques	28 December		
Bouffes-Parisiens	13 January		
Folies-Dramatiques	13 December	Die Tochter des Tambour-Majors	
Renaissance	30 October	Die schöne Lurette	Lurette
Opéra-Comique	10 February	Hoffmanns Erzählungen	
Renaissance Produced posthumously revised by Delibes (see *Grove*)	10 May		

Scapin et Mazetta
Le Mur

VOCAL WORKS (FRENCH)

1838   *Le Sylphe*, Catelin
        Le Pauvre prisonnier, Catelin
        Ronde tyrolienne, Catelin
1839   *Jalousie*, Ménestrel
        J'aime la rêverie, Ménestrel
1840   *L'Attente*, Heugel
1842   *L'Aveu de page*, Cotelle
        Fables de La Fontaine (Cotelle): *Le Corbeau et le Renard*
                                        Le Rat de ville et le Rat des champs
                                          Le Savetier et le Financier
                                          Le Loup et l'Agneau
                                          La Laitière et le Pot au lait
                                          Le Berger et la Mer
1843   *A toi*, Cotelle
        L'Arabe a son coursier, Cotelle
        La Croix de ma mère, Cotelle
        Dors mon enfant, Cotelle
        Doux Ménestrel, Cotelle
        Rends-moi mon âme, Ménestrel
        Virginie au départ . . ., Cotelle

List of Works

1844   *Meunière et Fermière*, Meissonnier

1846   *Le Moine bourru* or *les Deux Poltrons*, Meissonnier
         Le Sergent recrutateur, Meissonnier
         La Sortie de bal
         Sarah la blonde
         Le Langage des fleurs:

	La branche d'oranger
	La rose
	Ne m'oubliez pas
	La marguerite
	L'églantine
	La pâquerette

1850   *Sérénade du torero*, Chabal

1851   *Chanson de Valéria*, Mayaud
         Chanson de Fortunio, Heugel
         L'Étoile, Mayaud
         Si j'étais petit oiseau, Mayaud

1852   *Les Voix mystérieuses:*

	L'Hiver
	Chanson de Fortunio
	Les Saisons
	Ma belle amie est morte
	La Rose foulée
	Barcarolle, Heugel

1854   *Sérénade*, Heugel

1857   *Valse des animaux (les Petits prodiges)*
         La Chanson de ceux qui n'aiment plus

1860   *La Cigale et la fourmi*, Cotelle
         Bibi Bambou, Brandus

1862   *La Demoiselle de Nanterre (Et digue digue don)*, Dinguel

1863   *Ronde du Brésilien*, Brandus

1864   *Jeanne la rousse*, Brandus

1865   *La Pêche*, Chaliot

1873   *Chanson béarnaise*, Choudens
         Ronde savoyarde, Choudens

La Tambour du collège
La Fleur de Zirka
Ça ne s'est jamais vu . . ., Leduc
Sur la grève . . .
Deux fleurs . . .

UNPUBLISHED VOCAL WORKS (FRENCH)

Pauvre Cocotte (voice only)
La Tramontane (voice and piano, two versions)
Le Pâtre (voice, piano, cello)
Lève-toi (voice and piano)
Si j'étais la feuille (voice only)
Pablo (voice and piano)
Hier la nuit d'été . . . (voice and piano)
De ton pays, la plage désolée . . . (voice and piano)
Venez trinquer (voice and piano)
Minuit . . . (voice and piano)

Tristesse (voice only)
Comme une ondine (voice only)
Promenade du soir (voice and piano)
Un ange au doux visage . . . (voice, piano, violin)
Oui je t'aime . . . (duet, voice only)
Pâquerette jolie (voice and piano)
Près du lac bleu (voice only)
Ce que j'aime (voice and piano)
Seul dans le monde (voice only)
Absence (voice and piano)
Sur l'épine ou sur la rose (voice and piano)
Fanchette (voice only)
La Petite peureuse (voice and piano, 1838)
Roses et papillons (voice only)
Fi des amours (voice only)
L'Émir du Bengali (voice only)
S'il est . . . (voice only)
Ce noble ami (voice only)
Je suis la bohémienne (voice only)
Sous la blanche colonnade (voice only)
Pedrigo (voice only)
Duo des deux grenadiers (voice only)
Au pays qui me prend ma belle (voice only)
J'étais né pour être honnête homme (voice only)
C'est le bûcheron (voice only)
C'est charmant (voice and piano)
Le Mystère de minuit (voice and piano)
Aimons (voice only)
Le Ramier blessé (voice only)
Douce brise du soir (duet)
Qui frappe à ta porte? . . . (voice only)
Silence (voice and piano, 1847)
Nocturne à deux voix (voice and piano)
Mon bien-aimé n'est plus (voice and piano)
Valse pour Mlle Désirée (voice and piano, 1868)
Jobin
En répétant ce doux refrain
Gardez toujours le coeur fidèle

VOCAL WORKS (GERMAN)

Das Vaterland (1848), Schloss, Cologne
Bleib bei mir, Vaterlandlied, Spina
Leb wohl
Catherinen, was willst du mehr?
Was fliesset auf dem Felde
Lied des deutschen Knaben, Schloss, Cologne
Bleib mir treu
Ständchen
Im grünen Mai . . .
Mein' Lieb' gleicht dem Bächlein

List of Works

UNPUBLISHED WORKS (GERMAN)

O du mein Mond (voice and piano)

CHORUSES

Venise, barcarolle for 4 voices, Bernard Latte
Vive la Suisse
Der kleine Trommler (1863)

UNPUBLISHED CHORUSES

Introduction et ballade, (1846)
Valse du bal (1846)

PATRIOTIC SONGS

Dieu sauve la France, Heugel

UNPUBLISHED PATRIOTIC SONGS

Marche et Prière
Hymne

UNPUBLISHED RELIGIOUS MUSIC

Ave Maria (voice and organ)
Agnus Dei (voice and organ)
Le Cantique a l'Esprit-Saint
Espoir en Dieu
Près du Très-Haut
Gloire à Dieu

UNPUBLISHED ORCHESTRAL WORKS

Ouverture à grand orchestre, Cologne, September 1843
Hommage à Rossini (1843)
Le Désert (oratorio parody, 1846)
Concerto militaire (for violoncello, 1848)
Réminiscences de Robert le Diable (1852)
Réminiscences de la Lucie
Nuits d'Espagne (fragments)
Grande Scène espagnole (1840), Introduction, Prayer, *Zambada*, Serenade, *Boléro*, Op. 22

INCIDENTAL MUSIC FOR THE COMÉDIE-FRANÇAISE

Overture: *Le Bonhomme jadis*
Fantasy: *Le Barbier de Séville*
Overture: *Mademoiselle de La Seiglière*
Le Mariage de Figaro (incidental music)

List of Works

WORKS FOR VIOLONCELLO

Divertimento über Schweizerlieder, Op. 1
Introduction et valse mélancolique, 1839, Op. 14, Martin
Capriccio on *le Cor des Alpes* by Proch, Op. 15, 1841
Prière et Boléro, Op. 22
Musette (18th century ballet melody, Op. 24, 1843)
Quatrième mazurka, Op. 26
Caprice on the Romance from *Joseph* by Méhul, Op. 27
Les Chants du crépuscule, Op. 29:   *Souvenir du bal*
                                                  Sérénade
                                                  Ballade
                                                  Le Retour
                                                  L'Adieu
                                                  Pas villageois
La Sylphe (Op. 30)
Caprice sur *La Somnambula*, de Bellini, Op. 32
                I Puritani, de Bellini, Op. 33
Deux âmes au ciel (élégie, 1844), Richault
Las Campanillas (1847)
Trois grands duos concertants (for two violoncellos, Op. 43)
Cours méthodique de duos (for two violoncellos, 1847), Schoenberger Op. 49, 50, 51,
    52, 53, 54
    Trois duos dédiés aux amateurs
    Trois difficiles
    Trois très difficiles
Adagio and *Scherzo* (for 4 violoncellos)
Rêverie au bord de la mer (1849), Launer
La Course en traîneau (1849), Launer
Gaietés champêtres, Chabal
Harmonie du soir, Op. 68
Fantaisie sur Richard Coeur de Lion, by Grétry, Op. 69
                  Jean de Paris, by Boïeldieu, Op. 70
                  le Barbier de Séville, by Rossini, Op. 71
                  les Noces de Figaro, by Mozart, Op. 72
                  Norma, by Bellini, Op. 73
Fantaisie facile et brillante, Op. 74
Tambourin, after Rameau, Op. 75
Chant des mariniers galants, by Rameau, Op. 76, 1851
Vingt petites études pour le violoncelle, with bass accompaniment, Op. 77, Cotelle
Douze études pour violoncelle et basse, Op. 78
Marche chinoise
Harmonies des bois: Élégie *Le Soir*
                                         Les Larmes de Jacqueline
Fantaisies caprices sur: *Anne de Bolène* (Donizetti)
                                       La Dame blanche (Boïeldieu)
                                       L'Elisir d'Amore (Donizetti)
                                       Parisina (Donizetti)
                                       Béatrice di Tenda (Bellini)

MUSIC FOR PIANO: DANCES

Fleurs d'hiver (suite of waltzes, 1836) Serre

List of Works

Les Jeunes filles (suite of waltzes, 1836)
Brunes et blondes (suite of waltzes, 1837)
Les Trois Grâces (suite of waltzes, 1837) Catelin
Rébecca (suite of waltzes on Hebraic motifs of the fifteenth century, 1837)
Le Décameron dramatique (1854,
    dedicated to the artists of the
    Comédie-Française):

1. *Rachel*, grand waltz
2. *Émilie*, polka-mazurka
3. *Madeleine*, village polka
4. *Delphine*, redowa
5. *Augustine*, Scottish dance
6. *Louise*, grand waltz
7. *Maria*, polka-mazurka
8. *Élisa*, polka trilby
9. *Nathalie*, Scottish dance
10. *Clarisse*, varsoviana

Herminie, waltz, Maestro, London
Berthe, suite of waltzes
The Times, grand waltz, Cocks and Co, London
Les Feuilles du soir, waltzes (1864), Brandus
Jacqueline, suite of waltzes (1865), Brandus
Valse favorite
Les Roses du Bengale (six sentimental waltzes) Lemoine
Offenbach-valse (1876), Choudens
Le Fleuve d'or (1876), Choudens
Les Belles Américaines (1876), Choudens
Souvenir d'Aix-les-Bains, waltz
Polka des singes
Polka du mendiant, Bertin
Polka burlesque, Choudens
Kissi-Kissi, polka
Sum-Sum, polka
Schüler polka, Bote et Bock
Taxopholite, polka-mazurka, Cramer, London
Quatrième mazurka de salon
Postillon-galop, Heugel
Cachucha, Cateline
Parade militaire

MANUSCRIPTS
La Prière de Moïse (for 2 violins, piano and organ)

UNPUBLISHED DANCE MUSIC
Valse triomphale du château de Digoenne
Valse à quatre mains
Plaintes de la châtelaine
Les Cinq Soeurs (valses, suite, 1855):

Anna la sévère
Clotilde la coquette
Cécile la mélancolique
Élise la villageoise
Caroline la sautillante

List of Works

Polka des mirlitons (piano, trumpet and three kazoos)
Polka en mi majeur
La 'Chabrillan' polka
Polka en ut
Scottish (sic)

ORCHESTRATIONS OF SCHUBERT MELODIES

Barcarolle
Marguerite au rouet
Plainte de la jeune fille
Le Roi des aulnes
Sérénade

WORKS FOR VIOLONCELLO AND PIANO (with F. von Flotow)

SERENADES	REVERIES
Au bord de la mer	*La Harpe éolienne*
Souvenir du bal	*Scherzo*
Prière du soir	*Polka de salon*
La Retraite	*Chanson d'autrefois*
Ballade du pâtre	*Les Larmes*
Danse norvégienne	*Redowa brillante*

SOME STAGE WORKS BASED ON COMPILATIONS OF OFFENBACH'S MUSIC

1893   *Gaîté parisienne*, ballet, arr. Rosenthal.
1913   *Die Heimkehr des Odysseus* (The Homecoming of Odysseus), arr. Leopold Schmidt.
1918   *Die glückliche Insel* (The Happy Island), arr. Leopold Schmidt.
1919   *Der Goldschmied von Toledo* (The Goldsmith of Toledo), arr. J. Stern and A. Zamara.
1922   *Der Meister von Montmartre* (The Maestro of Montmartre), arr. Bretschneider and Klein. Later produced in Berlin as *Pariser Nächte* (Parisian Nights) and in New York as *The Lovesong*.
1929   *Das Hemd der Königin* (The Queen's Chemise), arr. Carl Rössler and Lion Feuchtwanger.
1965   *Not In Front Of The Waiter*, story and musical adaptation by Colin Graham, words by Viola Tunnard, orchestration by Vilem Tausky.
1976   *Christopher Columbus*, arr. Patric Schmid, libretto by Don White.
1977   *Bon Voyage*, based on *Le Voyage de M. Perrichon*, by Eugène Labiche and Eduard Martin, arr. Vera Brodsky Lawrence, libretto by Edward Mabley.

Vive Offenbach!, presented at the Opéra-Comique, Paris, in December 1979, was not a compilation in the sense used above, but a triple bill of three original Offenbach operettas, *Pomme d'Api*, *Monsieur Choufleury* and *Mesdames de la Halle*.

Bibliography

·⚓·

A. Biographies of Offenbach

Argus (pseud.). *Célébrités dramatiques: Jacques Offenbach*, Paris (Lachaud), 1872
Bekker, Paul. *Jacques Offenbach* (vols. 31–32 of *Die Musik*), Berlin, 1909
Bellaigue, Camille. *Études musicales et nouvelles silhouettes des musiciens*, Paris (Delagrave), 1898.
Brancour, René. *Les Musiciens célèbres: Offenbach*, Paris, 1929.
Brindejont-Offenbach, Jacques. *Offenbach, mon Grand-Père*, Paris (Plon), 1940.
Decaux, Alain. *Offenbach, roi du Second Empire*, Paris (Pierre Amiot), 1958.
Henseler, Anton. *Jakob Offenbach*, Berlin (Max Hesse), 1930.
Kracauer, Siegfried. *Offenbach and the Paris of His Time*, London (Constable), 1937.
Kristeller, Hans. *Der Aufstieg des Kölners Jacques Offenbach*, Berlin (Schultz), 1931.
Martinet, André. *Offenbach, sa vie et son oeuvre*, Paris (Dentu), 1887.
Mirecourt, Eugène de. *Les Contemporains: Auber, Offenbach*, Paris (Faure), 1867.
Schneider, Louis. *Les Maîtres de l'opérette française: Offenbach*, Paris (Perrin), 1923.
Wolff, Albert. *La Gloire à Paris: Jacques Offenbach*, essay in *Mémoires d'un parisien*, Paris (Victor-Havard), 1886.

B. Writings by Jacques Offenbach

Histoire d'une valse, Paris, c. 1872. Translated as 'The Story of a Waltz' in *The Theatre*, 1 October 1878.
Offenbach en Amérique: Notes d'un musicien en voyage, Précédés d'une notice biographique par Albert Wolff, Paris (Calmann-Lévy), 1877.
Orpheus in America, trans. Lander MacClintock, London (Hamish Hamilton), 1958. In this translation of the previous item Wolff's *notice biographique* is replaced by a new biographical introduction by the translator.
Foreword to: Mortier, Arnold, *Les Soirées parisiennes* (vol. i, 1874), Paris (Dentu), 1875.

C. Other Biographies

Boulenger, Marcel. *La Païva*, Paris (Trémois), 1930.

258

Bibliography

Chapman, J. M. and Brian. *The Life and Times of Baron Haussmann*, London (Weidenfeld and Nicolson), 1957.

Claretie, Jules. *Célébrités contemporaines: Ludovic Halévy*, Paris (Quantin), 1883.

Dean, Winton. *Bizet*, London (Dent), 1948.

Fantel, Hans. *Johann Strauss: Father and Son and Their Era*, Newton-Abbot (David and Charles), 1971.

Flotow, Freifrau von. *Friedrich von Flotows Leben, von seiner Wittwe*, Leipzig (Breitkopf), 1892.

Gregor-Dellin, Martin. *Wagner-Chronik: Daten zu Leben und Werk*, Munich (Hanser), 1972.

Hewett-Thayer, H. W. *Hoffmann, Author of The Tales*, Princeton (Princeton University Press), 1948.

Hughes, Gervase. *Composers of Operetta*, London (Macmillan), 1962.

Martin, Jules. *Nos Auteurs et Compositeurs dramatiques*, Paris (Flammarion), 1897.

Mirecourt, Eugène de. *Les Contemporains: Villemessant*, Paris (Faure), 1867.

Rouff, Marcel, and Casevitz, Thérèse. *La Vie de fête sous le Second Empire: Hortense Schneider*, Paris (Tallandier), 1930.

Roujon, Henry. *Artistes et amis des arts: Ludovic Halévy*, Paris (Hachette), 1912.

——————— *Quelques mots sur M. Ludovic Halévy*, Paris, 1888.

Schneider, Louis. *Les Maîtres de l'opérette française: Hervé, Charles Lecocq*, Paris (Perrin), 1924.

Schneider, Marcel. *Ernest Théodore Amadeus Hoffmann*, Paris (Julliard), 1979.

Séché, Léon, ed. *Alfred de Musset: Correspondance*, Paris (Société du Mercure de France), 1907.

Silvera, Alain. *Daniel Halévy and His Times*, New York (Cornell University Press), 1966.

Young, Percy M. *Sir Arthur Sullivan*, London (Dent), 1971.

D. Memoirs and Letters

Adam, Adolphe. *Souvenirs d'un musicien*, Paris (Michel Lévy), 1859.

——————— *Derniers souvenirs d'un musicien*, Paris (Michel Lévy), 1859.

Berlioz, Hector. *The Life of Hector Berlioz*, trans. K. F. Boult, London (Dent), 1870.

——————— *the Memoirs of Hector Berlioz*, trans. and ed. David Cairns, London (Gollancz), 1969.

Goncourt, Edmond and Jules de. *Journal* (6 vols.), Paris (Charpentier and Fasquelle), 1912.

Hanslick, Eduard. *Aus meinem Leben* (2 vols.), Berlin (Allgemeiner Verein für Deutsche Literatur), 1911.

Halévy, Ludovic. *Notes et souvenirs: 1871–1872*, Paris (Calmann-Lévy), 1889.

——————— *Carnets*, with introduction and notes by Daniel Halévy (2 vols.), Paris (Calmann-Lévy), 1935.

Hoffmann, E. T. A. *Selected Letters*, ed. and trans. Johanna Sahlin, Chicago (University of Chicago Press), 1977.

Houssaye, Arsène. *Les Confessions, souvenirs d'un demi-siècle 1830–1890* (6 vols.), Paris (Dentu), 1885–91.

——————— *Man About Paris*, ed. and trans. Henry Knepler, London (Gollancz), 1972.

Mortier, Arnold. *Les Soirées parisiennes* (11 vols.), Paris (Dentu), 1874–84.

Bibliography

Sardou, Victorien. *Les Papiers de Victorien Sardou*, ed. Georges Mouly, Paris (Albin Michel), 1934.

Scholl, Aurélien. *Mémoires du trottoir*, Paris (Dentu), 1882.

Véron, Louis-Désiré. *Mémoires d'un bourgeois de Paris*, (vols. 3–6), Paris (Gonet), 1854–5.

Villemessant, Henri de. *Mémoires d'un journaliste*, Paris (Dentu), 1867 and 1872.

Wagner, Richard. *Lettres françaises de Richard Wagner*, ed. Julien Tiersot, Paris (Grasset), 1935.

E. General

Blondel, Jean. *The Government of France*, London (Methuen), 1974.

Blunt, Wilfrid. *The Dream King: Ludwig II of Bavaria*, London (Hamish Hamilton), 1970.

Boutet de Monvel, Roger. *Les Variétés: 1850–1870*, Paris (Plon), 1905.

Brazier, Nicolas. *Chroniques des petits théâtres de Paris*, Paris (Rouveyre et Blond), revised ed. 1883, orig. publ. 1837.

Castellot, André. *Napoléon Trois: des prisons au pouvoir*, Paris (Perrin), 1973.

Cobban, Alfred. *A History of Modern France*, (3 vols.), Harmondsworth (Penguin), 1977.

Duncan, Barry. *The St. James's Theatre*, London (Barrie and Rockliff), 1964.

Gautier, Théophile. *Histoire de l'art dramatique en France depuis vingt-cinq ans*, Paris (Hetzel), 1859.

Gay, Peter. *Freud, Jews and Other Germans*, New York (Oxford University Press), 1978.

Grenville, J. A. S. *Europe Reshaped — 1848–1878*, London (Fontana/Collins), 1977.

Harding, James. *Folies de Paris: The Rise and Fall of French Operetta*, London (Chappell/Elm Tree Books), 1979.

Hobson, Harold. *French Theatre since 1830*, London (Calder), 1978.

Hoffmann, E. T. W. [*sic*]. *Weird Tales*, trans. and with a biographical notice by J. T. Bealby, London (Nimmo), 1885.

Janik, Allan, and Toulmin, Stephen. *Wittgenstein's Vienna*, London (Weidenfeld and Nicolson), 1973.

Labracherie, Pierre. *La Vie quotidienne de la Bohème litteraire au XIXe siècle*, Paris (Hachette), 1967.

Lasalle, Albert de. *Histoire des Bouffes-Parisiens*, Paris (Bourdilliat), 1860.

Lenôtre, G. *The Tuileries: The Glories and Enchantments of a Vanished Palace*, trans. Hugh Barnes, London (Herbert Jenkins), 1934.

Lyon, Raymond, and Saguer, Louis. *Les Contes d'Hoffmann: Étude et analyse*, Paris (Mellottée), 1948.

Maurois, André. *A History of France*, trans. H. L. Binsse, third (revised) edition, London (Cape), 1960.

Meilhac, Henri, and Halévy, Ludovic. *Meilhac et Halévy: Théâtre* (collected plays and librettos, 8 vols.), Paris (Calmann-Lévy), n.d. (c. 1900).

Musset, Alfred de. *Théâtre* (collected plays, 2 vols.), Paris (Garnier-Flammarion), 1964.

Nietzsche, Friedrich. *The Will to Power*, ed. and trans. Walter Kaufmann, London (Weidenfeld and Nicolson), 1968.

Popper, Karl R. *The Open Society and its Enemies*, London (Routledge & Kegan Paul), 1977.

Renaud, Madeleine, and Barrault, Jean-Louis. *Le Siècle d'Offenbach* (Cahiers de la compagnie Madeleine Renaud — Jean-Louis Barrault (no. 24), Paris (Julliard), 1958.

Richardson, Joanna. *La Vie Parisienne (1852–1870)*, London (Hamish Hamilton), 1971.

Sarcey, Francisque. *Quarante ans de théâtre*, Paris (Bibliothèque des 'Annales politiques et littéraires'), 1901.

Scholl, Aurélien. *L'Esprit du boulevard*, Paris (Victor-Havard), 1887.

Silbermann, Alphons. *Das imaginäre Tagebuch des Herrn Jacques Offenbach*, Berlin (Bote & Bock), 1960.

Thomson, David. *Europe since Napoleon*, Harmondsworth (Penguin), 1978.

Véron, Louis Désiré. *Les Théâtres de Paris depuis 1806 jusqu'en 1860*, Paris, 1860.

Zola, Émile. *Le Naturalisme au théâtre*, Paris (Charpentier), 1881.

     L'Argent, Paris (Charpentier), 1891.

     Nana, Paris (Charpentier), 1880.

     Mes Haines, Paris (Faure), 1866.

F. Musical Criticism and History

Berlioz, Hector. *Les Musiciens et la musique*, Paris (Calmann-Lévy), 1903.

Bruyas, Florian. *Histoire d l'opérette en France*, Paris (Vitte), 1974.

Cooper, Martin. *French Music*, London (Oxford University Press), 1951.

Debussy, Claude. *Monsieur Croche et autres écrits*, ed. François Lesure, Paris (Gallimard), 1971.

Oeser, Fritz. Foreword to the vocal score of *Hoffmanns Erzählungen*, Kassel (Bärenreiter/Alkor), 1977.

Raynor, Henry. *Music and Society since 1875*, London (Barrie and Jenkins), 1976.

Roger, G. *Le Carnet d'un ténor*, Paris (Ollendorff), 1880.

Saint-Saëns, Camille. *Harmonie et Mélodie*, Paris (Calmann-Lévy). 1885.

Soubies, Albert, and Malherbe, Charles. *Histoire de l'Opéra-Comique*, Paris (Flammarion), 1893.

Wagner, Richard. *Das Judentum in der Musik*, in *Sämtliche Schriften und Dichtungen* (Volks-Ausgabe), vol. v., Leipzig (Breitkopf), n.d.

Wechsberg, Joseph. *The Waltz Emperors*, London (Weidenfeld and Nicolson), 1973.

G. Periodicals and Journals

L'Artiste, Paris.
L'Art Musical, Paris.
L'Assemblée Nationale, Paris.
The Athenaeum, London.
L'Autographe, Paris.
Le Constitutionnel, Paris.
L'Éclair, Paris.
The Era, London.
Le Fouet, Paris.
Le Figaro, Paris.
La France Musicale, Paris.

Bibliography

La Gazette Musicale, Paris.
Le Journal Amusant, Paris.
Le Journal des Débats, Paris.
The Maestro, London.
Le Ménestrel, Paris.
The Musical Examiner, London.
La Musique en France, Paris.
La Nouvelle Revue, Paris.
Revue d'Art Dramatique, Paris.
Revue des Deux Mondes, Paris.
Revue et Gazette Musicale de Paris, Paris.
Revue et Gazette des Théâtres, Paris.
Revue Théâtrale, Paris.
Le Siècle, Paris.
The Theatre, London.
La Vie Parisienne, Paris.

Index

Compiled by Ann Melsom

·•✠•·

263

Index

Index

267

Index

Index

273